ENGLISH RECUSANT LITERATURE
1558–1640

Selected and Edited by
D. M. ROGERS

Volume 278

JOHN SWEETNAM
The Paradise of Delights
1620

ST. BENEDICT
The Rule of the Most Blissed
Father Saint Benedict
[1632]

JOHN SWEETNAM

The Paradise of Delights

1620

The Scolar Press

1976

ISBN o 85967 279 4

Published and printed in Great Britain by
The Scolar Press Limited, 59-61 East Parade,
Ilkley, Yorkshire and
39 Great Russell Street,
London WC1

NOTE

The following works are reproduced (original size) with permission:

1) John Sweetnam, *The paradise of delights*, 1620, from a copy in the library of St. Mary's Seminary, Oscott, by permission of the President. The title-page of this copy is badly damaged, and in the facsimile the title-page is reproduced from a copy in the British Library, by permission of the Board.

References: Allison and Rogers 804; STC 23531.

2) St. Benedict, *The rule*, [1632], from a copy in the library of Downside Abbey, by permission of the Abbot and Community. Page 35 of the second part of the *Statutes* is damaged in this copy, and in the facsimile this page is reproduced from a copy in the British Library, by permission of the Board.

References: Allison and Rogers 102; STC 1860/ [17552].

THE

PARADISE

OF DELIGHTS.

OR

The B. Virgins Garden of *Loreto*.
With briefe Difcourfes vpon
her Diuine Letanies, by
way of Meditation.

*For the comfort of all fuch , as be deuout
vnto her; and defyre her holy Pa-
tronage & Protection.*

By I. S. of the Society of IESVS.

Fulcite me floribus, ftipate me malis. Cant. 2.

Permiffu Superiorum, M.DC.XX.

TO THE RIGHT
HONOVRABLE
AND MOST
WORTHY ENGLISH
GENTLEMEN,
OF THE SODALITY
OF THE IMMACVLATE
CONCEPTION
OF THE EVER B.
VIRGIN MARY,
IN LOVAYNE.

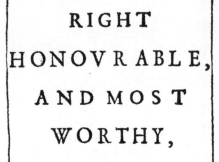

RIGHT
HONOVRABLE,
AND MOST
WORTHY,

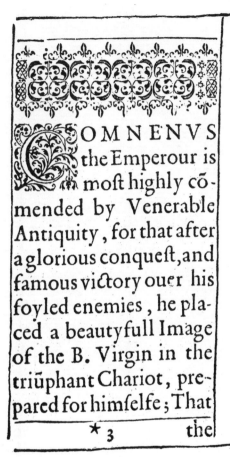

COMNENVS the Emperour is most highly cō-mended by Venerable Antiquity, for that after a glorious conqueſt, and famous victory ouer his foyled enemies, he placed a beautyfull Image of the B. Virgin in the triūphant Chariot, prepared for himſelfe; That

the Mighty Citty of
Rome , Lady and Mi-
ſtreſſe of the VVorld ,
might vvitneſſe , hovv
duely and faithfully he
did honour & reuerence
her, through vvhoſe ayd
and aſſiſtance (next after
God) he atchieued the
ſame. A greater victory
haue you obtayned ouer
farre more potent ene-
mies; and your gratefull
mindes & feruorous de-
uotions in aduauncing
the

the honor of the Blessed
Queene of Angells, and
povverfull Empresse of
the vvorld, vvill not on-
ly be a most faithfull re-
cognizing of her ready
help, to the full accom-
plishment of your spiri-
tuall Conquests; but al-
so yield a most svveet &
fragrant odour, of this
present age, to all true-
harted Catholikes; and
leaue a most memorable
example of your vertu-

ous endeauours to all Posterity.

Lib. de prouid. cap. 1.

Seneca vvorthily vvrites, that, *Inter bonos viros & Deum amicitia est, conciliante virtute* : Betvveene good men and God, there is a straite band of friendship, by reason of Vertue. Wherby it comes to passe, that by your Generous actes of vertuous life, hauing contracted, and (by your earnest seeking to ad-

uaunce

uaunce the honor of his
(Elected Mother) confir-
med this perpetuall lea-
gue of perfect Amity
vvith God; there muſt
needes follovv that fri-
endly & familiar com-
munication, that hea-
uenly comfort, and vni-
forme conſent of harts,
both vvith God, and a-
mongſt your ſelues, vn-
to vvhich they only are
vvorthily to be admit-
ted, vvho haue deſerued

to beare a part in this celestiall harmony, vvher-
by to be made truely
happy.

My vnvvorthynes
therfore finding you so
highly esteemed in this
melodious Quire, doth
present this little Trea-
tise vnto you; not much
vnlike to poore people,
vvho vse to offer trifling
Nevv-yeares-giftes vnto
Great men, thereby to
make their vnvvorthy

Presents

Prefents an humble pe-
tition of fome greater
guerdon, and revvard.
So if my flender labours
might gaine fo much
honour, and make me fo
happy as to be remem-
bred in your deuout, &
much refpected Com-.
munity, I should thinke
my felfe moft aboun-
dantly fatiffied. This my
vnpolished lynes doe
humbly requeft, not by
any vertue frō themfel-

ues,

ues, but for her sake of vvhom vve novv treate. In hope vvherof I rest,

Yours sincerely affected in Christ Iesus.

I. S.

THE

THE
PREFACE
to the Reader.

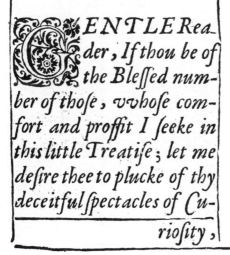

ENTLE Reader, If thou be of the Blessed number of those, vvhose comfort and proffit I seeke in this little Treatise; let me desire thee to plucke of thy deceitful spectacles of Curiosity,

riofity, and perufe my plaine lines vvith deuout fimplicity; othervvife thou art like to finde thy labour of as little effect, in regard of vvhat thou feekeft of me, as I fhal find my hopes of fmall expectation, for vvhat I defire to vvorke in thee.

Moyfes vvith admiration did fee the Bush, in vvhich Almighty God appeared, burning, but not confuming, vvhich

made

made him the more deſi-
rous to behold that great
and vvonderous viſion;
but yet vvas commaun-
ded to plucke off his ſhooes
before he might haue ac-
ceſſe. The like counſell I
find giuen by S. Bernard,
to thoſe vvho curiouſly deſire to behold the diuin mi-
ſteries, vvhich the Eter-
nall VViſdom of Almigh-
ty God hath vvrought in
this myſticall Buſh, the
moſt Bleſſed Virgin his
Mother.

Mother . Thou wilt not so much admire the Gedeon *Fleece besprinckled vvith devv, as to behold a vvoman clad vvith the sunne, yet not consumed vvith so great an heate .* Meritò quidem admiraris Moyses (*saith he*) & curiosiùs desideras intueri; verumtamen solue calceamenta de pedibus tuis , & inuolucra pone carnalium cogitationum , si accedere concupiscas . *Not vvithout*

Bern. serm. in Apoc.12

without cause thou dost admire (O holy *Moyses*) & more curiously dost desire to behold; but cast of thy shooes from thy feete, and bridle the inordinate desire of thy flesh, if thou desire to approach.

No curious conceite but a pure intention, no earthly affection, but true deuotion, no faygned loue, but a dutifull respect must bring thee to the presence of this sacred Queene, to the

⁂   sight

sight of this blazing starre,
into the most esteemed fauour of the euer Blessed
mother of God. Read ther-
fore vvith desire of proffit,
& my best vvishes shalbe
as my intention is, that it
may turne to the great honour of God, and his thrice
happy Mother, and to the
Eternall good of thy soule.
And in thy best deuotions
pray for me.

I. S.

A

A BRIEFE

INTRODVCTION

TO THE FOLLOWING

MEDITATIONS.

THE naturall con-
dition of mans wil
is such, that of
neceſſity it requireth the
help of the Vnderſtanding,
to the due performance of

her noble acts, according to that vulgar *Axiome* of Philosophers, *Nihil volitŭ, quin præcognitum*, Nothing can be desired, vnlesse it be first knowne, whereupon it comes to passe, that the Wil cannot work but according to the light that it hath frō the foresaid vnderstanding: and the greater that the knowledge is of the good apprehēded, the more doth the affection of the Will increase, and kindleth an earnest desire of the thing vve loue.

Wher-

Wherfore my intended purpose in these present Meditations, being to stirre vp the harts of al that rightly peruse them, and a reuerend respect, and deuout affection vnto the euer blessed and most happy Virgin Mother of God; I must first lay before your eyes, the greatnes of her excellent Vertues, & singular graces (as farre as my weakenes shalbe able) that the vnderstanding being once fully possessed vvith an impregnable conceipt of her vn-

spea-

speakable Perfections., the wil may be the more ſtrŏgly moued, to loue and reuerēce ſo beautiful a creature.

To this effect I haue made choice of her deuout Letanies of *Loreto*, wherin moſt admirable tytles, and moſt manifeſt arguments of her greatnes are propoſed vnto vs; by vvhich not only our Vnderſtanding, may be aboundantly enriched with diuine conceits, but alſo our Will may be greatly inflamed with vertuous deſires. From which

two

two well-grounded Roots, will spring the beautifull branch of Imitation, the chiefest and only scope of all vertuous myndes, and the last marke at which all true deuotion aymeth; and vvithout vvhich both deuotion is fruitles, or no deuotion at all, and the best purposes are without effects. Witnes that worthy saying of S. *Ambrose*, *Quisquis Mariæ exoptat præmium, imitetur exemplum*, Whosoeuer desireth the reward of the Blessed Virgin Mary,

Amb. l. 2. de Virgin.

** 4   let

let him imitate her exãple.
And S. *Bernard* giueth vs to
vnderſtand, that the per-
fect imitation of her excellent vertues muſt be the
only conduict to conuey
vnto vs her louing fa-
uours, *Vt impetres eius orati-*
onis ſuffragium, ne deſeras con-
uerſationis exemplum, that
thou mayſt attaine to thy
deſired effect of her prayers, leaue not to follow her
laudable Conuerſation.

Conſonant to this is the
doctrine of the burning
Lampe of Africke, & ſhi-
ning

Bern. ſu-
per Miſ.
ſi. s eſt.

ning light of the vvhole
Church, S. *Augustine*, who
writing of the true festiuity
of holy Martyrs, saith, *Ab* *Aug.*
eis Sanctorum in veritate festi- *serm.47.*
ua gaudia celebrantur, qui ipso- *de Sanc-*
rum Martyrum exempla sequi- *tis.*
tur. By those indeed festi-
uall dayes of holy Martyrs
are truly celebrated vvho
follovv the examples of
their vertues. *Fidelis sermo*
(saith S. *Chrysostome*) *& om-* *Chrysost.*
ni acceptione dignus &c. It is a *Tom. 3.*
faithfull saying and worthy *serm. de*
to be receiued by all men, *mart.*
that we should imitate in

** 5   our

our côuerſatiõ thoſe Saints whome we honour with ſolemne veneration.

And by reaſon of the excellent tytles which are moſt worthily giuen to the renowned Queene of heauen in theſe deuout Letanies , wherein her louing Children find exceeding Comfort and Delight ; I haue thought good to entytle this ſmall worke , *The Paradiſe of delights*, or ,*the B. Virgins garden of Loreto*. And for our better Collection , it will not be amiſſe to i-

imagine,

magine, a priuate Garden, adorned with all kind of delightfull flovvers, amiddeſt which the B. Virgin vſeth to vvalke, expecting the viſitation of her deereſt friends, and moſt deuoted Clyents. Vnto the gate of this myſticall garden, and Paradiſe, we muſt approach with all humility, deſiring to be admitted to the pleaſant vievv of thoſe celeſtiall flowers, whoſe dainty odours haue filled the whole world with their fragrant ſmell. And if our re-

queſt

queſt be gratiouſly granted
by the glorious Queene of
Heaué, & her Angels there
attending on her, humbly
proſtrate before her ſacred
feete, vve muſt deſire, that
whatſoeuer we shall gather
out of this delightſome Paradiſe, may be to the ho-
nour & glory of her ſweet
Sonne Ieſus, to the increaſe
of deuotion to her grati-
ous Selfe, and to the eternall happynes of our owne
ſoules. Then may we begin
vvith the firſt flovver of
this heauenly Garden, or

the

the firſt vvord of theſe
deuout Letanies *M A-*
R I A, the moſt venerable
name of the euer Bleſſed &
moſt happy Virgin *Mary*,
of which we may frame our
meditation; imploring firſt
her dayly ayde and aſſiſ-
tance in the manner following.

ORA-

ORATIO SODALITATIS
a singulis in admissione recitanda.

SANCTA Maria, Mater Dei & Virgo, Ego N. N. te hodie in Dominam, Patronam, & Aduocatam eligo; firmiterǵ statuo ac propono, me numquam te derelicturū, neǵ contra te aliquid vmquam dicturum, aut facturum; neǵ permissurum vt à meis subditis aliquid contra tuum honorem vmquam agatur. Obsecro te igitur, suscipe me in seruum perpetuum: adsis mihi in actionibus omnibus meis, nec me deseras in hora mortis. Amen.

THE

THE PRAYER
VSED TO BE

said by those, that be admit-
ted into the Sodality.

BLESSED Virgin Ma-
ry, Mother of God,
I N. N. do this day choose
thee for my Lady, Patro-
nesse, and Aduocate; and
I do firmely purpose & de-
termine, neuer to forsake
thee; nor euer to speake, or
do any thing against thee;
nor at any tyme to suffer
any thing to be done a-

against

gainſt thee, by thoſe that be vnder my care. Therfore I moſt humbly beſeech thee, to receaue me into thy perpetuall ſeruice and protection; be preſent with me in all my actions; and forſake me not in the houre of death. Amen.

THE

THE PARADISE
OF DELIGHTS.
OR
The B. Virgins Garden of Loreto.

THE I. MEDITATION.

Of the Venerable, and sacred Name of the most B. Virgin, MARIA.

MANY pious and deuout consideratiõs of the mysticall significa-tion of this most ve-nerable Name, *Maria*, haue beene

A   with)

with very great reuerēce set down
by the holy Fathers : and with
no lesse diligence learnedly colle-
&ed by the Reuerend Father *Cani-*
sius , in his memorable worke *Of*
the sacred Virgins prayses: which for
so much as at this present serue to
our purpose, we may not vnsitly
reduce to three .

First , *Maria,* is as much as
to say *Stella Maris, Illuminata* , or
Illuminatrix , that is, Starre of the
Sea , or North Starre, one that is
illuminated , or giueth light to
others. Secondly, *Maria* is *amarum*
mare, a bitter sea , or sea of bitternes . And thirdly, she is *Domina,*
Lady, or Mistresse . Out of the
which we may frame three points
in this manner .

1. How fitly this sacred Name
is deriued from *Light* ; and as the

North-ſtar is known by the name of the Sea-ſtarre, becauſe thereby the wandering Marriners direct their courſe, the better to attaine vnto their hoped and pretended Hauen: ſo this Beautious Queen of light in the Catholike Church is placed, whoſe radiant beames of vertuous life & heauenly conuerſation drawes the eyes of all thoſe who deſire to arriue at the happy Hauen of eternall bliſſe; which being fixed vpon her vnchangeable light, muſt needs eſchew the dangerous ſhipwracke of this wicked world, vnles they willfully forſake the infallible direction of ſo faire a Starre, and blindly run theſelues againſt the vnhappy rockes of vtter ruyne, and euerlaſting Death.

2. Moreouer ſhe is ſayd to be

Illumi-

Illuminata, endued with light, and this by reason of the diuine knowledge of most high and heauenly Misteries, the which so firmely and vndoubtedly she did beleeue, that not vnworthily she deserued to heare, *Beata qua credidisti*, blessed art thou who hast beleeued . And as all the beautifull stars do participate their borrowed light which we behold from the bright shyning lamp of the world the Sunne, according to their capacity and greatnes : euen so this sacred Queene being neerest vnto the bright Sunne of Iustice Christ Iesus, and most capable of his Celestiall influences , and heauenly blessings, did participate so much of his diuine light, that rightly she may be called *Illuminata*, indued with light .

Further-

Furthermore she is sayd to be *Illuminatrix*, one who giueth light vnto others : For that indeed is one of the chiefest effects of true vertue, as our Blessed Sauiour not obscurely did insinuate vnto his louing disciples, when he sayd, they were *Lux mundi*, the light of the world, and presently did an nexe their proper office and function, *Luceat lux vestra coram homi nibus* : let your light shine before men. This, I say, is a rare effect of true vertue, not only to be lightsome, yea delightsome in it selfe; but also to shine & giue light vnto others. And this being more apparant in the B. Virgin then in all other Saints togeather, I think none will deny, but that in a speciall manner, and that most fitly she hath this diuine *Epitheton* of

Matt.5.

A 3   *Illumi-*

Illuminatrix, one that giueth light vnto others.

2. The second Etimology, or deriuation of this Bleſſed Name *Maria*, is *amarum mare*, a bitter ſea, or ſea of bitternes, which well expreſſeth the ſorrowfull eſtate of the B Virgin, in the depth of her exceſſiue griefe, that ſhe ſuffered at the foot of the Croſſe, when with watry eyes, and moſt heauy hart, ſhe did behold her louing Sonne, the author of life, yea life it ſelfe wraſtling with death, euen till death: Which dolefull ſpectacle did fill her tender hart with whole floudes of ſorrow, whoſe bitter panges (as many holy Fathers haue left written to vs) did leaue her more then martyred. In which almoſt deadly agony, and ſtrong encounter with a ſea of

griefe,

griefe, we may behould this glittering Starre, almost ouerclouded with the thicke mist of grief, yet yeelding a most beautiful light by reason of her constant fortitude; notwithstanding we cánot choose but say, *Magna est velut Mare contritio tua; quis medebitur tui?* Thy Contrition or sorrow is like vnto a sea; who shallbe able to comfort thee? The abundant teares of *Iacob* for his murthered *Ioseph*, the vncessant griefe of *Anna* for her wandering Pilgrime, the harty sighes of *Ionathas* for his louely *Dauid*, the inward throbs of *Dauid* for his rebellious *Absalom*, the pittifull sobs and rufull lamentations of *Ieremias* for his sinnefull people, may well be shaddows (& but shaddowes) of her griefe.

O sacred Queen, in the mid-

Thren. cap. 2.

Gen. 37. Iob. 10. 1. Reg. c. 20. 2. Reg. 18. & 19. Thren. per totú.

dest

dest of these bitters stormes, shall I yet presume to call thee beautifull? Me thinkes I heare thee say with mourneful *Noëmi, Nolite vocare me Noëmi, sed vocate me Mara, quia amaritudinibus valde repleuit me Omnipotens*. Call me not *Noëmi*, that is to say *beautifull*, but call me *Mara*, that is *bitter*, because the Almighty hath filled me abundantly with bitternes.

Rutb. 1.

Another reason also may be why she should be compared to a bitter sea. Because as the Red sea prooued most bitter vnto *Pharao* & his wicked army, miraculously withstanding their passage, and hindring their pursuit to the great comfort & strengthening of the children of God, and to their own vtter ruine and destruction : So this B. Queene is a sea of bitternes

vnto

vnto the Diuell and his damned spirits (figured in that obstinate Tyrant & his impious followers) who like roaring lyons, neuer cease to persecute the chosen and beloued Children of God, seeking whome they may deuoure. In whose strong defence the powerfull Virgin is alwayes ready at hand, whose only Name is most terrible vnto them, and for these respects, she is most iustly intitled *amarum mare*, a bitter Sea.

3. Then lastly *Maria*, is as much as *Domina*, Lady, or Mistresse: & with great reason, for indeed she was euer Lady & Mistresse ouer all her actions, making alwayes her inward thoughts keep a most perfect cócord with her outward deedes; and both the one and the other directly to tend to the grea-

A 5   ter

ter honour and glory of God, the true and chiefest scope of all her vertuous endeauours.

Besides, she may be sayd to be *Domina*, a Lady, a powerfull Princesse, or mighty Empresse, by reason of the great power and authority she hath with her sweet Sonne, to help and succour sinners, as most deuoutly S. *Bernard* doth acknowledg, when he sayth *Amplectamur Mariæ vestigia, & deuotissima supplicatione beatis illius pedibus prouoluamur: teneamus eam, nec dimittamus donec benedixerit nobis, potens est enim*. Let vs imbrace the sacred footstepps of Blessed Mary, and with most deuout supplication, let vs fall at her blessed feet, let vs take hold on her, and neuer let go, vntill she vouchsafe to grace vs with her blessing, for

she

Beru. ser. in Apo. c. 12.

she is powerfull.

Thus hauing somewhat dif-
couered the hidden treafure wrap- The
ped in this happy Name of *Mary*; fruit of
it followeth that we ftirr vp our Meditation.
defires and inflame our harts with
moft feruerous deuotion and true
loue towardes fo beautifull a Lady. What foule in danger of eternall fhipwracke, beaten with the
rough billowes of finne, & threat-
ned with the furging waues of in-
ftant death, would not open his
deafe eares, and hearing the comfortable voyce of S. *Bernard* giue
attentiue eare, whileft he fayth,
Refpice ftellam, voca Mariam, looke
vp man that art in perill, view this
beautifull Star, call vpon the bleffed Name of *Mary*. What man fo
wretched; who hauing crucifyed
her only Sonne by his manifold

finnes

sinnes & grieuous offences, would
not run to the foot of the Crosse
where this sorrowfull Mother
standeth, and weep floods of tears
for his misdemeanour, and by her
powerfull intercession obtayne
forgiuenes of them . What sinfull
wight in distresse and misery ,
would not fly vnto so powerfull a
Lady, to obtaine new strength &
greater forces whereby to master
his vnbridled appetits , and ouercome his disordered passions ? Finally who would not be seruant
to so mighty a Princesse ? who
would not be suppliant to so louing a Mother , and wholy deuoted to so beautifull a Queene ?

Heerupon I wil in most humble manner desire the glorious
Queen of heauen, that henceforth
by her motherly help I may so keep

The Col-
loquium.

myne

myne eyes fixed vpon the bright
beames of her shining vertue, that
I vtterly hate all workes of darkenes, and so drown my soule in the
flowing streames of deuotion, that
I may wash away al the staynes of
my former offences , and neuer
more offend Almighty God : yea
that I may alwayes fly vnder her
protection, & that she wil vouchsafe to guard and defend me; *Sub
tuum præsidium confugimus sancta
Dei genitrix*, vnder thy protection
we flye , O holy Mother of God.
To conclude this Meditation ,
let vs with a firme and resolute
purpose dedicate our selues wholy vnto her, in all our necessityes
haue confident recourse vnto her,
and to the best of our powers ,
imitate her excellent heroical vertues , as the most true token of

our

our loue, and most louely pledg
of our endles friendship . For the
better obteyning whereof, let vs
heere deuoutly recite the *Salue
Regina* , or *Aue Maris Stella* ,
which in this place is more proper .

THE II. MEDITATION.

*Of the rare sanctity of the Blessed
Virgin .*

THREE famous workes we
read to haue beene most curiously accomplished by the wise
King *Salomon* in the old Law ,
which if we consider as types and
figures of what our true *Salomon*
Christ Iesus did afterward fullfill
in his blessed Mother , they will
help vs somewhat to declare the
vnspea.

vnſpeakable greatnes of the rare ſanctity of the holy mother of God which is indeed ſo far beyond all humane reach, as the wits & beſt vnderſtandings muſt be forced with S. *Auguſtine* to cry out, *Quid dicam de te paupere ingenio?* What can be ſayd of thee by the weake wit of man? Where the high conceits of learned S. *Auguſtine* came ſhort; vvhere the golden eloquence of fluent S . *Chryſoſtome* vvas not inough; vvhere the graue ſentences of renovvned S. *Ambroſe* craue pardon; vvhere the famous workes of learned S.*Hierome* confeſſe their weaknes; the piercing eye of enlightned *S . Anſelme* dazeleth ; the hony-flowing ſtile of Holy S. *Bernard* is dryed vp; the deuout hart of ſeraphicall S. *Bonauenture* is conſumed ; finally, where

where al the whole troope of worthy Writters doe acknowledge themselues vnable to declare thy vnspeakable prayse, I must needs say with S. *Augustine*: *Accipite itaq; quascumq; exiles, quascumq; meritis tuis impares, gratiarum actiones*, accept of these how euer so slender prayses, how euer so vnequall, vnto thy worthy merits.

Serm. 18. de Sanctis.

1. The first worke of this forenamed King, registred in holy Writ, is the building of the famous Temple of *Ierusalem*, which both for great cost and excellent workmanship may well be accoūted the Mirrour of all Ages, an earthly Heauen, where God himselfe chose to dwell, and of the which we read, *Nihil erat quod non auro tegeretur*, there was nothing that was not couered with gold.

3. Reg. 2. 6.

gold. If now we turne our eyes to
the sacred Temple of the Sonne
of God, to the diuine Tabernacle
of the Holy Ghost, and secret clo-
set of the blessed Trinity, the humble Virgin *Mary*, we shal find her
a worke beyond all admiration;
wrought by the eternall Wisedom
of Almighty God; adorned with
all kind of vertue; enriched with
aboundance of diuine grace, and
prepared as an vnspotted veyle,
wherein God himselfe should be
inwrapped, that so indeed she
might become the sacred Temple
of God, so enlightned with grace,
so inflamed with Charity, that al
the world might see & beare witnes, that *Nihil erat quod non auro
tegeretur*, there was nothing in
her, that was not couered with
golden Charity. Neither was the

B   famous

famous Temple of *Hierusalem*, e-
uer so frequented as is this Holy
Temple of God, because as S. *Ber-*
nard witnesseth, *omnibus sinum mi-*
sericordiæ aperit, vt de plenitudine
eius accipiant vniuersi : She layeth
open her mercifull breast vnto all,
that of her great aboundance euery one may take part.

2. The second worke of admiration recorded in the holy Scripture, we find to be a stately Pallace that King *Salomon* erected for
his owne vse. And this was finished by him, and brought to full
perfection in thirteen yeares. But
Wisedome it selfe built the house
of which we heere speake, and for
himselfe, *Sapientia ædificauit sibi*
domum, Wisedome built himselfe
a house, of which the Prophet *Isay*
spake when he sayd : *Erit præpara-*

tus

tus mons domus Domini in vertice
montium: There shallbe a moun-
tain prepared for the house of our
Lord in the top of Mountaynes.
Which words S. *Gregory* the great
expoundeth of the Blessed Virgin
thus: *An non mons sublimis Maria,*
quæ vt conceptionem æterni verbi at-
tingeret, meritorum verticē vsq; ad
solium Deitatis erexit: Is not this
Virgin a high & lofty mountayn,
who to reach to the Conception
of the Sonne of God she raysed the
height of her merits aboue the
quirs of Angels vnto the thron of
God. And as by the mountaine is
signifyed *Perfection*, she being placed in the top of mountaynes, giueth vs to vnderstand of how
great perfection and rare sanctity
she was, & is aboue al other Saints
and Angels: and all this the diuin

B 2   Wise-

in Reg. 1.

Wisedome had brought to passe in the space of thirteene yeares; for she was not full fourteene, when she was chosen the Mother of God.

Behold then, O my soule, this stately Pallace, ascend this holy mountaine, admire the diuine workemanship of all, and euery part of this famous building, and thou wilt be forced to say *Digitus Dei est hic*, this worke could only be done by the finger of God.

Exod. 8.

The third worke of fame, mentioned in Holy Writ, was a stately Throne, which King *Salomon* built for himselfe, & wherein he gloryed very much, of which the holy Scripture auerreth : *Non est factum tale opus in vniuersis regnis*: The like peece of worke was not made in the vvorld : it

vvas

was of Iuory, couered with the
best gold ; it was beset with princely Lyons in diuers places, and
there were six steps to ascend vnto it . By the Iuory Throne couered with beaten gold is signifyed the Blessed Virgin, by reason
of her chast purity , and the most
beautifull lustre of her golden
Charity . The six stepps signify
six vertuous acts, by which we
must ascend into the Blessed Virgins fauour , signifyed by these
Letters of her venerable Name
Mirjám, for *Sochath*, the Hebrew
word. The stepps be these ; *Mag-*
nanimity, *Inuocation Reuerence*, *I-*
mitation. *Affection*, and *Memory* of
her. *Magnanimity* bringeth forth a
firme & constant *Resolution* to be
truly hers. *Inuocation*, calleth vnto
her for ayde and succour , for the

B 3   better

better performance of this good
purpose. *Reuerence* cauſeth a deſire
of *Imitation*. *Imitation* breeds loue
and affection . *Affection* keepes a
perpetuall memory of what we
loue: & *Memory* is both a watchfull aduiſer of what we haue pro-
miſed, and a certaine Note-booke
of what we haue receaued.

These be the ſhaddows which
may in ſome ſort giue vs to vnderſtand the admirable ſanctity of
the euer Bleſſed Queen of Angels
and holy Mother of ſinners . For
greater was the Sanctity of this
excellent Virgin, then the ſanctity
of all Saints and Angells , iointly
conceaued , as both Fathers , and
Deuines do auerre. *Ceteris per par-*
tes, Maria autem ſe infudit tota gra-
tia plenitudo, ſayth *S. Hierome*: To
other Saints grace was giuen by

pàrts,

parts, but to this sacred Queene, all fullnes of grace was at once infused. And therefore most worthily she was saluted by the Angel when he brought his heauenly Embassage *Gratia plena*, full of grace, that of her fullnes (as before I sayd out of S. *Bernard*) we might all participate. Luc. 1.

Hauing thus by these three considerations grafted in our harts and minds the vnspeakable greatnes of her imcomparable sanctity and fullnes of grace, it resteth that as little children & tender Infants we haue recourse vnto her, who is louing, and therfore will not deny vs; who is our Mother, and therefore cannot be forgetfull of her poore distressed children, who with true deuotion seeke her. Let vs therefore cry, and call, *Sancta*

Maria ora pro nobis , Holy Mary
pray for vs. *Monstra te esse Matrem,*
shew thy selfe a Mother. And the
better to incline her louing hart ,
that she may shew her selfe a care
full Mother, let vs shew our selues
true & obedient children, giuing
attentiue eare vnto the diuine sentence, and healthfull counsell of S.
Peter : Quasi modo geniti infantes
rationabiles, sine dolo , lac concupisci-
te . As new borne children reasonable, without deceipt, desire yee
milke : not sweet alluring milke
of vayne pleasure & worldly va-
nityes , but the true nourishing
milke of a pure & vnspotted life ;
the delightsome milke of deuout
loue to the B . Virgin, in which
we may increase vnto eternall
happines .

　　　All haile , O sacred Virgin,
full

full of grace the Mirrour of Sanctity, and patterne of all perfection : Behould I most vnworthy of
al thy Children do heer prostrate
my selfe at thy feet, desiring from
the bottome of my hart that thou
wilt vouchsafe to take me vnder
thy protection, and with the a-
bundance of thy gracious fauours
so to enrich my needy soule, that
it may be gratefull vnto thy beloued Sonne, & pleasing vnto thee.
And being honored with so great
and high a Title as to be called
Thyne, I may endeauour to the vt-
termost of my power so to behaue
my selfe, that I may in all my actions shevv my selfe a true child of
such a Mother. Amen. *Salue Regina*.

*Collo-
quium.*

B 5 THE

THE III. MEDITATION.

Sancta Dei genitrix ora pro nobis.
Holy Mother of God , pray
for vs .

THIS most excellent Title of
Mother of God is giuen to the
Blessed Virgin, by the holy Euan-
gelists in diuers places. S. *Matthew*
recounting the genealogy of our
Lord and Sauiour Iesus Christ ,
deriueth it from *Abraham* , and
bringeth it to *S . Ioseph* , Spouse
of the Blessed Virgin , *De qua na-*
tus est Iesus, qui vocatur Christus ;
of whome was borne Iesus who
is called Christ. S *Iohn* speaking
of the wedding in *Cana* of *Gala-*
lee , sayth : *Erat mater Iesu ibi*, The
Mother of Iesus was there . And

at

at the death of our Blessed Sauiour making mention of her constant fortitude at the foot of the Crosse writeth : *Stabat iuxta Crucem Iesu Mater eius.* Iesus his Mother stood at the foot of the Crosse. In the Acts of the Apostles, S *Luke* also honoureth her with the same renowned title of the *Mother of God,* all which being inuincible testimonyes need no further proofe.

1. First then, I wil consider how this excellent title of *Mother of God,* is the chiefe ground & foundation of all her rare, and singular prerogatiues. Why should this heauenly Queen be called, and be both Mother & Virgin ? Because so it was fit for the B. Mother of God. Wherefore preserued from all spot, both of actuall and originall sinne? Because she was the B.

Mother

Mother of God. Why replenished
with grace aboue all other Creatures? For the same reason that
she was Mother of God . Why
more Holy then all Saints & Angells togeather? Because such sanctity was agreable to the renowned title of Mother of God. She
was elected the deuine Tabernacle of the most Highest , *Et sancti-*
ficauit Tabernaculum suũ altissimus ,
& thus he sanctifyed his holy Tabernacle. This most noble Title
therefore being giuen her, by reason of her profound humility, the
ground of all vertues, was the beginning of all the rest her singular fauours.

2. But to diue a litle further into botomles depth of this match-
lesse Title ; let vs consider the
greatnes therof. If there could be
                                 found

found some noble Lady on earth, whose Father should excell all the world in power, riches and authority; whose Sonne did go beyond all creatures in wisedome wealth, and nobility; and lastly whose Spouse did equall them both in all noble acts and vertuous proceedings: if such a Lady could be found for her singular vertues and rare qualityes, worthy to be acknowledged of such a Father, to be honoured by such a Sonne, and to be beloued of such a Spouse; what titles could this gracious Queene be honoured with, but such as both by Father, Sonne, & Spouse must needs be excellent? Consider then the euer Blessed & most happy Virgin *Mary*, daughter vnto Almighty God, Mother to his only Sonne, and Espoused

to the Holy Ghoſt; who for her
profound humility, Angelicall
chaſtity, moſt burning Charity,
and the reſt of her admirable vertues, is moſt worthily and tender-
ly beloued of them all. And ſhall
we not thinke they would honour
her with ſuch a title, as might
both anſwere the greatnes of them
that gaue it, and be moſt honourable to her that ſhould receaue it?
Yea doubtleſſe. And vvhat title
could this be but, *Sancta Dei Geni-*
trix, Holy Mother of God, *Mater*
Ieſu, Mother of Ieſus.

3. I will then conſider the great
dignity of this moſt noble Title.
For the better vnderſtāding wherof we may contemplate how in
the Eternal Wiſedome of God the
Father, the ſecond perſon of the *B.*
Trinity, was from all Eternity
borne

borne of his Father without a Mother, and at the decreed tyme being to be borne of a Mother without a Father, he made choise of the Blessed Virgin, which was the greatest dignity which any creature could be exalted vnto; as this sacred Queene did most humbly acknowledge and prayse God for the same, in her diuine Canticle, when she did also prophesy how for his cause all people should call her *Blessed*: *Ecce enim ex hoc beatam me dicent omnes generationes*: Behold from henceforth all generations shall call me Blessed. Therefore most worthily this honourable title is placed in the beginning of her Letanyes, as the chiefe ground of all the rest of her noble & deuout appellations. This I say is in the beginning, as the greatest

and

and most worthy to be engrafted
in the harts of all such as desire to
come vnto her, for the sweet milk
of true & cordiall deuotion . And
as little Infants neuer cease crying
and calling after their Mothers, or
Nurses, vntill they see them ; and
neuer content vntill they come to
sucke the full duggs, and imbrace
the paps from whence they draw
their sustenance : So ought we to
cry after this our louing Mother ,
and thinke our selues and soules
robbed vntill we both find her, &
tast the sweet milke of deuotion ,
of which S. *Augustine* spake, when
imagining himselfe betweene the
sacred wounds of Christ, and the
full duggs of the B . Virgin , he
sayd : *hinc pascor à vulnere, hinc la-
ctor ab vbere* . On the one side I am
fed with the precious bloud of
Christ,

Chrift, on the other with the de-
uotion-flowing teats of the Bleffed Virgin; of which two dainties
S. Bonauenture alfo gloryed, and
fayd he made himfelf a moft fweet
potion.

O euer Bleffed, and moft hap- *Collo-*
py Mother of God, who notwith- *quium.*
ftanding fo great a Title, and high
dignity, doft not difdaine to be
the Mother of finners; vouchfafe
to caft thy humble eye vpon a de-
folate and forfaken Orphane, who
cryeth with the Kingly Prophet:
Tibi derelictus eſt pauper; orphano tu
es adiutrix : Vnto thee the poore is
left, and thou wilt be a help vnto
the Orphane : *Ad te ſuſpiramus ge-*
mentes & flentes in hac lachrymarum
valle. Eia ergo aduocata noſtra, illos
tuos miſericordes eculos ad nos con-
uerte. Vnto thee, O facred Queen

C   we

we crye, groaning and lamenting
in this vale of miseryes . Come
therfore, O most Blessed aduocate
turne thy mercifull eyes towards
vs , heare our humble pititions,
Sancta Dei genitrix ora pro nobis : holy Mother of God pray for vs, that
we may escape the manifold dangers of this wicked life; that we
may follow thy diuine and humble footsteps; that we may not only in word and hart acknowledge
thee the Mother of God , but also
come to behould thy glorious
Crowne, which thou hast receaued , answerable to so worthy a
Title and so great a dignity . And
that so we may reioyce with thee
for all eternity, Amen . *Salue Regina &c.*

THE

THE IIII. MEDITATION.

Sancta Virgo Virginum, ora pro nobis.
Holy Virgin of Virgins, pray
for vs.

CONCERNING this *Epi-theton*, we may cóſider three
principal points. Firſt the dignity
of Virginity. Secondly why the
Bleſſed Virgin, is called *Virgo Vir-ginum*, Virgin of Virgins. Laſtly
of what eſteeme virginity is with
God, and our B. Lady.

1. The firſt conſideration of the
excellency of Virginity, we find
expreſſed & counſelled by Chriſt,
when in the myſticall parable of
the three kindes of Eunuches, the last, ſayth he, are ſuch as haue
made themſelues chaſt, for the

Mat. 19.

C 2   king-

kingdom of heauen : and to shew the difficulty in attaining to this excellent vertue, he addeth , *Qui potest capere capiat :* he that can reach vnto it, let him imbrace and follow it . The like proofe we haue of the dignity of virginall chastity , out of another parable, where Christ comparing his holy Church to a good land, whereof one part yealdeth fruit thirty fold, another sixty , and some an hundred : vnderstanding heereby, as some Fathers expound, the chastity of honest wiues, deuout widowes , and vertuous Virgins; amongst vvhich, as the chiefest , Virginity bringeth forth an hundred fold . S. *Paul* also much extolleth the quiet condition of virginall life , because as it is more free from troubles and vexations

of

Matt .13.

Luke 18.

Cypr . de hab.virg. Hier . l. 1. in Iou. August. de sancta virg . c. 44. & 45 .

1. Cor. 7.

of the flesh, so it is an estate more sequestred from earthly pleasures, and therefore more fit for the seruice of God.

Moreouer the excellency of this celestiall gift may be gathered out of the common and continual practise of the Church, and the high esteeme the holy Fathers euer had of this so pretious a iewel. S. *Ambrose* calleth it *Principalis virtus*, the chiefest vertue, adding that no vvit is able to comprehend the dignity thereof, because it exceeds the bondes of Nature, pierceth the clouds, passeth aboue the Stars, goeth beyond the quires of Angels, and taketh the Sonne of God for Spouse. S. *Cyprian* calleth virginity, the flowre of the Church, the grace, and ornament of spirituall fauour, the liuely i-

Lib. 2. de Virg.

De disc. & habit. Virg.

C 3   mage

mage of our Sauiour, deciphring
his sanctity, and the more illustrious portion of the Church and
flock of Christ. I omit others, for
by these we may sufficiently vnderstand the excellency & dignity
of virginity considered in it selfe.

2. Consider why, & with how
great reason the B. Mother of God
is called *Virgin of Virgins*. Where
we may contemplate, how this
sacred Queene was the first, that
euer offered her virginity to God
by Holy Vow; and this either in
the Temple at her Presentation
being of three years of age, where
she was brought vp vntil by diuin
ordination she was espoused to S.
Ioseph : or, as some thinke, she
made this laudable vow (being
preuented with the vse of reason)
in her Mothers wombe. Howso-

euer it was, all with vniforme cō-
sent agree that in this she was the
first, and therfore, most worthily
intitled the *Virgin of Virgins* .

Besides , she may most iustly be
named *Virgin of Virgins*, because in
her vnspotted life she was the most
perfect modell of all vertues , the
most exact patterne of virginity ,
& the most liuely example for all
Virgins, whereby to frame their
actions , and some their liues, as
S . *Ambrose* witnesseth : *Sit vobis*
(sayth he) *tamquam in imagine des-*
cripta virginitas, vitaq; Beatæ Ma-
riæ; de qua velut in speculo refulget
species Castitatis, & forma virtutis .
Let the virginity , and life of the
Blessed Virgin *Mary* be vnto you
as it were engrauen in an image,
from which as in a lookinglasse
the beames of Chastity, and the

Ambr.
l. 2. de
Virg .

C 4   forme

forme of vertue do yeald a moſt beautifull luſtre . For heere you ſhall find , both what to fly , and what to follow. And furthermore to ſtir vp in our harts an earneſt deſire to learne of ſuch a Miſtreſſe to follow ſuch a guide , and leuell our liues to ſuch a rule , he ſetteth forth her vertue and nobility as followeth : *Primus diſcendi ardor , nobilitas eſt magiſtri* , the firſt and chiefeſt motiue of the deſyre of learning , is the nobility of the maiſter: then further: *Quid nobiliùs Dei matre , quid ſplendidiùs ea quam ſplendor elegit ?* What more noble then the Mother of God , what more bright then ſhe whome brightnes hath elected and choſen for his Mother ? She therefore for nobility deſerues the Title of Miſtreſſe, and for her bright ſhining

vertue

vertue worthy the moſt exact patterne of all perfection.

Againe ſhe may be ſayd to be the *Virgin of Virgins*, becauſe vnto the honour of her virginity was ioyned the fruitfulneſſe of a Mother, neuer the like heard of before, neuer the like hoped for heereafter: *Virgo perpetua mater & Virgo* (ſayth *S. Hierome*) a perpetuall Virgin and Mother, or Virgin-Mother, and therfore *Mother of Virgins*, and *Virgin of Virgins*. This is the Eaſterne gate (as *S. Hierom* expoūdeth) alwayes ſhut, alwayes ſhining, mentioned by the Prophet *Ezechiel*, graced with the Title of Mother, yet without detriment or hurt of her vnſpotted virginity, alwayes remayning a Virgin: therfore we ought to call vpon her, and earneſtly to

C 5   cry

cry vnto her, *Sancta virgo Virginū ora pro nobis* . Holy Virgin of Virgins, pray for vs .

3 . The third point may be to consider, how gratefull this vertue is in the sight of God, and how pleasing vnto the Blessed Virgin. So highly esteemed in the sight of God, that being to effect one miraculous work, that should be the wonder of the world, that is, to wrap himselfe in the slender veyle of our humanity, & become man amongst men; he would not take that mantle, but of a Virgin, and a Virgin dedicated vnto himselfe by a perpetuall vow of chastity : *Virginitate placuit, Humilitate concepit*, sayth S. *Bernard* : By virginity she seemed pleasing vnto him, and by Humility she became his Mother, or (as S. *Chrysostom* saith)

by

by Chastity. This is that Altar of Perfumes, called *Altare Thymia-matis*, so pleasing vnto God. This is that dainty Rose of *Saron* springing from the pricky thornes of mortification: this that beautifull lylly of the humble vallies, which admitteth not the least touch or stain: it is that florishing flower of the field, which being roted in the B. virgin, hath now sprouted forth so many branches, that we may wel see and say, *Flores apparuerunt in terra nostra*: Flowers haue appeared in our Land; and being virginall flowers, and flowers of virginity, *Adducentur Regi virgines post eam*: After her, troops of virgens shall be brought to the King of Kinges, to Christ the true Spouse of holy Virgins. For, *Oleum effusum nomen tuum ideo Adoles-*

centulæ dilexerunt te. Thy name, O Lord, is oyle powred out, therefore young virgins loue thee, and following thy diuine steps they cry: *In odorem vnguentorum tuorū curremus*: We will runne after the sweet smell of thy pretious oyntements.

Virginity must also be most pleasing to the B. Virgin: for she knowing best the valew of such dainty flowers, and considering how much they are esteemed by her sweet Sonne, must needs haue a particuler loue therto, and a peculiar care therof that such choice flowers be not defiled, or trampled on by incursiō of bruit beasts. And as one that is the first founder of some holy & Religious Order, hath a most diligent care both to defend & aduance his religious

Institute,

Inſtitute, and taketh great delight in the increaſe and progreſſe therof: ſo the B Virgin being the firſt that euer found out this Angelicall life, the firſt that layd the ground and foundation of vowed Chaſtity, the firſt that diſplayd the banner, vnder which all chaſt virgins ought manfully to fight, & vnder which ſo many haue already winne the goale, gotten the victory, and worne the Crowne : She, I ſay, muſt needs take great delight in the groth of theſe ſo faire flowers of her louing Sonne, as he takes great content in gathering of them. Witnes thoſe beautifull flowers of virginity & conſtant pillars of renowned Chaſtity, tranſplanted by our Sauiours hand from this garden of miſery into the heauenly place of Paradiſe

S. C4

S . *Catherine*, S . *Agatha*, S . *Lucy*,
S . *Agnes*, S . *Cecily*, S . *Winifride*,
and thousands more in like man-
ner, who rather made choice to
loose their liues, then liue to be depriued of so rare a Iewel, and with
the vnspoted *Ermyn* seemed rather
to dye then be defiled .

And thus hauing viewed the
excellency of Virginity in it selfe,
the esteeme it hath in the sight of
God, the prize it beares vvith the
Blessed Virgin : and considering
hovv truly she is *Virgin of Virgins* ;
let vs stir vp in our selues a reuerend loue vnto this excellent vertue, and desire this Virgin of Virgins to pray for vs, that we may
euery one in his estate, and according to his calling imitate this
glorious Virgin, in keeping our
soules and bodyes as the chast ves-

sels

sels and chosen tabernacles of the
Holy Ghost, bringing forth fruit,
some thirty, some sixty, and some
an hundred fold , whereby we
shall be most pleasing to God, beloued of the B. Virgin, and shall
be of the happy number of that
select band, of so many thousands
of most holy & vnspotted virgins
whose priuiledge is to follow the
Lambe wheresouer, and whither-
soeuer he goeth:to which effect let
vs say, *Aue Maris stella &c.*

THE V. MEDITATION.

Mater Christi, ora pro nobis.
Mother of Christ, pray for vs.

HAVING contemplated the
excellent dignity of the Holy
Mother of God, let vs now consider

sider her as *Mother of Christ*, which although it be the same in effect, yet heere we will ponder some particuler points, as it were deriued from this word *Christ*, wherby it may the better appeare what dignity hath redounded to the B. Virgin by being called *Mother of Christ*. Christ therfore, is as much to say, as *Annointed*, because he was indeed the annointed of his Father, *Vnxit te Deus, Deus tuus*, O God, thy God hath annointed thee, and that *Oleo latitia præ consortibus tuis*, with oyle of gladnes aboue thy fellowes. By which diuin vnction is signifyed the abundance of heauenly grace, wherewith the sacred Humanity of Christ was beautifyed aboue al others.

Priests, Prophets and Kings
are

are wont to be annoynted, to signify the particuler grace which
they haue giuen them to perform
their functions : and Christ Iesus
being both Priest, Prophet, and
King, ought by al titles to be *Christ*
that is *Annoynted*, so that by christ
we vnderstand as it were the flowing fountain of all graces, from
whose fullnes we al receaue to sa-
tisfy our wants. Now if we seeke
the head of this diuine fountaine,
we shal find it hath one beginning
in heauen from all eternity of his
Father, another on earth *in fine
temporum*, towards the end of the
world, when being made **Man** he
came to pay the ransome of our
sinnes, and that is his blessed Mother, heere iustly intitled *Mater
Christi*, Mother of Christ.

*Homo in
fine tem-
porum.*

    Let vs now consider foure

propertyes of oyle, which will in
some sort declare vnto vs the
wonderfull effects of this diuine
oyle, whereby the greatnes of the
benefit we haue receaued of the
B. Virgin (who was Mother vn.
to this Annoynted Sonne of God,
and brought him into this world
among vs) may appeare the more.

The first property of Oyle is
to feed vs, and this S. *Bernard* no-
teth, and experience teacheth, &
Christ is he who is our true food,
without whom no soule can liue;
for vnles we eate his flesh, and
drink his bloud, we cannot auoyd
eternall death. The *Israelites* in
the desert were cloyed with the
heauenly *Manna*, and sayd, they
vvere vveary of so light meates;
therefore by the povverfull hand
of Almighty God they vvere soa-

rely

rely chaſtized with fiery Serpents,
the ſtinging wherof could not be
cured, but by the beholding of the
brazen ſerpent: So if we be cloyed
with this diuine food, vvhich the
Bleſſed Virgin hath brought vnto
vs; what can we expect but the
annoyance and byting of fiery
ſerpēts, that is of vnruly paſſions,
diſordered, and diſordinate luſtes
of the fleſh, neuer ceaſing to afflict
vs vntil we caſt our eyes vpon our
B. Sauiour nayled to the Croſſe,
figured in the brazen ſerpent;
which if we do vvith true deuotion, firme fayth, and harty repen-
tance of our ſinnes, we ſhallbe cured, and our ſoule ſhall find it ſelfe
refreſhed vvith the oyle of glade-
nes; for as S. *Auguſtine* ſayth: *de
peccato dolet, & de dolore gaudet*, a
ſinner grieueth for the ſinne com-

mitted, & reioyceth that he is sorrowfull for it .

The second property gathe-
red out of the same *S. Bernard* is,
that it giueth light : and as Christ
himselfe auerreth, he is the light of
the world, *Lux sum mūdi:* I am the
light of the world : therfore who_
soeuer findeth himselfe oppressed
with the darke cloudes of dull ig_
norance, let him haue recourse vnto this diuine lampe of burning
oyle ; and let him with the blind
man call vpon him and say, *Lord
haue mercy on me :* & if most bountiful Iesus shal demand what thou
wouldst haue? Thou shalt answere
Lord, that I may see light . What
light ? The light of thy celestiall
doctrine, of thy heauenly grace, of
thy eternall glory .

Another property of oyle is

to

to cure wounds, as the same Holy
Saint recordeth, of which we haue
an euident proofe out of the parable of the miserable man, who
descending from *Hierusalem* to
Hierico, fell into the handes of
theeues, & being sore wounded,
was cured by oyle and wine. The
precious bloud of Christ, is the
medicinable oyle powred forth
for the cure of our soules, & salue
of our soars; this must be the only
remedy of our bleeding wounds.

The last property of oyle is
(as S. *Gregory* writeth) to swim
aboue all other liquors, which is
the true effect of the grace of
Christ, to make them who are indued therewith to swim aboue al
waters of tribulation; and though
for a tyme they may seeme to be
cast down, because we see them

encoun-

encountred with so many changes
and chances ; yet they will come
vp to their naturall place againe,
& like the flourishing palme grow
the faster vnder the greatest bur-
den, for that is to florish like the
palme, as the Kingly Prophet writeth, *Iustus vt palma florebit*.

These are the foure excellent
propertyes of oyle which do shew
vnto vs the admirable cures that
Christ by his diuine grace vvor-
keth in our soules. And the Blessed
Virgin being called *Mother of
Christ*, if we vvant food to our
soules, we must call to her, that
she would vochsafe to pray vnto
her most louing Sonne to feed vs.
If we be destitute of light, that she
vvould intreate him to enlighten
vs. If we be wounded, that she
would desire him to cure vs. If we

be

be oppreſſed & ready to be drovv-
ned in the depth of miſery, that ſhe
vvould by her Motherly interceſſion pray him to releeue vs vvith
his mercy, that we faile not in his
cauſe, but like vnto oyle, alwayes
ſtriue to aſcend, that ſo we may
ſhew our ſelues to haue participation of that diuine oyle Chriſt,
vnto whoſe euer Bleſſed Mother
we muſt haue recourſe, ſaying:
Mater Chriſti ora pro nobis, Mother
of Chriſt pray for vs.

THE VI. MEDITATION.

Mater diuinæ gratiæ, ora pro nobis.
Mother of diuine grace, pray
for vs.

THIS Diuine Title may be
giuen to the Bleſſed Virgin

D 4   for

for three reasons, which yeald vs
three deuout points of Meditation .

1. The first reason why she is
called *Mother of diuine grace* , is ,
because she is the mother of Christ
who is the author of all graces ,
and fauours, and replenished with
such aboundance of grace , that
not vnfitly he may be called *Grace*
it selfe, whose Blessed Mother was
the Queene of Angells, of whom
we speake , and therefore most
rightly intitled *Mother of Diuine
grace* . For if we consider the me-
nifold benefits which we haue receaued from our Sauiour by his
comming amongst vs , and the a-
boundance of gracewe may draw
from the Holy Sacraments,which
he hath left as fountaines cōtinu-
ally flowing like the seauen-hea-

ded

ded *Nilus*, to which we may run at our pleasure, to refresh our needy and thirsty soules. These things I say, considered, & how he chose the Blessed Virgin to be the long desired ship, that could bring vs in, to our hauen at once such a precious Iewel, as might not only supply al our wants, but also make vs exceeding rich; we may with great reason say, *Mother of diuine grace, pray for vs*.

2. The second reason of this noble Title is, because of the great aboundance of spirituall graces, wherewith this sacred Queen was endowed, as partly we haue sayd in the former Meditations, and after shall more playnely appeare. She was saluted by the heauenly Embassadour *Gratia plena*, or as the Greeke word imports *Singu-* κεχαρι-τωμένη.

D 5 larly

larly gracious, becaule by reafon of her great merits, fhe was aboue all creatures pleafing vnto God , and for this great aboundance of grace produced in her bleffed foule , partly , by the gift of God , and partly by her owne cooperating thereto, fhe may fitly be called *Mother of Diuine grace*.

And if we confider with at-tention how this grace did incre-afe in the Bleffed Virgin, we can-not choofe , but acknowledge her to be the *Mother of diuine grace*. For as many Deuines affir me , the B. Virgin by euery act doubled the grace fhe had before receaued and this for the fpace of all her life which was 72. yeares (as the beft Writers do proue) vvhereby in the end of her life the grace wher-with fhe was indued, vvas almoft

infi-

infinite, & far surpasseth the weak
reach of humane reason to vnfold.
How rightly then do vve call her,
Mother of diuine grace?

3. The third reason of this ap-
pellation is, becaufe fhe is a perpetual Aduocate for vs vnto her beloued Sonne, & doth by her holy
interceffion obtaine grace & pardon for our fins. For as S. *Bernard*
deuoutly writeth, *Quidquid nos
habere voluit, id per Mariam transire
difpofuit:* Whatloeuer God would
haue vs to receaue, that vvould he
haue to paffe through the handes
of the Bleffed Virgin. And for this
caufe fhe is fayd to be as it vvere
the *Necke*, & *Throat* of the Church
and Chrift the *Head*. And as all
that maintaynes the body, paffeth
from the head through the Throat
to the chiefe parts of the body frō

the

the which it is duely diſtributed to all the reſt of the members : ſo all that commeth from Chriſt vnto his Spouſe the Church, he will haue to paſſe through the ſacred handes of the Bleſſed Virgin, vnto the whole body, & euery member of the Holy Church : & therfore we ſay, *Mater diuinæ gratiæ, ora pro nobis*, Mother of diuine grace pray for vs.

Collo-quium. O happy Mother of diuine grace, who by thy profound humility, vnſpotted chaſtity, vnſpeakable charity, and the reſt of thy excellent vertues, didſt bring into the world the author of grace & waſt thy ſelfe repleniſhed with all fullnes therof, and art as a perpetuall conduct to conuay his diuine fauours vnto vs; let vs ſo be ſtrengthned by thy diuine fauour

and

and holy interceſſion, that we may in ſuch ſort ſhew our ſelues true children of diuine grace, that thou maiſt not refuſe to be our Mother, or deny vs to be thy children ; but according to thy Name, as thou art called *Mother of mercy*, for the loue thou ſheweſt vnto repentant ſinners; ſo alſo ſhew thy ſelfe *Mother of diuine grace*, in obtayning for vs ſome portion of that celeſtiall gift which may make vs truly heyrs of that eternal Kingdom, of which this diuine grace is the only pledge, and ſureſt warrant. Amen. *Aue Maria*.

THE

THE VII. MEDITATION

Mater puriſſima, ora pro nobis.
Moſt pure Mother, pray for vs.

IN this Title of Purity we will not ſpeake of the Virginall purity of the Queene of heauen, of which we haue ſayd ſomewhat already in the Title of *Virgin of Virgins*, and ſhall adde more in the Meditations following: but we will now ſpeake of the vnſpotted Purity of the B. Virgin, from the blemiſh and ſtaine of ſinne.

1. Firſt therefore we may conſider, how free this B. Virgin did alwayes keep her ſelfe from the foule and vgly blot of all mortall ſinne. Our firſt Mother *Eue* vvas called the *Mother of the liuing*, but was indeed Mother of the dead,

for

for being seduced and subdued by
the serpents subtilty, she intised &
deceaued *Adam* to sinne also , by
whose disobedience we all remay-
ned subiect not only to death, but
also vnto thousands of miseryes .
But the B. Virgin *mutans Eua no-*
men, changing the name of *Eue* ,
did alwayes remayne vnited with
God , and so crushed and bruized
the Serpents head, that withal his
crafty guiles and subtile trickes he
could neuer supplant this gracious
Queene, to giue but the least consent vnto any vnlawfull act, or to
speake any hurtfull word, or haue
the least thought that might tend
vnto any mortall sinne : but she
alwayes kept her selfe most pure
in thought, vvord, and deed, and
therefore most vvorthily deserues
the shining Title of most *Pure* and

Vnspot-

Vnspotted; giuing vs alfo courage when the foule monfter and ene-my of mankind fhall affault vs, to caft our eyes vpon her, and fay, *Mater puriſſima, ora pro nobis*, moſt pure Mother pray for vs . For the Diuell being exceſſiue proud, and infolent, and hauing beene con-quered and foyled by thisglorious Queene, he dares not ſtay at the inuocation of her facred Name, nor can he endure to heare vs call for her foueraigne ayde and affi-ſtance, vvho is moſt pure, and moſt ready to help all thofe vvho truely call vpon her .

2. The fecond poynt yealdeth vs matter to meditate and ponder, how this pure and vnfpotted Vir-gin-Mother, did not only keep her felfe free from all tainture of mor-tall finne , but did alfo auoyd the

least

leaft blemifh of any venial finne,
into which ordinarily euen the
moft Iuft do fall, and that many
tymes a day, as holy Writ doth
witnes in thefe words: *Septies in
die cadit iuftus, & refurgit*: feauen
tymes a day the iuft man doth fal,
& rife againe, which is to be vn-
derftood of fmal finnes, and light
offences. Neither are they tear-
med light, becaufe we do carelefly
commit them, or make light of
them (for one of them ought not
to be committed to faue the whole
world) but they be fo called, becaufe they be of their own nature
fuch, as they do not extinguifh
the grace of God in the Iuft man,
nor are directly againft Charity,
& therefore may ftand both with
grace and charity, and may the
eafier be forgiuen. Yet I fay from

E   the

the little blemishes that taint euen
the best, this B. Virgin was alwayes free, euer so perfectly vnited with Almighty God, and so
wholy imployed in his diuine seruice, that the least blast of any venial sinne, could neuer stayne the
flourishing beauty of her excellent vertues. This consideration
made S. *Augustine* say, *Cùm de*
Aug. l. *peccatis agitur, nolo de B. Virgine*
de natur. *mentionem fieri,* When there is any
& grat. speach of sinne, I will haue no
cap. 36. mention made of the B. Virgin;
for right well he knew how free
she was, not only from the deadly wounds of mortall sinne, but
also from the least shaddow of a-
ny veniall sinne, and therefore
most pure and worthyly calledv-
pon by that Title, *Most pure Mo-*
ther, pray for vs.

3. The

3 . The third point is to contemplate the vndefiled purity of
the B . Virgin, euen from the generall ſpot of originall ſinne, vnto which all the children of *Adam*
were ſubiect, if they deſcended by
naturall propagation , as this ſacred Queene did ; yet by particular priuiledge was ſhe excepted
from that generall law . For the
infinite wiſedome of Almighty
God did not thinke it fit that ſhe
who was choſen from all eternity
to be the Mother vnto his only
Sonne, ſhould euer be ſayd to haue
been in the power of Sathan. And
therfore with his particular grace
did preuent the effect of the general curſe , whereby our moſt pure
Mother did remaine moſt beautifull in the ſight of God , pleaſing
vnto his Sonne ; and euen from

E 2   her

her first beginning, in her immaculate Conception, espoused vnto the Holy Ghost by heauenly
grace. And by this indeed the
Title of *Most pure* doth fitly agree
vnto her. For we may say she was
pure in that she fled all mortal sin;
yet more pure in that no veniall
sinne could euer taint her; but in
this most pure, that euen from
the spot of originall sinne she was
preserued, and by singular fauour
exempted from that curse, as indeed befitted the chosen Mother
of God.

O most pure, and vnspotted
Mother, cast thy diuin eyes vpon
thy deuout seruants, and let not
the impurity of our former sins,
defile vs. We must all confesse,
we are conceaued the children of
wrath, and borne in wickednes

Collo-
quium.

by

by originall sinne; yet, *Mater pu-
rissima ora pro nobis*, most pure Mother, pray for vs: That as we haue
by Baptisme drowned the one, so
we may, by true Pennance and
Contrition wash away the other,
that being sprinkled with the dew
of diuine grace, and made more
white then snow, we may appear
most ioyfully in the sight of thy
sweet Son, whose pretious bloud
hath beene the medicinable riuer
Iordan, to wash away our Lepro-
sy. Pray for vs, O sacred Queen,
that we may so imitate this thy
Angelicall purity, & be most pure
children of a most vnspotted Mother. Amen. *O gloriosa Domina &c.*

E 3   THE

THE VIII. MEDITATION.

Mater Castissima, ora pro nobis .
Most chast Mother, pray for vs .

VVE haue already in the fourth Meditation spoken of the excellency of the virginity of this powerfull Queene. Now are we to confider the renowned title of her fingular Chaftity, by which we falute her whē we fay, *Most chaft Mother, pray for vs* In this Angelical vertue of Chaftity, I find three degrees, which if we confider how eminent they were all in the B. Virgin, we fhall eafily perceaue how worthily fhe is called *Mater Caftiffima.*

1. The firft degree of Chaftity, is coniugall, that is, fuch as may

be

be kept betwixt man and wife, at least for a tyme, as S. *Paul* counselleth those that be maryed to do, that they might pray the better, and be the fitter for the seruice of God. This degree of Chastity, the B. Virgin had in the highest perfection; for although she were truly despoused to S. *Ioseph*, and was his vndoubted wife; yet as S. *Gregory* sayth, he was but *Custos integerrimæ Castitatis*, the keeper of her most pure Chastity. For as the sacred Text of holy Scripture doth lay open vnto vs, before they euer came togeather the mystery of the incarnation of Christ was knowne, though not as a Mystery; and therfore, as S. *Hierome* writeth, *Celabat silentio, cuius Mysterium nesciebat*, he couered with silence the mystery he

E 4   knew

knew not : So that the B . Virgin was a wife, but alwayes most chast, and therefore called a *Most chast Mother* .

2 . The second degree of Chastity is of holy Widdowes, who after the death of their husbands most earnestly imbrace this heauenly vertue. In this also the B . Virgin was most eminent : for it is very probable that *S . Ioseph* was departed this life before the Passion of our Sauiour. And therfore Christ commended his B Mother to S . *Iohn*, as himselfe witnesseth ; after whose death, the B . Virgin lead a widdowes life, and was the mirrour of all chast Widdowes. Besides she may be sayd to be a Widdow after the Ascension of Christ , in that, she was left as it were, *Viduata colum-*

ba,

ba, a doue without her mate, alwayes groaning, euer mourning
like the forsaken Turtle, vntill
she came to meet him againe in
the happy pallace of eternal blisse:
she therefore was a most chast
Widdovv, and that in a most re-
markable manner.

3. The third and most renovvned degree of this noble Vertue,
is called Virginal Chastity, which
is, vvhen Virgins wholy dedicate
themselues vnto Christ by holy
vow, and take him for their only
spouse, as the B. Virgin vvas the
first that euer did, binding her
selfe by vow of perpetuall chastity to be vvholy and only his;
after whose rare example so many
thousandes of holy Virgins haue
follovved vvith vndaunted courage, and many of them lost their

E 5   liues

liues in the iust defence of this
worthyly esteemed vertue. And
how eminent the B. Virgin was
in this, we may easily gather out
of that which hath beene sayd of
her *Chast Virginity* .

And by these three degrees ,
which we find most eminent in
the B. Virgin, we may easily conceaue with how great reason she
is intitled, *Mater castissima* , most
chast Mother. We must therefore
mooue our selues with an earnest
desire, & louing affection toward
this vertue, and no lesse towardes
the B. Virgin, who so greatly ex-
celled in it. And with these desires

Collo-
quium.

we must fall downe before this
chast Mother to implore her ayde
and help, for the better accomplishing what we desire, and say *Vir-*
go singularis, inter omnes mitis , nos

culpis

culpis solutos , mites fac & castos : Virgin without peere, & amongst all others most mild , we being cleansed from our sinnes by thy holy intercession , make vs also both mild & chast . Amen . Then we may conclude, to this effect, with the deuout Hymne , *Aue Maris stella* .

THE IX. MEDITATION.

Mater Inuiolata , ora pro nobis.

Vndefiled Mother, pray for vs .

BY this most worthy Title is signifyed vnto vs the admirable combination of the dignity of Virginity , ioyned with the honour of *Mother*; a thing naturally impossible, and only by the omnipotent hand of God to be broght

to

to paſſe . Therefore in this Title
we are to conſider this wonderfull worke of admiration, and to
prayſe the diuine prouidence of
Almighty God ; who to prepare
our hard hart to the great myſtery
of the Incarnation of his only
Sonne, would beginne with this
admirable Conception, long before diſcouered by the holy Prophet *Iſay* , *Ecce Virgo concipiet* , *&*
pariet filium : Behold a Virgin ſhal
conceaue, and bring forth a Son,
that is , neither the ſtrang conception, nor deſyred birth of that
miraculous Sonne , ſhould any
way impeach or diminiſh the dignity of Virginity, & yet he ſhould
bring with him the fecundity of
a Mother : therfore the ſayd Prophet as it were inuiting vs to admiration , ſayth , *Ecce* , behold .

And

And the holy Prophet *Hieremy* called it *Nouum*, a new thing, as indeed it was both ſtrang & new. She was a chaſt Virgin, yet a fruitfull Mother, and therfore a Virgin-Mother, *Mater inuiolata*, an vndefiled Mother. For how could ſhe be defiled, who conceaued by the worke of the Holy Ghoſt? how could ſhe be ſpotted, who as S. *Ambroſe* teacheth, *Corpus ſine corporis contagione concepit*, conceaued the ſacred body of Chriſt without any contagion of her owne.

Let vs therefore by this both prayſe the goodnes of God, for choſing the B. Virgin an inſtrument of this diuin miracle of miracles; and alſo congratulate our happieſt Queene, that ſhe was elected to ſo high a dignity, & of ſo great

Collo-quium.

great esteeme in the sight of God, and so the more powerfull to help vs, when we say, *Mater inuiolata ora pro nobis*, vndenied mother, pray for vs. For calling vpon her by this diuine Title, is as much as to say, for the loue of that diuine worke of admiration, wherin thou wert made Mother of God remayning a Virgin, pray for vs. For the ioy thou didst conceaue in this diuine Mystery, pray for vs. In honour of this vnspeakable combinatió of the venerable title of Mother, with the shinning lustre of virginity, pray for vs: & obtayne, that by thy powerfull prayers and holy intercession we may be worthy to conceaue thy Blessed Sonne sweet Iesus in our soules. Amen. *Salue Regina*.

THE

THE X. MEDITATION.

Mater Intemerata , ora pro nobis .
Vntouched Mother , pray for vs .

BY this *Epitheton*, we muſt có-ſider another excellent pro-perty of the B. Virgins chaſt re-nowne . For as in the former title we did contemplate how ſhe was Mother, yet without all ſtayne of her angelicall purity : ſo heere we may ponder the vnſpotted beauty of her chaſt virginity, not any whit diminiſhed , or ſo much as touched vvith that wonderfull acceſſe of this new title of *Mother*, and therfore moſt aptly ſhe is in-titled, *An vntouched Mother* .

The Lilly which is the chief ſymbole and figure of Chaſtity , is of it owne nature of moſt dain-

ty

ty condition . To the eye most
pleasing, to the smel most fragrāt;
but if it come to be handled , or
touched, it is so soon bleamished,
that it looseth both the exquisite
smell , and the excellent beauty :
so the renowned vertue of chast
Virgins will not admit the least
touch of any earthly affection, &
worldly loue, without a perpetuall stayne and vtter disgrace of so
rare a vertue . And becáuse this
beautifull *Lilly of the valleys*, the
B. Mother of God, was *Lilium inter spinas* , a Lilly a midst thornes;
yet euer vnspotted, vndefiled, &
vntouched, therefore she is called
Mater intemerata . Of this most
pure Virgin the holy Catholike
Church singeth: *Benedicta & vene-
rabilis es Virgo Maria, quæ sine tactu
pudoris inuenta es Mater Saluatoris.*

Blessed

Bleſſed & venerable art thou, O
Virgin Mary, who without any
touch of thy chaſtity didſt becom
the Mother of God .

    Let vs ſee further how this
admirable worke was effected .
She, as the moſt beautifull flower
of virginity, was repleniſhed with
great aboundance of grace , and
ſo ſaluted by the heauenly Em-
baſſadour , when he denounced
vnto her that ſhe ſhould become
Mother of God : yet our ſacred
Queene replyed, in the behalfe of
her vnſpotted purity, asking how
that could come to paſſe , being
ſhe was a vowed Virgin ? To
which the Angell anſwered , that
it was a worke to be accompli-
ſhed by the diuine help of the holy Ghoſt ; and therefore the child
ſhe was to beare, was to be the

F Sonne

Sonne of God . The humble obedient Virgin, diuing in the depth
of her owne nothing , answered
withall submission, and most perfect resignation, *Ecce Ancilla Do-*
mini, fiat mihi secundum verbum tu-
um : Behould the hand mayd of
our Lord, let his wil be fulfilled in
me, according to thy speach. And
so by this humble consent, by this
admirable *fiat*, she became indeed
Mother of God. Behold then how
she was made Mother , yet with
the integrity of her virginall chastity . By a word, with a *fiat*, the
heauens were created, the Sunne,
the Moone, and all the glittering
light of heauen ; by a word, with
a *fiat* the earth was made, the Sea,
the Land, and all thinges els that
sea and land contaynes : now (O
miracle of miracles) by one word
by

by one *fiat* of a Virgin, God himfelfe is made Man, conceaued
by a chaſt conſent, borne of a
pure and vnſpotted Mother, *Ma-*
ter intemerata.

O diuine Mother, let the
ſweet perfumes of this Angelicall
vertue, ſo enter into our ſenſes, ſo
wrappe our vnderſtanding, and *Collo-*
quium.
ſo rauiſh our will, that we may
admit no other thought, or ima-
gination, no other affections or
deſires, but ſuch as may bring
forth this ſweet ſmell, this fragrant perfume of purity; that we
may be gratefull in the eyes of our
Creator, pleaſing in the preſence
of our Redeemer, and in thy ſight
worthy to be beloued. Amen *Aue*
Maris ſtella.

F 2   THE

THE XI. MEDITATION.
Mater amabilis, ora pro nobis.
Louely Mother, pray for vs.

MANY causes may be assigned & many reasons found why the B. Virgin is sayd to be *louely*, which I will endeauour to reduce to three general heads, because I will not exceed my wonted breuity.

1. The first cause or reason, which both maketh her louely, & moueth vs to loue her, may be her excellent beauty, which did so abound in this *louely* Queen, as the like hath not beene found in any other. For as our Sauiour was the most beautifull of men according to the kingly prophesy, *Speciosus forma prae filijs hominum,*

beauti-

beautifull and comely in shape beyond the sonnes of men : so the
B. Virgin was most beautifull of
all the daughters of women; that
whosoeuer should behould them
both, might say, she could not be
Mother, but of so fayre a Sonne,
nor he Sonne, but of so beautifull
a Mother. And this beauty of the
B. Virgin (of externall beauty
& comlines we speake) did consist in a most perfect proportion
of all the lineaments of her sacred
body, whereby she was *pulcherima
mulierum*, the most beautifull of
women, and therfore most *louely*
in that respect. Neither was her
virginal comelynes such as vsual-
ly doth stir vp wanton lustes, or
inflame bad desires; but altogeather so far contrary, that who so
should behold the beautifull blush

of her modeſt and virginall countenance, could not choſe , but be
inflamed with moſt chaſt deſires
and feruent loue towardes this
vertuous Queene .

This then may be giuen for
the firſt reaſon of this louely title,
Mater amabilis. And in this beauty I include her grauity in ſpeach,
her modeſty in countenance , her
grace in conuerſation, & the due
proportion of all her actions , being alwayes guided and gouerned
by her inward vertues, of vvhich
heereafter we ſhall haue occaſion
to ſpeake more . *Iudith* being to
worke the ouerthrow of proud
Holofernes, in defence of her citty
and people , adorned and decked
her ſelfe withall the richeſt iewels
and beſt ornaments ſhe had , and
made herſelfe as beautiful as with

her

her beſt skil ſhe could, ouer which
Almighty God caſt a ſplendour,
of which holy Writ telleth vs: *Cui
Dominus quoq; contulit ſplendo-*   Iud. 10.
rem, vnto which beauty our Lord
alſo added a luſtre. And ſhall we
not then thinke of the B. Virgin,
vvhoſe figure *Iudith* did beare,
that after nature had ſhewed her
ſelfe in this admirable worke, that
our Lord alſo added the chiefeſt
grace of her excellent beauty?
How then could ſhe be but *louely*,
and therfore, *Mater amabilis.*

2. The ſecond cauſe, and more
chiefe reaſon of her comelynes
(which ſhall be the ſecond point)
is her invvard beauty, that is, her
excellent vertue, by the vvhich
deſeruedly ſhe may be ſayd tvvice
beautifull, and ſo in the Canticles
ſhe is, and that vvith a kind of ad-

miration , *Quàm pulchra es amica mea, quàm pulchra es* ! Hovv beautifull thou art my beloued, hovv beautifull! Beautifull by reason of her outward comelynes , but much more by reason of her invvard vertues : For *Omnis gloria filiæ Regis ab intus*, all the glory of the Kings daughter is from within.

Heere therfore we must consider the singular grace & comely meeting of all vertues in this gracious Queene ; her profound humility ; her humble obedience ; her shining purity ; her vnspeakable modesty; her burning charity; and most perfect resignation of her selfe into the handes of God , withall the rest of her excellent vertues in due tyme and place, in the best manner, guided by rea-

son, with exact obseruation of e-
uery circumstance, and as it were
Castrorum acies ordinata, an army
of souldiers well ordered . This
considered as an harmony of perfect musicke , where no voyce
misseth his right note and tune,
no instrument iarreth, no sound
out of order , must make vs of
force to stand amazed at the rare
composition of her inward beauty , the singular concord of her
matchles vertues, & thus be moued to loue & affect her most worthy person, wherin we find them
so perfectly vnited, and by which
indeed she is *Mater amabilis* , a louely Mother .

3 . The last generall reason , and
the third point, is to meditat how
much we are beloued of her , and
in how princely and bountifull

manner fhe dealeth with vs . For
nothing moueth more to loue ,
then to know we are beloued, &
fince loue can neuer be repayed
but by loue, feeing fhe hath fhew-
ed her felfe fo louely a Mother vnto vs, we are bound in all gratitude and dutifull refpect, to the
vttermoft of our power, to requite
it . She had but one only Sonne,
whome fhe loued far more then al
the Mothers in the world loue
their children ; yet was fhe content that in his infancy he fhould
be our companion, at his laft fup-
per our food, at his death the price
of our Redemption, and now fhe
continually prayeth for vs, that he
may be our endles ioy, and happines . How could fhe fhevv her
felfe more louing, or hovv more
louely, then like another *Abraham*

to

to offer vp her owne beloued Son
at the commandment of Almighty God, only for our good ? Let
vs therefore louingly and deuoutly say *Mater amabilis ora pro nobis,*
louely Mother, pray for vs.   *O
gloriosa Domina &c.*

THE XII. MEDITATION.

Mater Admirabilis, ora pro nobis.

Admirable Mother, pray for vs.

IN this admirable title we must
first suppose the force of this
world *Admirable*; for it doth import some strange and wounder-
full thing which is cause of admiration : and from hence miracles
do take their name, because being beyond our naturall reach ,
they make vs admire. But if we
                              well

confider the vertuous life, the miraculous death or departure, & the exceffiue glory of the B. Virgin, we fhall not only fee hovv iuftly this Title is applyed vnto her, but alfo vvith how great reafon we may fay, *Mater admirabilis*, admirable Mother pray for vs.

1. Firft then, in a briefe and compendious manner, we are to call to mind the admirable life of the B. Virgin. Admirable was her cōception, obtayned by prayer and vow, denounced by an Angel, of aged & barren parents, without the fpot of originall fin: all thefe thinges are great caufes of admiration. Admirable was her ftrang Natiuity, borne in the field (as S. *Iohn Damafcen* witneffeth) in a certaine grange of her Fathers, among the fweet tu-

ned

ned notes of innocent bleating
Lambes, as one who vvas to be
the Mother to the immaculate
Lambe of God, defigned to be
flaine for ranfome of vs all; or as
one who vvas to bring vs the true
fheep-heard of our foules, vvho
would haue moft tender care of
vs. Admirable, in that fhe vvas
preuented vvith the vfe of reafon
either in her Mothers wombe, or
at the third yeare of her age, whē
fhe vvas offered vp and prefented
in the Temple. Admirable in her
life and conuerfation, and aboue
al admirable in that fhe vvas both
Mother and Virgin. Admirable
alfo in her conftancy, at the foot
of the croffe, admirable in knowledge, in grace, and in all kind of
vertue. Thefe thinges, and the
like confidered, will giue vs perfect

fect vnderstanding how she is indeed *Mater admirabilis*, an admirable Mother.

2. The second point is to ponder the admirable departure of her Blessed soule out of her sacred body, and out of this life. For she liued 72. yeares, dyed not of any disease, or distemper of disordered humors, but of pure loue and longing desire to be with Christ her dearest Sonne, which was an admirable death. Besides, all the Apostles then liuing were miraculously gathered togeather at her departure, and most solemnly performed the dutyes of her exequies. After three dayes, our Sauiour descended from heauen accompanyed with his Quires of Angells, and assumpted her into heauen body and soule, where she

vvas

vvas seated in such maiesty, and crowned with so great glory, there to raigne for euer.

3. The third point, shallbe to admire this Elected Queene of Angells passing through the Blessed company of Virgins, leauing behind her the constant Confessors, glorious Martyrs the holy Apostles, Patriarkes, and Prophets; mounting aboue the nine Quires of Angells, seated aboue the Cherubims and Seraphims in a Royall Throne by her selfe, as best befitted so glorious & admirable a Mother. And if we will at length come to the height of admiration, let vs behould this diuine Empresse vested with the Sunne, crowned with stars, and treading the Moone vnder her victorious feet, that is, in exceeding

great

great glory, anſwerable both to her admirable titles, and ſingular vertues. For as we haue already meditated, ſhe was enriched with more grace and ſpirituall gifts, then al Saints and Angels beſides, and therfore muſt haue a Crown of glory anſwerable thereunto; which muſt exceed the glorious crowns of them all. And by theſe three points we ſee how ſhe was admirable in life, admirable in her departure, admirable in glory, & ſo moſt worthily called *Mater admirabilis*, an admirable Mother.

O moſt admirable, and euer happy Mother, who art in all points ſo much to be admyred; be now vnto vs a powerful aduocate that we may (as far as our weaknes will permit) imitate thy admirable vertues in our life; that

Collo-quium.

vve

we may find comfort at our death
and deserue to receaue a Crown
of glory with thee in heauen for
all eternity . Amen . *O gloriosa
Domina.*

The XIII. Meditation.

Mater Creatoris, ora pro nobis.

Mother of the Creatour, pray
for vs .

MANY of these Titles are
the same in effect, with *Mother of God*; yet we will so consider them, that we may conceaue
some particuler reason of this , &
the like titles , whereby the great
dignity of the B. Mother of God
may the more appeare . For although sometymes we vse to attribute Omnipotency to God the

G   Father

Father, Wisedome to the Sonne,
and Bounty to the holy Ghost;
yet being all but one God, they
are all equally Omnipotent, Wise,
and Bountifull : And because in
their outward actions (as the Deuines speake *ad extra*) they work
inseparably, so that whatsoeuer
the one doth, they are sayd to
worke all three togeather; Creation is as well attributed to the
Sonne, as the Father, and in this
sense the B . Virgin is called *Ma-*
ter Creatoris, Mother of the Creatour . For indeed so he was, since
as *S . Iohn* sayth, *omnia per ipsum*
facta sunt, all thinges were made
by him . Heere therfore we are
to consider how the infinite wisedome of God found out so sweet
meanes to communicate himselfe
to man, as to shut himselfe within

the

the B. Virgins sacred wombe, whereby we worthily say, *Quem cæli capere non poterant, tuo gremio contulisti*: He whome the wide heauens could not contayne, thou hast inclosed in thy sacred womb.

2. Secondly consider, that the B. Virgin being mother of our, & her Creatour, she is the fittest Patronesse for all sinners to chose, that the worke of their creation may not be frustrate; seeing then that God hath created all thinges for vs, and our selues for himself, let vs make recourse to the Blessed Mother of the Creatour of all things, that by her powerfull intercession, we may vse them according to the end for which they were created, & make of them a ladder to clime and ascend to the height of that dignity, for which

G 3   vve

we vvere ordayned by the eternal
Prouidence of God.

3. Thirdly we may contemplat
how Creation is nothing els , but
the making of a thing of nothing;
and this can only be performed
by the Omnipotent hand of God:
we then considering our selues
to be nothing , we may say with
the Kingly Prophet , *Cor mundum
erea in me Deus , & spiritum rectum
innoua in visceribus meis* : Create a
cleane hart in me , O God, and
renew a right spirit in my bowels
since of this nothing of ours, he is
able to make most excellent work
by the sending his diuine spirit a-
mongst vs . For as we see the
scorched fields in the middst of
Summer refreshed by some gentle
shower ; or the face of the earth
after a long and tedious winter,

renew-

renewed by a pleasant spring : so
doth the presence of this diuine
spirit make vs all new againe.
Therefore if we feele our vertues
dying, or our resolution fayling,
let vs not cease to cry, *Emitte spi-*
ritum tuum & creabuntur, & reno-
uabis faciem terræ : Send forth , O
Lord, thy holy spirit, & al things
now turned to nothing wil receaue another being, and thou wilt
renew the face of the earth : and
to obtayne our petition of the
Creatour of all thinges , let vs
not be vnmindfull of his Blessed
Mother , but with this worthy
title say, *Mater Creatoris ora pro*
nobis , Mother of our Creatour
pray for vs.

G3   THE

THE XIV. MEDITATION.

Mater Saluatoris, ora pro nobis.

Mother of our Sauiour, pray
for vs.

THIS most Venerable Title
doth inuite vs to contemplat
a while vpon the sweet name of
Iesus; for Iesus and Sauiour are
the same; and to be Mother of
our Sauiour is to be the Mother of
Iesus : let vs therfore vvith atten-
tion diligently ponder the greatnes of the gift, that our deuotion
towardes the giuer may increase
the more.

1.   First then let vs consider
how vve vvere all lost, in perpetuall boundage, in euerlasting
thraldome and captiuity of sinne,
vntill this B. Mother brought vs
forth

forth a Sauiour , a Redeemer,
vvhose most pretious bloud vvas
the only ransome of our sinnes ,
vvhose death vvas vnto vs life ,
and vvhose bleeding woundes
vvere the only cure and most soueraigne balme of our festred
soules . For darke night she
brought vs cheerefull day ; for a
hard and sharp winter, a svveet &
pleasant spring ; for our mortall
vvounds, immortall medicines ;
for our pining soules,bread of life;
and lastly for all our misery , the
Father of mercyes . This the glorious Angell song vnto the seely
sheep-hards , in the happy night
of his Natiuity, *Natus est vobis ho-*
die Saluator, qui est Christus Iesus :
You haue this day born vnto you
(of the B . Virgin) a Sauiour ,
which is Christ Iesus . Our lost

taſt by this ſvveet Name muſt be
reſtored, for he is hony in the
mouth : our eares accuſtomed to
iarring diſcordes, muſt be reformed by this ſvveet muſicke, for he
is melody in the eare : our harts
oppreſſed vvith grief & ſorrovv,
muſt be repleniſhed vvith ioy, for
he is gladnes in the hart.

2. Secondly to diue yet deeper
into the greatnes of this benefit,
conſider vvhat ioy a poore priſo-
ner vvould find in his hart, if cō-
demned to a moſt ignominious &
cruell death, one ſhould come &
louingly offer him his pardon?
What comfort ſhould one find if
being by ſentence iudged to perpetuall baniſhment, a fauourable
ſentence ſhould recall him, and
place him again in his former honour and ancient dignity? Then

let

let vs apply this to the B. Virgin,
vvho brought vs forth a Sauiour
after the sharp sentence of death,
to pronounce vs a fauourable pardon; and after the doome of perpetual banishment, from the sight
of God, for hauing incurred his
high displeasure, he hath brought
vs backe againe, & made vs Sons
of his heauenly Father, & fellow-
heires in this ovvne kingdome.

3. Thirdly vve are to consider
the great part our B. Lady had in
this happy vvork of our Redemption, being chosen by Gods eternall Wisedome to be his Mother,
and the floyving conduit of all
happynes to vs, that vve might
vvith great deuotion say, *Mater Saluatoris ora pro nobis*, Mother
of our Sauiour, pray for vs.
And vvhat better petition can

we make vnto her, but that vve
may be gratefull for so great a benefit, that now the price of our
Redemption being payd, we neglect not to make our best profit
and commodity thereof, that he
may be truly and indeed a Sauiour vnto vs, as she truely was a
Mother vnto him. For how great
might our ingratitude be accounted, if after so long seeking vs, &
so deare buying vs, we should neglect his bountifull mercyes, and
seeme to be carelesof his vndeser-
ued liberalityes.

Colloquium.

O most Blessed & euer hap-
py Mother of Iesus, assist with thy
holy prayers, we beseech thee, thy
deuout suppliants, that thy sweet
Sonne Iesus may bevnto vs Iesus,
that is a Sauiour. Behold vve cal
vpon thee, Mother of our Sauiour

to

to be saued, Mother of Iesus to be healed, Mother of God to be made his true and faythfull children by thy powerfull intercessió, throgh the infinite merits of the Blessed fruit of thy holy wombe . Amen.

THE XV. MEDITATION.

Virgo Prudentißima, ora pro nobis.

Most prudent Virgin, pray for vs.

THAT we may the better vnderstand the reason why the B. Queene of Angells is called *Most prudent*, we will produce three or foure examples of prudét Matrones in the old Testament, who may seeme to haue borne the type and figure of this prudent Virgin.

1. The

1. The first we read in the booke of *Iudith*, where this vertuous & prudent matron, seeing the extreme affliction of her beloued nation to increase in such sort that the wisest of them were thinking it best to yeald themselues vnto the merciles handes of their proude enemyes; she prudently by the direction of Almighty God behaued her selfe with such prudence and fortitude, that she both foyled her enemies, and got her people a most famous and triumphant victory: for which she was by the high Priest, and chiefest of the people denounced blessed, and all the vulgar sort answered, Amen. This no doubt was an act not only of inuincible fortitude, but also of admirable prudence. But if we turne our eyes

vnto

vnto the sacred Virgin, we shall
find that she hath deliuered vs
from a stronger enemy, preserued
vs from greater danger then temporall death, foyled & ouercome
a prouder foe then *Holofernes*; and
therefore with great reason we
may say , *Tu gloria Hierusalem, tu
latitia Israël, tu honorificentia popu-
li nostri* : Thou art the glory of
Hierusalem, thou the ioy of *Israël*,
thou the honour and renowne of
our Nation. She bedecked with
the pricelesse ornament of vertue,
her soule adorned with the splendor and beames of diuine grace,
and assisted by the potent hand of
Almighty God, came to tread our
ancient enemy Sathan vnder her
conquering feet.

2. The second act of admirable Prudence, we read in the

Heſt. 5.

booke of *Heſter*, how for the good of her Nation, ſhe aduentured to enter before the King, was inuited by his golden Rod, wherwith her great prudéce ſhe ſo wrought the King, that ſhe obtayned not only the liues of her deare Countrymen, but alſo great and ample priuileges for them; yea & ſeuere chaſtizement of thoſe that ſought her, and her Countryes deſtruction. No leſſe the B. Virgin, after Sathan had conſpired the ouerthrow of mankind, entring before the King of heauen, with her profound humility, ſo prudently ſhe behaued her ſelfe, that ſhe became Mother vnto his only Son, who both deliuered vs from eternall perill, and made vs of the happy number of the children of God, and heyres to the kingdom

of

of heauen, which by our disobedience we had lost, and therefore
most worthily she is called *Virgo*
Prudentissima , a most prudent
Vigin.

3.   The third and fourth ex-
ample we haue in *Iahel* & *Abigaël* Iud. 4.
the one vanquishing proud *Sisira*
the fierce enemy of the Iewes; the 1. Reg.
other appeasing the fell wrath of 35.
King *Dauid* , against her foolish
husband , vvhen he was in danger of his life . But hovv often
hath this most prudent Virgin deliuered vs from our cruell perse-
cutors, who like roaring Lyons
seeke day and night whome they
may deuoure, & how many times
hath she appeased the iust wrath
of God , kindled against vs for
our foule offences, & brought vs
againe into his gracious fauour .

O most

Collo-
quium.

O most prudent Virgin, by this we see, how fittly this Title doth agree vnto thee ; wherefore as by thee we are deliuered from so manifold dangers, & by whose holy intercession we receaue so many & gracious fauours, let thy most prudent counsell so direct vs, that we may auoyd all danger of sinne, & keep our selues in the fauour of thy B. Sonne. Amen.

THE XVI. MEDITATION.

Virgo Veneranda, ora pro nobis.

Venerable Virgin, pray for vs.

THIS worthy Title, doth manifest vnto vs the honour due vnto the B. Virgin, which beeing threefold, doth yield vs three substantiall groundes for

this

this present Meditation.

    The first kind of honour is called *Ciuill*, which is due vnto great Personages, by reason of their Nobility, Place, Estate, or the like. The second is *Religious* worship or honour, which belongeth to vertuous and holy men, as they are indued with excellent vertues, eminent graces, and supernaturall gifts. The third is *diuine* and *supernaturall* worship appertayning to God, and his Saints in heauen as we shal after declare.

    1.   First therefore to consider the B. Virgin according to her lineall descent, we shall find her worthy to be honoured withall Ciuill honour and dutifull respect. For if we should demaund vvith holy S. *Bernard, Quid ergo sidereum micat in generatione Ma-*

Bern. ser. c. 12. in Apoc.

H   *ria?*

ria? What star-like splendor doth shine in the generation of the B. Virgin Mary? We may take his owne answere in the same place, that she sprung from Kinges, of the seed of *Abraham*, of the stocke of *Dauid*, that she was foresignifyed by Figures, foretold by Prophets, and by mysticall Oracles insinuated vnto vs; therefore if we respect her Nobility, vve shall find that she is worthy of ciuill honour, in the highest degree, and so in this respect *Virgo veneranda*, a Virgin worthy to be honoured.

2. Secondly if we weigh the great aboundance of her singular graces, the greatnes of her excellent vertues, the number of her supernaturall gifts, and lastly the dignity of Mother of God, we

shall

ſhal find her as worthy of Religious honour aboue all others, as
ſhe doth exceed them all in her
ſingular vertues and vnſpeakable
gifts For as the diuine Wiſedome
pronounceth of the prudent wo-
man, *Multæ filia congregauerunt* Parab. 31,
diuitias, tu ſupergreſſa es vniuerſas,
Many daughters haue gathered
riches togeather , but thou haſt
gone beyond them all; for we
may iuſtly ſay of this ſacred
Queene, That many Holy Ma-
trons in the old law, many ſacred
Virgins in the new haue been in
dued with rare vertues , ſingular
graces, and meruailous fauours;
but when this glittering ſtar appeared, ſhe did as far exceed them
all, as the leaſt ſtar is in light inferiour to the Sunne , and therefore
moſt worthy of Religious honour

H 2   and

and respect , *Virgo veneranda*.

3. Thirdly if we come to the diuine and supernaturall worship belonging to God, and his Saints in heauen, we shall find her to be preferred before all Saints, & Angels, and installed next vnto God; for as the diuine worship of *Latria* (so the Dauines terme it) is due, and giuen to none but to God alone: so vnto his Saints is due the worship of *Dulia*, which belongs vnto them, as friends & seruants of God, the most eminent degree whereof is called *Hyperdulia*, which most iustly is giuen to the B. Virgin. Loe how vvorthily we do giue vnto her honour and reuerence in all the senses aforenamed: and why should we not confidently fly vnto her in our necessityes and troubles, saying *Vir-*

go

go. Veneranda ora pro nobis, Venerable Virgin pray for vs.

Heere we ought to ſtir vp our affection towards this happy Queene, and earneſtly to deſyre, that this honour ſo iuſtly due vnto her, may be giuen her by al true Chriſtians, and endeauour to the vttermoſt of our forces to aduance it moſt carefully, procuring that by our negligence it be not hindred: to which effect we muſt deuoutly implore her Motherly help, and powerfull hand. Then may we conclude with this diuin Hymne, *Aue Maris Stella*.

Collo-
quium.

H 3 THE

THE XVII. MEDITATION.

Virgo Prædicanda, ora pro nobis .
Virgin worthy of prayse, pray
for vs .

IN this laudable Title, the B
Virgin is denounced to be worthy of prayse and commendation,
worthy to be called *Blessed throgh-*
out all Generations : but becaufe
Prayfe may be giuen vnto this B.
Creature three manner of wayes
therfore we will a while contemplate this threefold branch or tri-
ple head of her deferued prayfe .

1 . The firft manner of fetting
forth the B. Virgins prayfe, is in
hart, when with a true and cordiall affection we defire that fhe
may be honoured and prayfed of
all people ; & that we do inward-

ly

ly reioyce from the bottom of our harts of her eternall glory and e-uerlasting happynes, praysing the diuine prouidence of Almighty God that hath chosen and elected her to so great felicity; and in this deuout cogitation we may wish and desire for her greater honour the vnderstanding of Cherubims & the burning loue of Seraphims, the better to blaze her worthy prayse throughout the whole world, and to inflame the harts of all people to loue and affect her: and in this first manner of prayse the first ground and foundation of true deuotion doth consist.

2. The second máner of prayse is by word, where first we may consider how little we are able to perform in respect of what is due vnto her. For how many learned

Fathers, holy men,& great Saints
haue serioufly imployed their hap
py tongues in setting forth, to the
view of the vvorld her rare excel-
lencyes, and yet they haue beene
forced to fay, that they could fay
nothing at all in comparison of
what her heroicall actions haue
deferued . What then fhal we prefume (moft holy Virgin) to fpeak
of thy prayfe, where fo many deuout feruants of thyne haue acknowledged themfelues vnworthy ? Yet B. Queene we know
thou doft not ponder the words,
but the will, not the gift, but the
loue,as thy B. Sonne did with the
poore,yet truly affected vviddow
who with fo great deuotion offered her little mite among the reft,
and therefore by him iudged to
haue giuen more then all the reft.

There-

Therefore no gift so smal, but being offered with true deuotion, will be gratefull vnto thee, o B. Virgin. And since we neither haue those words which may be fitting vnto thy greatnes, nor the sincere deuotion which may supply them; yet let these weake desires of ours by thy holy intercession, so increase, that it may bring forth some fruit worthy to be presented vnto thee, and gratefull in thy sight.

3. The third manner of prayse is *by Worke*, that is, when our workes be such, as they redound to the honour of our B. Lady. For as it vvere not inough for the Iewes to say they vvere the Sons of *Abraham*, but they must also shevv the workes of *Abraham*, to be the truest signe and best token

of their progeny : so it will little auayle vs to say we are the deuout children of the B. Virgin , if our life and conuersation be not conforme to the rule & square of her directions , which are the right patterne & true forme of perfect life; and which vvhen vve follow , vve greatly comend in her. S *Iohn* not content our loue one towardes another should be in wordes only, but that it should also appeare in deeds, vvriteth, *non diligamus lingua, & sermone, sed opere & veritate* : let vs not loue in the tongue, & speach (as vve say from the teeth outvvard) but indeed, and in truth : for works are the surest testimony vvhich speak the best language for all men to vnderstand.

O thrice happy they, vvho

Colloquium.

haue

haue their vvits and vvills, their
minds and harts, vvholy imployed in the B. Virgin prayses! It is
fayd, there is a tree called *Persea*,
that hath leaues like a tongue, and
fruit like a hart, which some wise
men haue applyed to the beautifull concord betwixt the hart &
the tongue, whé the tonguespeaks
what the hart thinkes. But how
far more beautifull a concord wil
there be, when not only the hart
and tongue, but also the outward
works shall sound forth the sweet
musicke of the B. Virgins prayses.
Doubtles it wil be such as the heauenly Quires will not disdayne to
beare a part; & these be the three
wayes by which euery deuout
child of the B. Virgin, ought to
sing her prayse. O Blessed Virgin
worthy of greater prayse, then
humane

humane or Angelical tongue can giue vnto thee, graunt that by thy holy intercession we may so imploy our thoughts, wordes, and workes in this diuine harmony of thy prayse, that they may turne to the glory of God, to thy honour, & to the profit of our poore and needy soules. Amen. *O gloriosa Domina.*

THE XVIII. MEDITATION.

Virgo Potens, ora pro nobis.

Potent Virgin, pray for vs.

IN this Title we doe acknowledge the great power which the B. Virgin hath both in heauen & earth: in heauen to obtayne vs graces and fauours, in earth to defend vs from perils & dangers.

1. First

1. First then let vs consider her power in heauen : for the better vnderstanding whereof, we will consider the noble and heroicall act of *Salomon* the Wise, who seated in his throne of State, caused his mother to be placed on his right hand, and sayd vnto her, Aske what thou wilt, I will not say thee nay. If King *Salomon* had this dutifull respect vnto his Mother, to make her so potent, that whatsoeuer she demaunded, she should be sure to obtaine; vvhat may we thinke our B. Sauiour vvould say vnto his louing Mother, when she was seated by him in heauen, but aske whatsoeuer thou wilt my deerest Mother, for I vvill not deny thee. For hovv should she be denied who neuer knevv how to aske but wel? And

hovv

hovv ſhoud he deny, vvho neuer
could deny what vvas asked wel?
Could Queene *Heſter* be ſo gratefull in the ſight of King *Aſſue-*
rus that he bad her aske vvhat ſhe
vvould, if it were the halfe of his
kingdome, it ſhould not be gaine-
ſayd · and ſhall we not perſwade
our ſelues, that our B . Lady is
more gratefull in the ſight of the
King of heauen, more pleaſing to
her only Sonne, and therefore
more potent to demaund without
deniall ? Could a vvicked * King
for a vvanton Daunce make the
like promiſe of halfe his Kingdom
and ſhall vve not beleeue that
Chriſt vvould be more bountiful
to his deareſt and Bleſſed Mother,
vvho neuer diſpleaſed him ? Let
vs then conclude this point vvith
this vndenyable truth, that the B.

Herod.

Vigria

Virgin is so potent in the Court of Heauen, that vvhatsoeuer she demandeth of her Sonne she shall obtaine, and therefore let vs say, *Virgo potens, ora pro nobis* : Povverfull Virgin, pray for vs.

2. The second point may be to contemplate her great povver on earth, vvhich is nothing els but the execution of her povver in heauen. For as there her Motherly care and tender loue tovvardes vs, is to obtayne fauours for vs; so heere it is to effect, that vve be not fruftrate of them, vvhich is by defending vs from our proud enemies, and ftrong aduerfaryes the vvorld, the flefh, and the Diuell; for as the grace of God is the chiefeft benefit vve can enioy on earth; fo that is the marke at vvhich our fubtile enemy doth

most

most ayme, thereby to bereaue vs
of the right and title we haue to
the kingdome of Heauen: where
the B. Virgin is most watchfull
vvith her potent prayers to defend vs, and to put him to flight,
if we deuoutly, as we ought, call
vpon her, when we find our selues in danger. For as a valiant &
stout Champion vvould be asha-
med euen to heare the Name of
that Woman, who shold haue cō-
quered and foyled him in playne
field : so this monster of Pride,
Sathan, hauing always beene
vanquished by her mighty power,
dares not abide so much, as the
naming of that sacred Name of
Mary. Therefore as we haue often sayd before, let vs fly vnto her
as to a Citty of Refuge, & Tower
of defence, for she is able to defēd

*Collo-
quium.*

Vs;

vs; and if we be true Children, she will neuer fayle vs. Hereupon we may conclude this meditation, *Collo-quium.* defyring that in our temporall Crosses and spirituall tentations, we may be myndfull of so sure a refuge, so sweet a succour, so strong a Castle, and so powerfull a defence. *Salue Regina.*

THE XIX. MEDITATION

Virgo Clemens, ora pro nobis.
Clement Virgin, pray
for vs.

CLEMENCY is as it were a branch of compassionat mercy, by which title we do call vpon the B Virgin, that she may take pitty and compassion of our miseries, and commiseration of our

I   necessities

neceffities, notwithftanding our
vnworthynes, wherby fhe makes
her felfe moft like vnto her fweet
Sonne, who came into the world
to forgiue the fault, and pardon
the offender : and by how much
greater the fault is proued which
is cōmitted; by fo much more the
greatnes of the Clemency doth
appeare in him that pardoneth.
If therfore we confider the iniury
done vnto the B. Virgin, when
we offend her fonne; we fhall fee
her high Clemency both in par-
doning, of her part, the fo hey-
nous offence ; and alfo her Mercy
in intreating before the mercy
feate for the life of him who hath
fo often deferued death.

   1.   Firft let vs confider, how
much the obftinat and ftony harted Iewes did againft all iuftice,

law,

law, and conscience; they abused
her only Sonne, reiected, scorned,
and put him to an ignominious
death: yet when she heard the pittifull voyce of Christ vpon the
Crosse, crying to his Eternall Father to pardon them, she also forgetfull of all wrong said; *and I thy
mother, do also forgiue them* . Behould the rare Clemency of the
tender bowells of the B. Virgin,
whome no wrong could moue,
no rage stir vp , nor any fury
driue from her wonted Clemency, & most mild behauiour. And
if thus she prayed for the professed
enemyes of Christ , why should
not they who loue him , and desire only to serue him, confidently
implore her gratious help , & say,
Virgo Clemens ora pro nobis , Myld
Virgin pray for vs .

Salmerõ.

2. Secondly

2. Secondly, let vs ponder the Ingratitude of man, after ſo much knowledge of Chriſt, that he doth not ceaſe, (as much as in him lyeth) to crucify him againe by euery mortall ſynne that he committeth as S. *Paul* writeth. Neither doth he this abuſe of ignorance, as Chriſt pleaded for the Iewes ; but after the firme beliefe of his Godhead, his Incarnation, Death and Reſurrection, yea after he knowes him to be aſcended and ſeated in heauen, whence he ſhall come to be our terrible Iudge : yet forgetfull of al, he ceaſeth not to offend him, and ſtill his bleſſed Mother doth interpoſe herſelfe, as a wall for *Ieruſalem*, that is, for him who will truly repent, and call for mercy in tyme, with a firme purpoſe and ſtrong

reſo-

Heb. 6.

resolution neuer againe to offend
him.

O incomparable Clemency
of this B. Virgin, who desireth
nothing, but to do good euen vnto those vvho are most vvorthy
of exceeding great punishment!
vvho vvould be so carelesse of his
owne good, vvho so negligent of
his saluation, as not to fly vnto
this Sanctuary, as not to runne
vnto this fountaine, as not to imbrace this sweet remedy. The
poore blind man cryed to Iesus
for sight, and vvould not cease
(though some rebuked him for it)
vntil he obteyned the effect of his
desire: so let vs call vpon this clement and meeke Mother, hovv-
soeuer others repine therat; let vs
cry vnto this mild Virgin; Let vs
not cease to say, *Virgo Clemens, ora*

*Collo-
quium.*

I 3   *pro*

pro nobis, Clement Virgin pray
for vs .

THE XX. MEDITATION.

Virgo fidelis, ora pro nobis .
Faithfull Vigin, pray
for vs .

FAITHFVLLNES may be
taken diuers vvayes, and therfore diuers vvayes doth yield vs
copious matter of the B. Virgins
prayſe.

1.   Firſt therfore vve may
conſider *fidelity* as it doth import
an excellent act of ſupernaturall
beleefe, in vvhich vve ſhall find
the ſacred Virgin to excell, as in
all other vertues, & by the togue
of the holy Ghoſt, for the ſame
canonized a liuing Saint, and cal-

led

led *Blessed: Beata quæ credidisti quo-niam perficientur in te quæ dicta sunt tibi à Domino:* Blessed art thou who hast beleeued, because in thee shalbe perfected those mysteries vvhich were declared vnto thee from our Lord. For doubtlesse she had most excellent actes of faith, concerning the high Mystery of the Incarnation especially , and therfore as one truly faithfull vve may inuocate her holy and wil-ling assistance , saying , *Virgo fidelis ora pro nobis,* faithfull Virgin, pray for vs .

2. Secondly we may consi-der Fidelity as it doth import a certaine kind of assurance of one friend towards another , wherby the one is fully perswaded of his friends loue & help in all things , so long as he keepeth himselfe

I 4   within

within the bonds and limits of a true friend. And of the fidelity of our B. Lady, and louing mother, we need not doubt, who is most ready to help & comfort vs in all our miseries, tribulations, and afflictions, if our selues by our ingratitude, and little respect vnto her, deserue not the repulse. Therfore keeping our fidelity with her sweet Sonne, and herselfe, we may assure our selues of her fidelity towards vs, at all tymes, in all occasions, and in all our busines we shall alwayes find her *Virgo fidelis*, a faithful Virgin.

3. Thirdly we may conceaue fidelity as it doth signifythe faithfull accomplishing of all busines committed to our charge : in which sense our Sauiour speaketh in the Parable of the talents, con-

gratulating

gratulating the diligent labours
of his faithfull seruant, *Euge serue*
bone & fidelis ,quia in pauca fuisti fi-
delis , super multa te constituam :
Well , good and faithfull seruant
because thou hast byn trusty ouer
a little , I will make thee steward
ouer much. And in this sense how
worthily the B. Virgin is said to
be *faithfull*, will easely appeare, if
vve consider aright hovv profi-
tably she did imploy al her rare talents , wherwith her blessed Sóne
had endued her. For what guifts
either of Nature or Grace, what
talents either naturall or supernaturall (in all which she did a-
bound) did she not fully imploy
in the seruice of God , and profit of her neighbour , whose only study was to please the one ,
and help the other,& therfore had

the only priuiledge neuer to offend him, or be wanting to them?
So as we knowing her loue no
leſſe towards vs now, then it was
vvhilſt ſhe liued, and her povver
far greater, do confidently ſay,
Virgo fidelis, ora pro nobis, faithfull
Virgin, pray for vs.

4. Laſtly we may contem-
plate hovv Fidelity doth ſignify
the ſtrict band of true loyalty bet-
vvixt true and lawfull ſpouſes:
which if we côſider in the B. Virgin towards *S. Ioſeph*, it may ſerue
for a mirrour to all vertuous and
godly ſpouſes: but if vve weigh
the matcheleſſe example of her
conſtant fidelity towards the Holy Ghoſt, to whome by ſpeciall
grace, and holy vow, ſhe was eſ-
pouſed; it will ſo farre paſſe the
ſhort reach of our weake vnder-

stan-

standing , that we shall be no
more able to view the perfection
therof , then the seely Bat, or har-
melesse owle is able to gaze vpon
the glittring beames of the sunne;
yet may we with all humility say,
Virgo fidelis, ora pro nobis, faithfull
Virgin , pray for vs ; since in all
those senses of Fidelity , vve find
her to haue the chiefest place.
Aue Maris stella.

THE XXI. MEDITATION.

Speculum Iustitiæ , ora pro nobis .
Mirour of Iustice, pray for vs.

IVSTICE in this place doth
not so much import the speciall
vertue of *Iustice*, as a generall collection of all vertues togeather ,
wherby a man doth perfectly con

forme

forme himselfe to the will of God in all things, and is therfore said to be *Iust*. In which sense to call our blessed Lady *Mirour of Iustice*, is as much as to say, the perfect patterne of all vertue, because in her (as out of S. *Ambrose* we haue noted)*velut in speculo refulget species castitatis & forma virtutis*: as in glasse the beauty of Chastity, and forme of all vertue shineth.

Ambr. lib. 2. de Virgin.

1.   Wherfore in this tytle we are to consider the *B. Virgin* as the perfect modell of all our actions, because by this we shall most euidently see, what is to be followed, what to be eschewed, what to be imbraced, what reiected: finally how to order our liues and actions to the greater honour & glory of God. We must therfore look

into

into this Glasse, not for curiosity
to behold our beauty, but with
earnest desire to améd our faults,
we mnst consider her excellent
vertues as the aboue named Saint
did, when he wrote, that she *was
humble in mind, graue in speach prudent in iudgment sparing in words,
studious in reading, reposing her hope.
full trust not in the vncertainty of
riches, but in the deuout prayers of
the poore : she was willing to worke,
bashfull in speach, accustomed to seeke
not men, but God, for the arbiter of
her mind; she hurt no man, she wished
well to all, respecting her elders, not
enuying her equalls, flying boasting,
following reason, and louing vertue.*
This and much more to this effect
doth S. *Ambrose* write, wherby we may see, that most worthily the B. Virgin is said to be, *Speculum*

*Ambr.
vbi su-
pra.*

culum Iustitia, the Mirrour of Iustice.

2. How carefull would any
gentlewoman be, if she were to
speake in the presence of a great
Person, to view herselfe in a glasse
once, and many tymes, least any
spot or blemish in her face, any
fault or disorder in her attyre,
might make her lesse gratefull in
his sight, then either he deserued,
or she could wish : and shall not
we, when we go to speake with
the King of Kings, for the better
and more decent attyring of our
soules, looke in this glasse of all
perfection, and learne to decke
& adorne our selues in such sort,
that we may not óly with Queen
Hester deserue to be inuited with
the golden Rod of Gods Mercy,
vnto his diuine presence, but

                                    also

alſo be made worthy to obtaine
of him, what we moſt deſire?
Yea, let vs not looke only into
this myſtical glaſſe, but alſo let vs
vſe it as a powerful help to obtain
our wiſhed ſuite and petition : let
vs frame our actions according
to the liuely portraict of her excellent vertues, that we may with
greater confidence implore her
powerfull ayde : let her be our
Patterne and Patroneſſe in life
and death : let vs deuoutly ſay,
Speculum Iuſtitiæ, ora pro nobis.
Myrrour of al perfection, pray for
vs. *Aue Maris ſtella.*

THE

THE XXII. MEDITATION.

Sedes Sapientiæ, ora pro nobis.
The seate of wisdome,
pray for vs.

IT is written by the diuine in-
stinct of the holy Ghost, and
left for our instruction, that *Wisdome built himselfe a howse, vnder-
propped and borne vp with seauen
stately Pillars*, which not vnfitly
we may apply vnto the Eternall
Wisdome of the Sonne of God, in
beautifying and adorning the B.
Virgin for his mother, and making her indeed *Sedes sapientiæ*, the
seate of Wisdome.

Let vs therfore consider the
seauen stately Pillars which our
Sauiour did erect in this his spiri-

tuall

tuall Soule, his mysticall seate, for
doubtlesse they were the seauen
guifts, & seaue-fould grace of the
holy Ghost, to wit, *Wisdō, Vnderstanding, Counsell, Fortitud Science,
Piety, & feare of our Lord,* al which
how eminent they were in our B.
Lady, no true Christian wil cal in
question; wherby she became the
worthy *seate of VVisdome,* the princely throne of the true *Salomon,* &
the holy mother of God.

1. And for two reasons we
may cal the B. Virgin the *Royall
seate of VVisdome.* First, in that she
was the most blessed, and selected
Creature chosen amongst, and a-
boue all women, to be his holy
mother; in whose sacred wombe
he was to take his nyne moneths
rest, and then to be most louingly
folded in her tender armes, and

K   seated

seated on her lappe, with all respect vnto him, as her God, and
no lesse loue as to her Sonne; and
therfore was the *seate of VVisdome*.

2. The second reason why she
may be so intytled, is because, if
wisdome be taken for the grace
of the holy Ghost, or the spirituall
dwelling of Christ in a soule, we
shall find that neuer in any pure
Creature the like aboundance of
wisdome was found, the like
graces, fauours, & supernaturall
gifts. And because she so carefully kept these gracious guifts, that
she alwayes deserued to keep God
in her blessed soule; therfore she
may more properly be said to be
the *seate of wisdome*. For although
Christ many tymes visiteth most
mercifully the vnworthy howse
of our soules; yet by reason of our

strange

strange ingratitude, wee do not
esteeme as we ought, the heauély
company of so worthy a ghest,
& the singular fauours of so speciall a friend, but by our offences
we expell him from the howse of
our soules, and yeild his rightfull
seate vnto his vsurping enemy.
But our blessed Lady was alwaies
constant, euer true vnto him, and
therfore his perpetuall seate, according as our Sauiour witnes-
seth of euery iust man, *ad eum ve-* Ioan. 14.
niemus, & mansionem apud eum fa-
ciemus : vve vvill come vnto him
and make our mansion or place of
abroad with him.

O Blessed and euer most hap-
py Virgin Mother, the Regall seat Collo-
of Eternall wisdome; Let thy po- quium.
werfull intercession so preuayle,
vvith thy louing Sonne, that vve

K 2   may

may in such sort receiue him, into the hovvse of our soules, that
vve do not vngratefully cast him
forth againe; but vvithall honour
and respect so serue him in this
life, that vve may deserue to
dwell in those heauenly mansions
of Eternity. Amen. *Salue Regina.*

THE XXIII. MEDITATION.

Causa nostra latitiæ, ora pro nobis.

Cause of our Ioy, pray for vs.

HEEREVVE are to consider
the great ioy vvhich the B.
Virgin brought into the world at
her sacred birth, according to that
which we read in the office of her
Natiuity, *Natiuitas tua Dei Geni-*
trix Virgo, gaudium annunciauit
vniuerso mundo: Thy Natiuity, O
Virgin

Virgin Mother of God, hath been the long defired meffenger of ioy to all the world : for ot thee is borne the fome of Iuftice, who deftroying the former curfe, brought a generall bleffing vnto vs all. Yet for the better vnderftanding of the greatnes of the ioy we all receiued by her happy comming, it vvill be good to make vfe of this contemplation.

1. Imagine after a long and tedious vvinter, hovv gratefull the approach of a pleafant fpring doth feeme, not only vnto man, but euen vnto brute beafts & feely birds, yea in fome fort to the very plants, and the earth it felf, vvho vefteth herfelfe in nevv apparell to vvelcome the neere approach of the gladfome Sunne, & the pretty birds in their láguage,

K 3   do

do the like, to fhevv the greatnes of their ioy, vvith their beft muficke.

2. Or els confider how gratefull is the beautifull breaking of a fayre morning after a darke tempeftuous night, telling vs vvith a gladfome blufh, that the ioyfull Planet, the Sunne, is neere at hand.

3. Ponder moreouer hovv comfortable vvas the comming of *Iudith* to the forrovvfull gates of befeiged *Bethulia*, vvhen fhe brought them certaine nevves of their prefent deliuery, and future fafety. Then apply all this to the B. Virgin, caufe of our ioy, who after fo long and tendious a winter of finne, and vvickednes, by her happy comming into this world, did fignify vnto, vs that

the

the Lambe of God who taketh a-
vvay the sinnes of the world, was
novv neere at hand, & that the
bright shyning lampe of heauen,
would spread ere long his beautiful beams of light vpon the earth,
& that the *Sunne of Iustice* would
shortly appeare vnto vs; that it
might be fulfilled as the Prophet
had foretold: The people that sate
in darkenes, saw great light; and
to them that dvvelt in the region
& shaddovv of death, light is risen. Her happy birth was the fore
runner of greater light, and her
appearing in this world, the ioyfull dawning of a blessed day: her
prudent demeanour, and religious cariage of farre more profit
and comfort vnto vs, then the
wonder, and vvonderfull acts of
Iudith to the *Bethulians*. She to

one people only was the cause of ioy; our B. Lady vnto all Nations: she vnto one Citty, the B. Virgin vnto al the world brought ioy and gladnes.

Collo-quium.

Let vs therfore not only acknowledge this great benefit, but let vs encourage our selues, with greater confidence to inuocate her blessed Name, and say, *Causa nostræ lætitiæ, ora pro nobis:* Cause of our ioy, pray for vs: that as by her perso̅, the Sonne of God became man for our redemption; so by her holy intercessio̅ we may profit our selues by so pricelesse a ransome. *Salue Regina.*

THE

THE XXIIII. MEDITATION

Vas Spirituale ora pro nobis.
Spirituall veſſell , pray
for vs .

HEERE we call vpon the B.
Virgin by the name of *Spirituall veſſell* , to ſignify the great a-
bundance of her ſpirituall Graces
and bleſſings , wherwith ſhe was
repleniſhed. We will therfore cõ-
ſider the ſweet odours of this diuine veſſell . It is ſaid ,

*Quo ſemel eſt imbuta recens, ſeruabit
odorem, teſta diu ,* ———

with what ſent , or ſauour a veſſel
is firſt ſeaſoned , it will conſerue
the ſmell therof a long tyme . If
thẽ we conſider the firſt ſauour of
diuine Grace wherwith this ſpirituall veſſell was ſo aboundantly
K 5   ſeaſo-

seasoned in her first Conception, which was neuer after lost, but increased almost without measure; we shall not meruayle at this tytle of *Spirituall veßell*, or diuine Tabernacle of the Holy Ghost. For albeit she was full of grace when the Angell came to deliuer his heauenly Embassage; yet the cōming of the holy Ghost was promised vnto her, and the protection of the most high to defend her. Moreouer the day of *Pentecost* the same holy Spirit descended vpon her in more ample manner then any of the rest, being indeed a vessell more capable of such diuine influence, then any els, and therfore most worthily intytled *Vas Spirituale*, a Spirituall vessell.

They vsed in the Temple certeine

teine confecrated veffells dedicated vnto the feruice of God, and
could not be applyed to any prophane vfe without the cryme of
Sacriledge; and the like is now of
the confecrated Chalices and o-
ther holy veffells. Our B. Lady
was a *Spirituall veffell* confecrated
only to the feruice of God, and
would haue deemed it a great prophaning of his diuine veffell, if
fhe fhould haue admitted the leaft
cogitation of any thought that
might haue been vnfeemely in his
eyes.

How great was the cryme of
Nabuchodonofor, that tooke fuch
veffells from the holy Temple of
Hierufalem; and how feuerely his
fon *Baltaffar* was punifhed for the *Dan.5.*
prophane vfe he put them vnto,
let the Scripture be witnes. But

far

far greater punishment may we
assuredly perswade our selues is
layd vp for such as eyther shall a-
buse this sacred Vessell, or not
giue that duely deserued respect
vnto her which they ought. For
if God so seuerely punished the
prophaning of his vessells of gold
and siluer; what will he do when
his holy mother shalbe robbed of
her right, and the most worthy
vessell in the world be abused?
And on the contrary side, vvhat
benefits shall they receiue at his
bountifull hands, who, with all
religious reuerence and duty call
vpon her, and esteem her as she is
indeed a Spirituall vessell, a con-
secrated Temple, a diuine Comfort, a gratious Queene, a louing
mother and a powerfull Intercessor for all sinners, who deuoutly
come

come vnto her Sonne by her. Let
vs by this spirituall tytle call for
her ayde, *Vas Spirituale, ora pro
nobis*, Spirituall vessell, pray for
vs; that we may be alwaies of the
number of those, who loue & defend thee, and who desire to aduance thy holy name, to the honour of thy blessed Sonne sweet
Iesus. Amen. *O gloriosa Domina.*

THE XXV. MEDITATION.

Vas Honorabile, ora pro nobis.
Honorable Vessell, pray
for vs.

THIS Honourable tytle doth
many and diuers wayes de-
monstrate vnto vs the dignity of
our B. Mother. For if we looke
with S. *Paul,* to the powerfull act

of

of Predeſtination, we ſhall find
ſome veſſells of Gold, ſome of
Clay, ſome of Honour, others of
Contumely, ſome Elect, ſome
Reprobate: amongſt the which
elect we ſhal find the Bleſſed Virgin moſt highly ſeated, & therfor
by a certaine kind of excellency
ſhe may be ſaid *Vas Honorabile*, an
honourable veſſell.

Furthermore ſome veſſells
there are which be dedicated only to the Emperours, or Kinges
vſe, and therfore honorable veſſells: and ſuch we ſhall find the
B. Virgin to be, and ſo much the
more honourable, by how much
the Emperour and King of heauen (whom ſhe only ſerued) is able to aduance her to more noble
ſeruices. If they be called *Ladies
of Honour*, who attend about the

Queenes

Queenes perſon;how much more the *B. Virgin*, who attended on God himſelfe,ſhould be eſteemed Honourable, and as ſo pretious a Iewell be accounted worthy of Reuerence & Honour.

Againe,if the word *Honorab'e* be taken in that ſenſe vvhich vve ſpake of, when we treated of the honour due vnto her in Heauen, we haue already declared in the X V I. Meditation, what degree of honour belongeth vnto her a-boue all other Creatures; ſince therfore by ſo many tytles, Ho-nour is due, vnto her, all equity and reaſon commands, that vve ſhould not be ſlacke in rendring honour, *cui honor debetur*, vnto vvhome honour is due.

O diuine veſſell of honour, predeſtinate from all Eternity,

and choſen to be the elected mother of him vvho is moſt worthy
of all honour; be our faithfull aduocate before his diuine Maieſty
that we may be alwayes ready to defend thine honour, and
yield all honour due vnto thee,
as the Honourable veſſell of the
holy Ghoſt, and the moſt bleſſed of all women. Amen. *Salue
Regina*.

THE XXVI. MEDITATION.

Vas inſigne deuotionis, ora pro nobis.
Noble veſſell of deuotion,
pray for vs.

BY this worthy Tytle we are
taught, what deuotion we
ought to haue towards the bleſſed
Queene of Heauen, and mother
of

of God, who is indeed the fource, fountaine, and veffell of deuotion. In the Booke of Kings mention is made of a Veffell of oyle belonging to a poore widdowe, which did not only remaine full it felfe, but alfo filled full many other veftells: which not vnfitly doth refemble the bleffed Virgin, where barren and dry foules may fully refrefh themfelues, and vve fhall find her fo liberall and bountifull a mother, that fhe will not ceafe to communicate fpirituall bleffings vnto vs, fo long as vve haue veffells capable to receiue them.

If a veffell fhould be placed in the midft of a market, full of gold with free licence for al poore and needy people to repaire thither to releeue their wants: if

4. Reg. 4.

L   any

any fhould be found fo negligent
and carelefle as not to feeke this
only meanes, to make himfelfe
truly rich; he fhould not only be
iudged worthy to liue in his former mifery, but rightly be con-
demned of floth and folly . But if
we caft our eyes vpon this diuine
and noble veffell, the B. Virgin,
we fhall fee that Almighty God
hath placed her firft in his mili-
tant, thē in his triūphant Church,
as a miraculous veffell of deuotion, vnto whome all that want
fuch heauenly liquor, may with
confidence approach ; and not
only befprinckle, but euen po-
wre full fhowers of deuotion v-
pon their dry & thirfting foules,
which do, and euer will moft
fweetly flow from this wonderfull veffell of deuotion .

In

In this Celestiall vessell the ancient Fathers dipped their learned, and deuout pennes, when they left vnto vs so many, & most worthy monuments of their dutyfull seruice to her bountifull liberality towards them. With this deuotion to this sacred Queene, the vndaunted spirit of *S. Ignatius* was confirmed; the diuine cōceits of *S. Denis* graced; the witty sentences of *S. Augustine* adorned; the graue sayings of *S. Ambrose* beautified; the learned writings of S. *Hierome*, honoured; the illuminated mind of S. *Anselme* enlightned; the mellifluous Sermons of S. *Bernard* sweetned; the burning hart of the Seraphicall doctor S. *Bonauenture*, inflamed; finally the learned men of al ages, were besprinkled with this

L 2   heauenly

uenly dew. Let vs not therfore by
our owne wilfull blindnes loose
so great a treasure , and depriue
selues of so soueraigne a remedy ;
but let vs deuoutly, or with desire
of deuotion, say, *Vas insigne deuo-*
tionis , ora pro nobis , Noble vessell
of deuotion pray for vs. *Aue Ma-*
ris Stella.

THE XXVII. MEDITATION.

Rosa mystica, ora pro nobis .

Mysticall Rose , pray
for vs .

OMITTING many proper-
ties of the Rose which might
most aptly be applyed vnto the
B . Virgin , I will only insist v-
pon three or foure, not to exceed
my wonted breuity .

1 . First

1. First the Rose is most beautifull to behould, and most pleasing to the eye, especially being bedewed with some sweet morning shower, which if we apply to our Blessed Lady, we shall find that, in naturall beauty none came neere vnto her, or could be compared with her, as we haue already proued. And for the aboundance of heauenly graces, and wholsome showers of blessings powred vpon her, we haue also declared how farre she did, and doth excell all other creatures.

1. The second property wherin our blessed Queene resembles the Rose, is in the sweet fragrant smell: for as the Rose is as it were the Queene of flowers, by reason of it sweet perfuming smell; so the B. Virgin, aboue all women

L 3   was

was moſt gratefull vnto God , &
the fragrant odours of her rare
vertues , as a moſt excellent ſmell
haue filled the whole Church
with ſweetnes , according to that
ſaying of S. *Paul* , *Chriſti bonus o-*
dor ſumus in omni loco : we are the
good odour of Chriſt in euery
place : which is verified chiefly in
the Queene of heauen .

3 . The third reſemblance of
this dainty flower is in colour: for
as ſome are white , ſome red , o-
thers damaske ; ſo our holy Mother the Church doth preſent our
Bleſſed Lady vnto vs, ſometymes
white , as in her imaculate Conception ; ſometymes red , as in
her vnſpotted purification; when
as old *Simeon* did propheſy vnto
her , that the ſword of Griefe
ſhould pierce and wound her B .

soule,

foule, to wit the bitter paſſion of her louing Sonne, for whome ſhe grieued ſo much, that as many learned Wryters witnes; *plus quàm martyr fuit*, ſhe was more thē martyred. Other whiles ſhe appeares in damaske, as in the admirable Annunciation, where doubtles with a comely bluſh ſhe pleaded with the Angel about the conſeruation of her Chaſt Virginity, which when ſhe vnderſtood it ſhould be kept vnſpotted, ſhe moſt willingly admitted of the Embaſſage.

4. Laſtly a Roſe hath it birth, or as we ſay, ſpringeth from thornes, and amongſt them it groweth vp to perfection: which may be applyed to our bleſſed Lady in two ſenſes. Firſt, that ſhe ſprong from the race of ſinners,

ſicut

ſicut lilium inter ſpinas, as a lilly, or roſe amongſt thornes. For
albeit her parents were holy people; yet not ſo holy, as they could
altogeather auoyd the name of
ſinners, the only priuiledge of
Chriſt and his Bleſſed Mother.
Secondly, as the roſe groweth a-
mongſt ſharpe thornes; ſo the B.
Virgin grew vp in vertue, amidſt
many harſh and ſharpe mortifications and heauy Croſſes: in ſo
much that ſhe is compared to the
Roſe-bed, *quaſi plantatio roſæ in
Hierico*: like the planting or plan-
ted bed of a roſe in *Hierico*; for the
roſe tree the longer it groweth,
the greater and ſharper are the
pricks it beareth; and the Bleſſed
Virgin the longer ſhe liued, the
more her mortifications did increaſe, that ſhe might well ſay,

that

that all her life was *Crux & martyrium*, a Crosse and martyrdome. And by these properties it may easily be gathered: how fitly the patterne of all perfection, and the model of patience is compared to the dainty rose, and therfore mystically we say, *Rosa Mystica, ora pro nobis*, Mysticall Rose pray for vs. Amen. *Salue Regina*.

THE XXVIII. MEDITATION.

Turris Dauidica, ora pro nobis.

Tower of Dauid, pray
for vs.

IN the fourth Chapter of the *Canticles* the vnspotted beauty of the Holy Church in diuers places is described; and in the fourth verse her *Necke* is compa-

L 5   red

red to the Tower of *Dauid*, built
for defence: and moreouer it is
said, *Mille clypei pendent ex ea, om-*
nis armatura fortium; a thowsand
sheilds hange theron, all the armour of strong and valiant men.
Now let vs see, for what reason
our Blessed Lady is called *Turris*
Dauidica, the Tower of *Dauid*.

1. The first may be, because
heere we read that the *Necke* of
the Church is compared to a Tower; and we haue said before
that as Christ is the *Head* of the
Church, so the B. Virgin is the
Necke, through which all spirituall food descendeth to the whole
body of the Church: therefore
this Tower of *Dauid* is most fitly
applyed vnto her, and she most
worthily said to be the tower of
Dauid.

2. Secondly

2. Secondly this Tower of *Dauid* was a Tower built for defence, and therfore a thowsand shields did hāg on it, & al kind of armor for strong men ; which if we accomodat vnto this holy Mother the B Virgin , we shall find that she was a stately Tower , by reason of her height in vertue , & strong by reason of her Constancy which neuer fayled ; and for this she is said to tread the *moone vnder her feete*, which is the symbole of Inconstancy . A thousand shields are alwaies ready and prepared ; becaufe as the diuell hath a thowsand crafty sleights to deceiue; so hath this Blessed Tower as many diuine plotts to preuent him , which by her rare example she hath left vnto vs, with al kind of Armor, both offensiue and defensiue

fenfiue to withftand the might &
force of our ftronge aduerfary,
vvho, as the holy Patriarch *Iob*
vvitneffeth, is fo potent, that no
povver on earth can be compared
vnto him. Therfore vvith great
reafon vve fly vnto this ftrong &
inuincible Tower, to cal for ayde,
to feeke vveapons, to arme our
felues, againft the fierce affaults
of fo cruel an enemy, faying once
and many tymes, *Turris Dauidica, ora pro nobis*, Tower of *Dauid*
pray for vs.

3.   Another reafon vvhy the
bleffed Virgin is named *Turris Dauidica*, the Tovver of *Dauid*, is,
becaufe as it is faid of the Church
in generall; fo it may be applied
to euery iuft and vertuous perfon
in particuler, and efpecially to the
B. Virgin, who in all vertue and

Religion

Religion was most excellent; yea so, *per excellentiam*, as we say, that she may be called the Tovver of *Dauid*, for the reasons aforenamed.

Wherfore O Blessed Virgin, O strong and mighty Tower, vnder the shadovv of thy defence we fly for succour. Holy Mary, help those that are in misery, strengthen those that faint, comfort those that grieue; finally pray for vs all, that vnder so stronge a tower vve may be able to defend our selues from our deadly enemies, the world, the flesh, and the Diuell. Amen. *Salue Regina.*

Collo-quium.

THE

THE XXIX. MEDITATION.

Turris Eburnea, ora pro nobis.

Tovver of iuory, pray
for vs.

THIS tytle declareth the excellency of the Blessed Virgin . For as Iuory is rare and precious, and therfore a Tower built
of it , must needs be of great esteeme and strength; so the Blessed
Queen of heauen is of very great
esteeme and account ; not only in
the sight of God , (which is truly
to be great) but also in the sight
of Angells and men, worthy to be
admired . But because we haue already spoké of the Tower, we wil
novv consider vvhy she is compared to *Iuory* .

1. Iuory amongst other properties hath this for one, that the
older it is, the more it turnes to a
beautifull red, or ruddy colour;
as vve read in prayse and commendation of the old *Nazarets*,
that thy vvere *rubicundiores ebore*
antiquo, more ruddy then the ancient Iuory; vvhich property be-
fitts best the Blessed Virgin, who
the longer she liued in this mortall
life, the more she suffered; and as
her Crosses did increase, so the
more she drevv to the ruddy colour of Martyrdome: and the nee-
rer she came vnto so high a degree
of loue and fortitude, the more
her golden Charity did shine
throughout the vvorld; and therfore most fitly she is compared
not only to *Iuory*, but euen vnto
the ancient *Iuory*, vvhen it is in

greatest

greateſt beauty and vvorth.

2. Another excellent vertue of Iuory is, to expell poyſon from the infected vvaters, vvhich is the cauſe (as ſome do vvrite) that the other beaſts vvhere the vvaters often be poyſoned by venemous ſerpents, vſe not to drinke vntill the Vnicorne hath dipped in his horne which expelleth al poyſon, and leaueth the waters as wholſome as before: which property, if we apply to the Bleſſed Virgin, we ſhall ſee that no waters of tribulation can be hurtfull to thoſe who ſet her Heroicall example of Patience before them. For as the wood that *Moyſes* caſt into the bitter vvater, made it ſvveet and ſauoury; ſo no Croſſes ſo bitter or diſtaſtfull, but by meditation of her excellent life, will be made

ſvveet

sweet and pleasant.

O Bleſſed Virgin , be our *I-uory* Tovver of defence , be our Citty of Refuge, for, *ſub tuum præ-ſidium confugimus* , vnto thy holy protection vve fly ; let not the ſtrong aſſaults of our enemies daunt vs, nor the fierce encounters of our aduerſaryes diſcourage vs; but with thy powerfull interceſſion help vs , that to the greater glory of thy ſweet Sonne , and further profit of our own ſoules , we may ſtand immoueable in the ſeruice of God , & dayly increaſe in deuotion towards thee. Amen. *O glorioſa Domina.*

Collo-quium.

M   The

THE XXX. MEDITATION

Domus aurea, ora pro nobis.

Golden howſe, pray
for vs.

IN this pretious tytle, the golden Charity of the B. Virgin
is inſinuated. For, as we haue already proued, the famous Temple
of *Ieruſalem* built by *Salomon*, and
all couered with gold, was a type
or figure of the bleſſed Virgin.
And as that Temple was a Golden Howſe, built for God himſelfe; ſo was the Bleſſed Virgin a
ſpirituall and myſticall howſe, ordeyned and adorned for the diuin
Temple of the holy Ghoſt, and
Bride-chamber of Chriſt; yea
for an elected howſe and hoſpitall

for

for the Bleſſed Trinity. She is alſo ſaid to be of gould, by reaſon of
her burning Charity, and infla-
ming loue, ſignified by gould.
And as Gould excelleth all other
mettalls : ſo doth the Queene of
Angells, ſurpaſſe all other pure
Creatures.

By this we may gather, how
different are the wayes of God
from the wayes of men, and how
far diſtāt his thoughts from ours.
Herod had his ſtately Pallace a-
dorned richly in outvvard ſhevv;
Chriſt his poore mother richly
bedecked with inward vertues.
The eies of men iudge by the outward face; the eyes of God by the
inward hart ; therfore the famous Pallace of *Herod* is left; this
celeſtial howſe of God choſen; for
though the Sonne of the Bleſſed

M 2   Virgin

Virgin had howſe to hide his head , (as himſelfe witneſſeth) ſpeaking of an earthly habitation; yet he neuer wanted this Golden Chappel,this worthy howſe, his deuout mother , to intertaine him , with all loue and tender affection .

　　　Since therfore we haue in this world , no permanent howſe of aboad, no certaine Citty to inhabite, and dwell in , for any long tyme (as S. *Paul* wryteth;) let vs endeauour all to follow the vertuous life of this ſpirituall and myſticall howſe , that we may alſo deſerue to be a howſe , wherin Chriſt may reſt : that intertayning him in our ſoules by grace , in this life,we may be made heires of glory in the next. Amen. *Aue Maris ſtella.*

THE

THE XXXI. MEDITATION.

Fœderis arca , ora pro nobis.
Arke of the Couenant,
pray for vs.

IN the old Law in diuers places
is mentioned the *Arke of the
Couenant* , made by *Moyses* , and
by Gods expreſſe Commaund ,
the forme, ſcituation , and all the
reſt belonging vnto it : we will
briefly conſider, what wood it
was made of , and how it was couered with gold , what was kept
in it , and ſome properties therof,
which we will apply to this our
myſticall Arke , the Bleſſed Virgin .

1.   Firſt *Moyses* made this   *Deut.10.*
Arke of *Settim* wood , which is

M 3   called

called incorruptible, by reason of
the longe tyme that it remayneth
vncorrupted, and this Arke by
Gods ordināce was to be couered
all ouer, both within and without, with pure Gold. Heere vve
may confider how fittly this figured bleſſed Virgin, who though
made of the corruptible Maſſe
wherof all men be compoſed ; yet
by the Eternall wiſdome of God
preſerued from all taint of Cor-
ruption, both in body and ſoule ;
couered ouer with pure Gold,
within and without, becauſe her
burning Charity within did giue
ſo faire a luſtre to all her outward
actions, that ſhe did ſeeme to exceed the fayreſt Gold. And as o-
uer the Arke was a Crown of the
ſame pure and maſſy gold; ſo ouer
the bleſſed Virgins heauenly head

did

did hang that vnſpekable Crown of Glory, from all Eternity prepared for her, which ſhe now enioyes.

2. Secondly, we may conſider, that in the *Arke of the Couenant* were kept the Tables of the ten Commaundments, as a witnes againſt thoſe that ſhould afterward rebell; and alſo there was kept a certain meaſure of the *Manna*, in remembrance of ſo great a benefit done vnto the Choſen people of *Iſraell* : So in the Bleſſed Virgins ſacred breſt was layd vp the table of thoſe ten Commaundements which ſhe alwaies kept moſt inuiolable, againſt thoſe who ſhall deny, that they are able to be kept by any.

And as for the *Manna*, we know ſhe had the keeping of the

Deut. 10.

Exod. 16.

M 4   Celeſtiall

Celestiall *Manna*, Chrift Iefus,
the true food of our hungry
foules, and a memoriall of his
trueft loue, and one of his greateft
benefitts done vnto vs.

3 . Befides this, the Arke
coming into the watersof *Iordan*,
they gaue place for the Children
of Ifraell to paffe ouer without a-
ny danger: which fignifies the B.
Virgins powerfull help, ftaying
the waters of tribulation from
the hurtfull purfuite of the Children of God, making them to
paffe as fecure as if they walked
on dry land.

4. And laftly the Arke with
it prefence made the Idoll *Dagon*
fall flat downe before it; it was
a terrour vnto the enemies of
God; and the curious beholders
of it, were not a little punifhed

for

for their fault: so the Blessed Virgin hath, and is the destroyer of Idolatry, the terrour vnto the enemies of the Church, and a seuere Chastizer of those who be more curious then wise, in matters belonging to her.

Behould then, how fittly she is compared to the *Arke of the Couenant*, who is also ready to help vs , to keep the Couenant vve haue made with God , both in the spiritual generation of Baptisme, as also in our good purposes, vowes , and all other deuotions wherein we giue our selues to God Let vs therfore deuoutly cal vpon her holy Name by this worthy tytle, & say , *Fœderis Arca, ora pro nobis* , Arke of the Couenant pray for vs . *Salue Regina.*

THE XXXII. MEDITATION.

Ianua Cæli , ora pro nobis.

Gate of heauen , pray
for vs .

THIS Metaphoricall speach
doth signify vnto vs, that as
into stronge walled Citties there
is no hope of entrance, but by the
gate: so he that pretēdeth to enter
into the glorious Citty of the heauenly Hierusalem , must knock
at this beautifull gate the Blessed
Virgin, who therfore by the holy
Church is so intytled , as in that
diuine hymne *Aue Marris stella*,
she is said to be *Felix cæli porta*, the
happy gate of heauen : and in the
Anthym *Aue regina Cælorum* , we
say, *Salue radix salue porta, ex qua*

mundo

mundo lux est orta : All hayle o B. roote , all hayle o heauenly gate. And conformable to this in thefe deuout Letanies compofed in her honor , we falute her by the name of *Ianua Cæli,* gate of heauen.

1. Firft therfore we may meditate hovv vve are created for Cittizens of heauen , where all our chiefeft treafure is layd vp ; by finne the gate was fhut againft vs , as rebells againft Gods facred Lawes , vntill Chrift by his Omnipotent power did open it again vnto vs , and left this beautyfull gate patent vnto all ; that who fo vvould enter into this blisfull paradife , fhould firft haue this Gate vvell knovvne , by vvhich he might freely enter into Eternall happines; and therfore fhe is called *Felix cæli porta* , the happy gate

of

of heauen .

2 . Secondly vve may confider , that if this gate be ſhut a-
gainſt vs , vve can haue but little
hope to be able to attain vnto our
longing deſire of entrance into
the Citty ; that is , if our life ,
manners & conuerſation be ſuch
as may hinder our acceſſe vnto
this ſtately Gate , vve can haue
but ſmall hope of her holy interceſſion ; eſpecially if we ceaſe not
to offend her Bleſſed Sóne , which
is the only cauſe that vvill bread a
deniall to our approach vnto that
ſhyning gate , vvho vvith her beautifull beames of light inuiteth
al men frō the works of darknes ,
to the fountaine of light ; from the
ſnaresof death to the fruits of life ,
& from the valley of extreme miſery , vnto the height of all goodnes .

O

O let vs not be so blind, as not to see this light; let vs with holy *Moyses* put off the shooes of our earthly affection , and vvith deuout *S. Bernard* fall before her feete; and as these deuout Letanies doe teach vs , let vs say *Ianua Cæli* , gate of Heauen pray for vs : and *Felix cæli porta* , o happy gate of heauen , be not shut against vs, who so much desire to enter by thee and to reigne with thee , for euer . Amen . *Aue Maris stella* .

THE XXXIII. MEDITATION.

Stella matutina, ora pro nobis.

Morning starre, pray
for vs .

FOR the better vnderstanding
this worthy tytle , we must

con-

confider firft what the *Starre of
the morning* doth denote vnto vs,
and alfo the tyme of its appea-
rance, by which we fhall eafily
perceaue how fittly the Bleffed
Virgin is called *Stella matutina*, the
morning ftarre.

1. Firft as this bright fhyning
ftarre of the morning, appearing
vnto vs, giueth vs to vnderftand
that the darke night is ended, &
the cheerfull day at hand; & therfore the difmall clouds of the
night were fhortly to be difperfed
by the comming of a glittering
light, to wit the Sunne : Euen fo
the firft appearing of the Bleffed
Virgin in this world, was a fore-
running of that great light, her
fweet Sonne Chrift Iefus, whofe
ioyfull beames were to expell the
myfty darkenes of former ignorance

rance with his shyning light of doctrine.

2.   Secondly this morning starre doth not only foretell the comming of a light, that should be the ending of a sad and melancholy night, but also the beginning of a most ioyfull day : so the happy birth of the Blessed Virgin, did foretell vnto the world, that happy day, that now was at hand, when the Angell should denounce vnto the whole world, and first vnto the poore watchfull sheepheards, *gaudium magnum quod erit in omni populo*, the great ioy which should not be confined ned to the land of *Iury* only, but should be common to al Nations, *omni populo*, to wit, the birth of Christ, Sauiour and redeemer of mankind.

3.   Againe,

3. Againe, the day-ſtarre appeareth more bright and light-
ſome, then the reſt of the ſtarrs
that ſhyned before in the night:
and the Bleſſed Virgin was in
brightnes of ſanctity and cleernes
of vertues, beyond all Stars, that
is, all the Saints that went before
or came after her (her Sonne alwaies excepted, as in al ſuch ſpea-
ches is moſt fit:) and thus by this
glittering light, we may eaſily ſee
& truly ſay, *nox præceſſit, dies autē
appropinquauit*: that, the night is
paſt and the day drawes nigh; &
therefore vſing the holy Apoſtles
Counſell, let vs caſt away the
workes of darknes, and arme our
ſelues with light; and as at myd-
day, let vs walke honeſtly in ſight
of all the world, for in ſuch works
we ſhall be ſure to haue this B.

ſtarre to guide and conduct vs;
which God graunt. Amen. *Aue
Maris ſtella.*

The XXXIIII. Meditation.

Salus infirmorum, ora pro nobis.
Health of the ſicke, pray
for vs.

ALL manner of ſicknes may
be reduced to two kindes of
Infirmities; the one corporall,
that vexeth and ſometyme taketh
away the life of the body; the o-
ther ſpirituall, which weakeneth
and ſometyme extinguiſheth the
life of the ſoule: of both which,
we may eaſily perceaue the Blef-
ſed Virgin, to haue been, and dayly to be a ſoueraigne remedy, by
which ſhe is iuſtly ſaid to be *Salus*

N   *infirmo-*

infirmorum, the health of the infirme, or ficke.

　1. Firſt then to conſider the
Bleſſed Virgins bounty and liberality towards ficke perſons, vve
need no further perſuaſion then
the manifold examples written
by graue Authors of the almoſt
infinit miraculous cures wrought
by the Bleſſed Queene of Angels,
vpon diſeaſed perſons of all ſorts,
and of the deuotion of the places,
yet extant, with the frequent con-
courſe of ficke and weake people
vnto them, with miraculous re-
ſtoring of their health, when it is
more conuenient for their good,
or the honour of God. This I ſay
may ſerue for ſufficient proofe of
this point, for all ſuch as are deuoutly diſpoſed towards the B.
Virgin.

　2. Con-

2. Concerning spirituall diseases, it is not vnknowne to any Catholike, how many miraculous Conuersions haue beene wrought by her holy intercession; how many therby haue been brought from the very gates of hell, to the happy gate of heauen; euen such as haue almost beene swallowed vp in the desperate gulfe of despaire; which is an euident signe and token that she is *Salus infirmorum*, the health of the diseased; by her holy intercession obteyning the perfect Cure both of body and soule; giuing vs therby full assurance, that if vve confidently haue recourse vnto her, we may obtayne the like benefit, if we haue the like deuotion. *Salue Regina*.

THE XXXV. MEDITATION.

Refugium Peccatorum, ora pro nobis.

Refuge of finners, pray
for vs.

IN the old Law there were many
Citties ordeyned by Gods expreſſe commaundment, whither
men guilty of certaine Crymes,
might fly to ſaue their liues, as
now in the new Law our Sanctu-
aries are, where offendours may
be ſafe from the purſuing enemy.
And becauſe the Bleſſed Virgin is
a common Refuge, to whome all
finners may fly, to hide themſelues, vntill the wrath of God be
paſt; therfore ſhe is called and
rightly intytled the Refuge of finners.

The

The summe of this Meditaton may be, to consider, That these forenamed Citties of Refuge were ordeyned for such as casually did murther their brethren; for if wilfully they did commit any such cryme it auayled them nothing at all to fly to the said Citties: So whilst our sinnes, be of infirmity and weakenes, we may with confidéce fly vnto her; but if they proceed of obstinacy and malice, and so contynue, we can expect no fauour at her hands, yet in this she so excelleth all the foresaid Citties of Refuge, that although the sin be of this latter sort of obstinate malice; yet if they will informe their vnderstanding, and conforme their will, she is ready to take them vnder her protection, and with her powerfull pray-

N 3   ers

ers obtaine them pardon, & bring them againe into the fauour of God. Since therfore she doth not disdaine to be called *Refuge of sinners*, let vs not be so vngratefull and blind, as not to make vse of so friendly an offer, so stronge a Refuge, and so potent an intercessor, but let vs deuoutly fly vnto her saying, *Refugium Peccatorum, ora pro nobis*: Refuge of sinners pray for vs. *Pater & Aue.*

THE XXXVI. MEDITATION.

Consolatrix afflictorum ora pro nobis.

Comfortresse of the afflicted, pray for vs.

VVE haue seene before that this heauenly Queene is a soueraigne remedy of the sicke, the

the diſeaſe being either corporal or
ſpirituall: now we are to conſider
how ſhe is a cōfort to the afflicted,
which will appeare many waies.

1.   Firſt it is a comfort for
one that is in affliction, to knovv
that ſome others haue paſſed the
ſame way; and farre greater to
vnderſtand that they paſſed not
only vvithout hurt, but vvith
great renowne: So in our greateſt miſeries and calamities if vve
looke vpon this comfortable ob-
ject, & conſider the rare example
ſhe hath left vs, we ſhall find that
all we ſuffer or can ſuffer, is but a
ſhaddovv to that which ſhe hath
vndergone. This then may be the
firſt cauſe of comfort to the afflicted.

2.   Secondly it is a great comfort to thoſe that are afflicted,

to haue some deare and louing friend to take compassion of their misery, where they behould as it were, the image of themselues, suffering in their friends hart: And doubtles the Blessed Virgin hath such perfect loue vnto her true Children, and such tender compassion of their afflictions, that she cannot choose but in a manner suffer with them; which is exceeding comfort to haue a partaker of our sorrowes. For albeit these passions be not in heauen, yet she hath perfect notice of our troubles, and as a most louing mother seeketh to remedy our afflictions when it is conuenient for vs.

3. Thirdly, it is a great refreshing to the afflicted, to know they haue a friend who is able to

de-

deliuer them , if they giue him notice of it , and shew that they desire it . And such is the Blessed Virgin alwaies ready to giue vs all comfort , if confidently and de-uoutly, as vve ought , vve fly vnto her. For so povverfull is her intercession , that what she asketh for vs she obteyneth ; and so great her wisdome is, that she vvill aske nothing but what is conuenient for our eternall good . If therfore in our afflictions , she doth not always succour vs, we may perswad our selues , that they are more a-uaylable for our spirituall good , then al the comforts in the world. And by these considerations vve may see , how truly the B. Virgin is, *Consolatrix afflictorum*, the comfortresse of the afflicted . *Salue Regina* .

THE XXXVII. MEDITATION.

Auxiliū Chriſtianorum, ora pro nobis.

The help of Chriſtians,
pray for vs.

BY this title all true Chriſtians do acknowledge the power-full help of the Bleſſed Virgin in their neceſſities, eſpecially when they vndertake any worthy exploit for her Bleſſed Sonne; as the conuerſion of Nations, the redeeming of Chriſtian Captiues, or the iuſt defence of their owne Country, againſt the treacherous inuaſions of barbarous people and Infidells; for in ſuch worthy imployments, as the Chriſtians hiue alwayes vſed, to ſhew their ſingular deuotion, in the inuoca-

tion

tion of our Blessed Lady : so she
hath neuer fayled in shewing par_
ticuler fauours towards them .

Besides , we haue other eni-
mies both stronger and subtiler,
against whose assaults we haue
more need of her ayde and assistance ; I meane, the Capitall enemy of mankind , who neuer cea-
seth to deface the very image of
God in vs , & who by her powerfull intercession and holy prayers
is put to confusion, yea by the on
ly naming of our B. Lady, which
he is not able to endure. And lastly, though we were free from all
outward foes ; yet shall we neuer
want a domesticall enemy, whose
disordered appetites & dishonest
desires do seldome, or neuer beare
sway in those, who are truely deuoted to the B. Virgin .

To

Bern. super Missus est.

To conclude as S. *Bernard* wryteth, Let vs in al tribulations, in all ſtraites, in all dangers, call vpon her Bleſſed name, and vve ſhall proue in our ſelus how rightly ſhe may be, and is intytled *Auxilium Chriſtianorum*, the ayder and helper of Chriſtians: But that we may the better inioy this ſoueraigne help, we muſt examin our ſelues, that we be not, as *Saint Auguſtine* ſaith, *nomine Chriſtiani, re vani,* in name Chriſtians, but indeed vayne, and deuoyd of all true Chriſtianity: for ſuch haue put a clowde before the bright beames of her fauour, that they cannot ſhine vpon them. Therfore O Bleſſed Virgin help vs, that we may be truly ſeruāts of Chriſt and true Chriſtians; for then we ſhall neuer be deſtitute of thy lo-

uing

uing help, who art the thend of
all good Chriſtians . *O glorioſa
Domina* .

THE XXXVII. MEDITATION.

Regina Angelorum, ora pro nobis.

Queene of Angells, pray
for vs .

IN theſe tytles following our B.
Lady is called *Queene of An-
nells*, *Queene of Patriarks*, *Queene
of Prophets*, and the like . Wherefore we will briefly aſſigne ſome
one or two reaſons, why ſhe may
be ſaid to be their Queene, for
ſome excellency that did ſhine in
her, in that kind . As in this preſent Meditation ſhe is intytled
Queene of Angells, by reaſon of
her vnſpotted and chaſt behaui-

                                    our,

our, wherin she did excell and lead, as we vse to say, an Angelicall life on earth.

Secondly as she is now crowned Queene of Heauen, she may most fitly be called *Queene of Angells*, because they be the chiefest assistants in that heauenly Court, where she, as Queene and Em-presse, sits exalted aboue them all, and they no doubt most prompt and obedient at her will; and by this vve salute her in this place, & call her, as indeed she is, *Regina Angelorum*, Queene of Angells. *Aue regina Cælorum*.

THE

THE XXXIX. MEDITATION.

Regina Patriarcharum, ora pro nobis.
Queene of the Patriarkes,
pray for vs.

OVR blessed Lady may be called *Queene of Patriarks* in this
respect, that the high mystery of
the Incarnation was fulfilled in
her; and the chiefest Promises
made vnto them had their effect
in this Blessed Queene. Besides,
her excellent faith of all the
mysteries of our faith, did far exceed that of the *Patriarkes*; her
zeale was greater, her expectation more feruorous, her desires
more ardent:that whatsoeuer was
in them prayse-worthy, was in the
B. Virgin in a farre more high
degree,

degree, and therfore moſt worthily we ſay, *Regina Patriarcharum,*
ora pro nobis, Queene of the Patriarks, pray for vs.

THE XL. MEDITATION.

Regina Prophetarum, ora pro nobis.
Queene of Prophets, pray
for vs.

THE holy Prophets, as by
their writings we may vn-
derſtand, (and their names import as much) had great light
from Almighty God, concerning
the myſteries of our faith; the
conuerſion of the world; the order of the Church; the Birth,
Death & Reſurrection of Chriſt,
with the reſt belonging to our
faith: but the light that was com-

municated

municated vnto our blessed Lady,
did go farre beyond them , her
guiftes and prophesy greater ,
her grace more aboundant, and
was indeed the shyning star , at
which they in their prophesies did
but point, as the Prophet *Isay* witnesseth when he saith , *Ecce Virgo
concipiet* , behold a Virgin shall
conceaue : and by this she is said
Queene of Prophets . *Aue Maria.*

THE XLI. MEDITATION.

Regina Apostolorum , ora pro nobis.

Queene of the Apostles , pray
for vs .

B Y greater reason, she is said to
be the *Queene of the Apostles,*
then either of *Patriarkes* or Prophets , being (after the Ascension
of Christ) left amógst them as a

O   Queene

Queene to gouerne and direct
them, to their exceeding great
comfort and confolation. For although the holy Ghoft was indeed their chiefe Directour and
Rectour; yet it is like that they did
many things by her meanes; as it
is thought, that *S. Luke* did write
his Ghofpell, efpecially concerning the infancy of our Sauiour
by her direction, though gouerned otherwife by the holy fpirit
of God. And therfore when fhe
paffed out of this life, they all
came togeather miraculoufly conioyned, to celebrate with due reuerence and deuotion, the Fu-
nerall rites of their foueraigne
Queene. Behold therfore, hovv
deferuedly fhe is called *Queene of
the Apoftles. Salue Regina*.

THE

THE XLII. MEDITATION.

Regina Martyrum, ora pro nobis.

Queen of Martyrs, pray for vs.

MOST worthily she is enty-
tled *Queene of Martyrs*, &
that for many reasons.

1. First because in her life
she suffered more then any, yea
then all the Martyrs togeather,
as I haue already proued.

2. Secondly she may be called
Queen of Martyrs, by reason of the
rare example that she left them.

3. And lastly, because in
their agonyes and passions, no
doubt they had particuler help &
comfort from her, whome they
called vpon, as we do, *Regina
Martyrum, ora pro nobis*, Queene
of Martyrs pray for vs.

THE XLIII. MEDITATION.

Regina Confessorum, ora pro nobis.
Queen of côfessours, pray for vs.

CONFESSOVRS are they, who though they cannot attaine to the sublime dignity of Martyrdome, yet with their good life & vertuous actions they confesse Christ to be true God and Man, and are ready to dye, if so it should please him, in defence of the least article of his holy doctrine. And because the Blessed Virgin in this point hath gone so farre beyond them all, and left them so memorable examples of Constancy and Fortitude; therfore she is not only sayd to be their comforter, as we haue already meditated; but also their Queene,

Regina,

Regina Confessorum , Queene of Confessors .

THE XLIIII. MEDITATION.

Regina Virginum , ora pro nobis .

Queene of Virgins , pray
for vs .

OVR Blessed Lady hauing re-
mayned euer a perpetual Virgin , and being the first that dedicated herselfe vnto God by holy
vow of Virginity ; became the in-
uentour & foundresse of this Angelicall life; and therfore by great
reason, she is said to be the *Queene
of Virgins,* and by which title we
daily call vpon her saying, *Regina
Virginum , ora pro nobis ,* Queene
of Virgins pray for vs .

THE

THE XLV. MEDITATION.
Regina Sanctorū omniū ora pro nobis.
Queen of all Saints, pray for vs.

BRIEFLY in this tytle we may
consider, that what vertue or
excellent guift soeuer hath beene
eminent in any Saint, hath shy-
ned farre more in our blessed Lady; yea whatsoeuer naturall, or
supernaturall guift or grace, hath
beene in them all togeather, hath
byn all at once in this B. Queene;
& therfore most worthily we salute her by this renowned tytle,
of *Queene of all Saints*, and by this
desiring her powerfull prayers,
and holy intercession, we say,
*Regina Sanctorum omnium ora pro
nobis*, Queene of all Saints pray
for vs. Amen. *Aue Maris stella*

THE

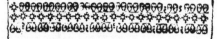

THE

CONCLVSION,

WITH AN APOSTROPHE

to the euer B Virgin.

MY intention (Right Ho-
nourable, and moſt worthy)
in theſe ſhort meditations, vvas
not to delight your eares with flowing eloquence, which is both
beyond my reach, & paſt my skil;
but my chiefe purpoſe tending
only to the encouragement of ſo
Noble a C O N G R E G A T I O N, ſo
happily inſtituted in Honor of the
Imaculate Virgin Mary, Mother
of God, & the ſatisfaction which

I hoped many other of her deuout Childrē by reading therof, would find ; I was the more willing to let it come to your view in the simple attyre wherwith it is vested.

For albeit, of it selfe , it be scarce worthy to be read of any ; yet for her sake, of whome it treateth, I desyre it may diligently be perused of many. Wherfore if any thing heerin be found worthy of commendations , let the praysе be giuen to the true deseruer ; for al that is blame-worthy, is wholly myne ; for which I craue , both your pardon for my errour and boldnes , and allso your prayers, for my future diligence , and a-mendment.

And thou thrice-happy and euer B. Virgin, Mother , Queene & Empresse of Heauen & Earth ,

whose

whofe Honour, next after thy
fweet Sonne I moſt intend, in
thefe my willing, but weake labours; be thou a Starre to enlighten thofe that read them; a Miſtreſſe to inſtruct them, a Patroneſſe to defend them, and a fafe
Guide to direct them, to the hauen of Eternall bliſſe, and euerlaſting happines. Amen.

THE

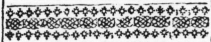

THE TABLE
OF THE CONTENTS.

The

Of the Contents.

OF THE CONTENTS.

The

FINIS.

ST. BENEDICT
The Rule of the Most Blissed
Father Saint Benedict
[1632]

THE RVLE

OF THE MOST BLISSED

FATHER

SAINT BENEDICT

PATRIAKKE

OF ALL MVNKES.

Tu iuxta Regulam Patrum viuere stude: maxime autem
Confessoris Sancti B E N E D I C T I, ne declinas
ab ea quoquam, nec illi addas quidquam, nec
minuas. Totum quod sufficit habet &
numquam minus habet. *Gregorius*
Mag. in manuscripto.

Indeuour to liue conformable to the Rule of the Fathers,
Butt especially of the Confessour Saint Benedict, do
nott swarue any way from itt, neither add you
any thinge to itt, nor take any thinge a way; for
itt hath that which sufficeth, and is in no-
thing defectiue.

Printed at Gant by I o o s D o o m s.

TO THE HONORABLE,
RIGHT REVERENDE
AND HER MOST RESPECTED LADY
THE LADY

EVGENIA POVLTON,

A BBESSE
OF THE ENGLISH MONASTERY
OF THE HOLY ORDER

OF S. BENEDICT
IN GANT.

Honorable, and Right Reuerende Madame

NEVER doe the newe ri-
singe sunne spreede forth his
beames , without a newe comfort
to the behoulders ; neither doth the
splendours yealded to so many
dayes, yeares, and ages , any whitt
deminish the accustomed solace taken by the newe Spectatours. And
can I doubt this glorious sunne ,

(2)

our Rule, a bright beame of diuine light, newely raised to shine in this place, by your lady shipps predicessour ãd your indeuour, bringe lesse them wonted ioy to the inioyers, ãd though itt hath illustrated the worlde, for many dayes, yeares, ãd ages, with so cleare beames of Illustrious sanctity, cannonizinge with glorious triũph more thẽ 3000 sainctes; brought frõ the obscurity of idolitry, to the light of faith, 33 nations; adorned the Church with 15000. Bishopps 7000 Archbishops 2000 Cardinalls, and twentye foure Popes, most of which shined vnto the world, as brightest starres hauinge taken ther lustre and light, as from the sunne, from this glorious Rule. Not to number

the

the innumerable florishinge monasteryes, the shininge and illustrious
Doctours, and writters, the intyre
and purest Virgines, fruites, which
this holy rule, as a most comfortable
sunne, hath produced, fostered, and
brought vp to inlighte ãd illustratt,
both with word, writinges and examples, of singuler sanctitye, the
whole Occidentall church, Can I (*as*
I say) yet douht, that the vigour
ther of, is any whitt deminished,
butt rather *as an experienced and*
an eye wittnesse can I auere, newe
comfort, ioy, ãd solace, raysed in the
mindes, and hartes, of the newe
Embracers, who vnder your lady-
shipps gouerment, happely doe *a*
newe inioy the splendour of that
light, and most comfortably do per-

(:)   take

take the fire of charity, which with herbeames, she doth inkindle in our hartes. Giue me therfore leaue, most Respected Madame, though after many ages , to lett this so holy a rule spreed her rayes a broade in our English tonge, vnder your ladishippes protection , that as you instill the loue of it in our hartes , so you would make itt obuious to our Eyes, and a monge the rest to hers, who desires to remaine as she this day is become.

Your Ladishipps.

Professed and vowed child,
ALEXIA GRAY.

THE

THE BREVE

OF

S. GREGORY POPE

FOR THE CONFIRMATION

OF THE RVLE

OF

SAINT BENEDICT.

I *Gregory Prælat of the holy Romane Church haue writt, the life of Saint Benedict, and reade the Rule which the Saint hath written with his owne hand, I haue praysed itt, and I haue confirmed itt in a Holy Counsell, and haue comanded, that through sundry partes of Italy, and wheresoeuer the Latine toung is vsed, itt should hee exactly, obserued by all whosoeuer to the end of the worlde, should come to a retyred life. And I also confirme the 12. Monasteryes the holy Saint erected.*

Ex originali in Monasterio sublacensi,

THE

THE BVLL
OF
ZACHARY POPE

Successor to Saint GREGORY
THE GREATE FOR THE
APPROBATION
OF THE RVLE
OF THE MOST HOLY
S. BENEDICT,

ZACHARY Byßhop, seruant of the seruantes of God. To all redeemed by the bloode of Christ, wisheth health and Apostolicall Benediction. VVee giue thankes to Almighty God, whose mercy is more deare then life, that he is glorious and admirable in his Saintes, and bistoweth with vnspeakeable bounty his vertues, ãd gistes. For he hath putt the most Blessed BENEDICT to bee the Father of all Munkes. He through the meritts of this Saint, hath made the monastery of Cassina placed in the grounde of Tertullus Patritius, to bee aboue all the Monasteryes in the worlde, where the Saint writt the Rule of Munkes, which our predicessour of holy memory Greg. hath aboundamly approued ãd praysed in his booke of Diologs, ãd wee approue and prayse, and declare itt to bee holy, and in the dedication of that holy church while wee are ther with therteen Arckbishoppes, threscore and eight Bishopes doe ordaine appointing that whe soeuer shall dare to contradict itt, bee excõmunicated

FINIS.

THE RVLE

OF OVR HOLY

FATHER S.' BENETT.

THE PREFACE

HARKEN *daughter to the commaundmēt of God thy Master : and inclyne the eare of thy hart, and willingly receaue the admonition, of thy pittifull Father, and put it in execution; to the end thou mayst retourne againe vnto him by the labour of thy obedience; from whom thou deddist depart by the negligence of thy disobedience. To thee therefore, which*

A   *dost*

doſt renounce thyn owne will with
intention to fight vnder Chriſt the
true king, and to take vppon thee
the ſtrong armour of obedience thes
wordes are addreſſed; firſt of all
deſire thou by moſt inſtant prayer,
that that good worke which thou
purpoſeſt to begin, in the may bee
perfected, that hee who hath vouch
ſafed to accoūt vs in the numbre of
his Children might not bee contri-
ſtated by our miſdemeanour; and
ſoe wee muſt alwayes obey him with
thoſe good parts that are in vs, that
not onely hee may not at any tyme
like an angry Father deſinheritt vs
his childrē, nor like a dreadfull lord
prouoked by our offences, adiudge

vs

vs as naughty seruants to perpetuall punishment, which would not
follow him to his Glory; Now therefore at lenght lett vs rise, the
holy Scripture exciting vs saying.
Now is the hower to rise out of sleep
and with open eyes and attentiue eares let vs behould the deuine
splendor, and heare that which the
voyce of God dayly crying doth
admonish saying. If this day you
shall heare his voyce harden not
your hartes. and againe: hee which
hath eares to heare lett him heare
what the spirritt sayth to the Churches; ād what sayth it. Come hether
Children giue eare to mee, I will
teach you the Feare of our lord God

Runn while you haue the light of
life , left the darcknesse of death
ouerreach you. And God seeking
his labourour amongst the Comon
sort of people , sayth furthermore :
what man is hee that wisheth life
and hath a desire to see gooddayes?
and if thou hearing this doft make
an sweare saying, I am hee. God
sayth vnto thee againe , it you wilt
enioy a true euerlasting life refray-
ne thy tonge from euill and thy
lipps from vttering lyes and de-
ceipts , shunn ewill and doe that
which is good, seeke peace and pur-
fue it; and at what tyme you shall
doe this , myne eyes shall watch
ouer you, and myne eares shalbee
at-

attentiue vnto your prayers &
before you shall call vppon mee I
will say vnto you, be hold I am present, what thing deare Sisters can
bee more pleasant to you, then this
voyce of God which thus doth in
vite you behould how our lord of
his Bounty, hath Vouchsafed to
shew you the way of life; hauing
therefore our loynes girt with
fayth and the obseruance of Good
VVorkes, and our Feete shodd by
guydance of the Ghospell, lett vs
goe forware in this way, that wee
may deserue to see him in his kingdome whoe hath bestowed vppon
vs this holy Vocation; In the Tabernacle of whose kingdome if wee

A 3   desire

desire to dwell, lett vs laboure
earnesly to doe good workes ; for
none commeth thither, but by meanes of their good deseruing ;
lett vs demaunde of God, saying
vnto him with the holy Prophet ,
lord whoe shall dwell in thy Tabernacle or whoe shall rest in thy
holy hill ? after wee haue asked
this questiõ, lett vs giue eare vnto
God ansaearing , and shewnig vs
the way, leading vnto this Tabernacle saying , hee that walketh
without blemish of Sinne, and doth
that which is most iust and righteous , who speaketh truth in his
hart , and forgeth noe Guyle in
his toung : who doth noe wrong to
his

his *Neighbour*, and receaueth noe
reproath against his *Neighbour*,
who hath cast out of his harte
that wicked *Tempter* the deuill
with all his perswasions, and hath
brought both him and his sugge-
stions to naught, ād hath taken his
Cogitations whyle they were new
and little, and hath dashed them
against the *Rooke*, which is *Christ*
who fearing god take not pride
in their well doing , but beleiuing
that the good they haue proceedeth
not of any power of theirs , but rather from our lord , and therefore
they prayse and gloryfy him , thus
working in them saying with the
Prophett. Not vnto vs lord not

*vnto vs , but giue Glory vnto thy
holy name, as S. Paul the Apostle
attributed not vnto him selfe, that
followed of his preaching , for hee
sayth , by the grace of God I am
that I am , and moreouer hee addeth, hee that will glory , lett him
glory in our lord. And therefore
our lord sayth in the Ghospell ,
euery one that heareth these my
words and doth them , shalbee li-
kned to a wise man, that buylt his
house vppon a Rocke , the Floods
came the winds blew , and they
beate against the house and it fell
not, for it was founded vppon a
Rocke, our lord proceeding with vs
in the same manner dayly expe-
ctecth*

Eteth that wee should bee correspondent to his holy admonitions; and therefore the dayes of this present life are afforded vnto vs in a manner of a truce, that there in wee might amend our wickednesse as the Apostle sayth, knowest thou not that the benignitie of God bringeth thee to Penance., for our morcifull lord sayth, I will not the death of a Sinner but that hee should be couerted ãd liue, therefor my good sisters when wee haue Demaunded of God, that person which is to dwell in his holy Tabernacle, wee vnderstand the precept annexed to that habitation, soe that if wee full fill the duty of

Inhabitants wee shalbee Inheri-
tours of the heuenly kingdone,
Come therefore ãd lett vs prepare
our harts and bodyes to serue in
the holy obedience of his Comma-
undements, and that which nature
is not able to worke in vs, lett vs
beeseech Almighty God that hee
will assist vs with his holy grace, ãd
if wee desire to Fly Hell Paynes,
and to attayne vnto euerlasting
life, whyle now wee may, and
that wee are in this mortall life,
that wee may atchiue all these
things by the light of grace, now
must wee run, now must wee
labour for that which may bee ex-
pedient for vs for euer hereafter
                                    wee

wee muſt therefore ſett vpp a
Schoole to teath the Seruice of
God therein , wherein wee hope
nothing ſhalbee tought by vs to
rigerous or to heauy , but if wee
proceede ſome what the more
ſtricktly according to the Rule of
Reaſon, for the correcting of Vice
and Conſeruation of Charitie ,
thou muſt not therefore vppon
Feare fortwith abandon the way
of thy Saluation , which cannot
bee begun but by a narrow Entrance , not with ſtanding after
ſome tyme ymployed in this Conuerſation at pleaſure thou ſhalt
run in the way of Gods Commaundements , hauing they hart
                              dilated

dilated by true Fayth and with vnspeakeable sweetenesse of Charitie, in such sort as wee neuer forsaking the Schoole of God, but persisting in his Doctrine, perseuering there in euen vntill death in the Monastery, wee may bee made pertakers of Christs paynes and Passion. soe that hereafter wee may deserue to bee his Compartners in his glorious kingdome.

HERE

HERE BEGINNETH THE RVLE OF OVR HOLY FATHER S. BENEDICT.

OF FOVRE SORTS OF RELIGIOVS.

CHAP I.

T is manifest that there are foure sorts of those which lead the monasticall life ; the first are Cenobites that is to say Conuentuall, trayned vp in a Rule vnder an Abbott or Abbesse. The second is of Anachorites that is to say, of Hermites, these are those that with noe Nouitiall feruor or heate of their new Conuersion, but after long triall of the Monasticall life, haue learned by the ayde and hartning of many to sight against the deuill, and being well armed may securely without the Consolation of any (only assisted with the Grace of God) by there owne force alone, proceede from their Fraternall Army, to vndertake the betayle against all their vices of their Flesh and Cogitations ; The third sort and that very pernitions, is of those which are called Sarabaites, who tried by noe Rule, which

is

is the Mistresse of experience, they seeme
like vnto the gould of the fornace, but yet
like vnto soft lead, still by their workes ad-
hering to the world, are knowne by their
tonsure how vnfaythfull and dissoyall they
are vnto God, whoe by twoes or threes or
alone by themselues without any Pastour or
Sheapherd shutt vpp in their owne Foulds,
and not in the Fould of our Lord, they take
the pleasure of their owne Wills, liking for
their Law, in accounting for holy whatsoeuer they shall thinke to bee good, or of what
soeuer they shall make election, and that to
bee only vnlawfull which is not according
to their Tast ; The Fourth sort is of thofe
whoe are called. Vagabonds which spend
all their life in running vp and dawne indi-
uers Prouinces, and lodge for two or three
dayes in diuers Monasteryes, allwayes walking and neuer setled, but at all tymes and at
all places subiect to their owne pleasures
and Gluttony; foe as thy are in all things far
worse then the Sarabaits whose miserable
kinde of life it is better to passe ouer with
Silence then to make any longer discourse
of the same. Omitting therefore allthese, lett
vs by the ayde of God come to sett downe
the order of the Cenobites which is the
strongest and durablest sort of all.

VVhat

VVhat a Kinde of Perſon the Abbeſſe ought to bee.

CHAPTER 2.

THE Abbeſſe which is worthy to haue the care of the Moneſtary, ought allwayes to beare in mynde her calling, and to expreſſe in her actions that which by her name is ſignified: for ſhee is to beare Chriſts perſon in the Monaſtary, ſeing ſhee hath his title as the Apoſtle ſayth, you haue receaued the Spirit of adoption of Children of God, in which wee call him Abba Father; wherefore the Abbeſſe ought not to teach, ordaine, or commaunde any thing which (as God for bid) ſhould bee againſt the Commaundements of our Lord, but her doctrine and commaundements ought to ſeaſon the harts of her diſciples as though it were the Leauen of Gods deuine Iuſtice, lett the Abbeſſe allwayes remember that an examination muſt bee made of her doctryne, and of her Schollers obedience, and that both together in the dreadfull day of iudgment of Almightie God. And lett the Abbeſſe vnderſtand that it is imputed to the Paſters fault, what want of proffitt ſoeuer the Lord and Maſter

may

may happen to finde in his sheepe, yet not
with standing shee shalbee freed, if she hath
bestowed all her dilligence vppon her vnquiett and disobedient Flocke, and that all
her care hath beene ymployed to heale
their corrupt and diseased meanners, soe
their Pastors being sett free in the Iudgment
of God, may say with the Prophett to our
lord, I concealed not thy Iustice in my hart
I Declared thy Truth ad Saluation, but they
contemning despised mee, and vppon the
Sheepe which disobeyed her care and solli-
citude, iust punishment shalbee inflicted, to
witt, death it selfe; when there fore any taketh vppon her the name of an Abbesse,
she ought to gouerne her Schollers, with
two sorts of Doctrynes, that is to say rather
to shew them all goodnesse and vertue, or
holynesse in her life, then in her words; that
shee propose in words alone the Commaundements of God to those that are capable
of Instructions, but to those that are harder
harted or more simple, shee must shew the
the will of God by her life and externall
behauiour; Therefore what soeuer shee shal
teach to bee hurtfull to her Schollers, lett
her shew by her owne actions, that they
must in noe case admitt it; lest she preaching
well vnto others, should bee found herselfe
to bee a Reprobate; and lest God might say
vnto

vnto her. offeuding in this manner,why declarest thou my Iustices , and takest vppon thee by thy Mouth,to talke of my law ? thou hast hated all disciplyne and hast cast my words behinde thy backe , and thou which diddest see a Straw in thy Brothers eye, didst not espy a Beame in thyne owne ; By her lett noe difference of persons bee made in the Monastery , lett not one be more fauored then an other , except itbee such ā one who shee shall finde to be better then the rest in her good behauiour and obedience,lett not the noble bee præferred before her,which was before her Conuertion of a base or seruile Condition ; except there shalbee some reasonable cause besides;And if soe bee, that vppon iust Consideration it shall seeme good to the Abbesse, lett her soe behaue her selfe in the seuerall degrees of each person : for otherwise lett euery one keepe her owne place;for wheter bond or Free;wee are all in our lord and Sauiour Christ,and wee beare the burthen of equall Seruitude vnder one and the selfe same lord , for there is noe exception of Persons with God,herein wee bee distinguished by him of wee bee found better then others in our well doing and of more humilitie;therefore lett her beare an equall affection to all,let one manner of disciplyne bee

B

bee obferued towards, all according to their merits and deferts. The Abbeffe in her manner of teaching ought allwayes to obferue that manner and Forme of the Apoftle , according to whith hee fayth, conuince, intreate sharpely, reprehend. that is tempering one tyme with another, fayre words with sharpe threatnings , lett her shew the feueritie of a Miftreffe, and againe the louing affection of a Mother , that is to fay she ought to reprehend sharpely the vnquiett , and thofe that will obferue noe dilcipline; and by intreaty to Deale with the obedient meeke and patient, that they will labour to goe ftill forward; But wee aduife her that shee reprehend sharpely and cor-rect thofe that are negligent and defpifers of dilciplyne; Neither lett her winke at the faults of thofe which offend, but as foone as any Vice beginnes to fpring lett her cut it of by the Rootes with all her forces poffible bearing allwayes in mynne the perilows punishment of Hely the Preift in Silo. lett her reprehend with onely Words the more honeft and docible natures for the firft and fecond tyme, but lett her punish with bo-dyly punishment and blowes the ftubborne hard harted and dilobedient, fo foone as euer they haue offended , knowing that it is written; the foole with words will not bee amended,

amended and againe ftrike thy Ghild with
the Rodd, and thou fhalt deliuer his Soule
from death; The Abbeffe ought to Remember allwayes whoe shee is, and what her
name imports, and to know that to whom
the more charge is committed, the more of
them muft bee exacted; and lett her confider
how hard and important a matter shee hath
taken in hand, as the gouerement of Soules,
and to accommodate her felfe to foe diuers
humours, and that shee muft conforme her
felfe to euery one, to this Sifter with fweete
in treating, to another with hard threatnings
to another with forcible perfwafions according to the Condition and Capacitie of
euery one that not onely shee fuffer noe do-
mage in the Flocke committed to her charge; but that shee may take Ioy in the dayly
increafe and augmentation of her good and
vertuous Troope: but aboue all lett her take
heed left with diffemblyng, and litle eftee-
ming the good of Soules committed vnto
her change, shee haue not too much care of
things that are tranfitory, earthly, and mortall; but lett her aboue all beare in mynde
allwayes that shee hath taken in hand the
gouernment of Soules, for which one day
shee muft render an account; and that shee
may not complayne of the flender Subftace
of her Monaftery lett her remember what

is written;First seeke the kingdome of God
and the ustice of him , and all o her things
shalbee giuen you besides ; and againe nothing is wanting to those which feare him;
And lett the Abbesse consider with herselfe
that as shee hath taken vppó her the charge
of other folkes Soules,soe must shee prouide
to giue vpp an account for them , and see
how many Sisters are vnder her direction,
soe lett her most certaynly know that shee
must giue a reckning to our lord in the day
of Iudgment for their Soules,and that without all doubt besides the Reckning shee
must make for her owne Soule ; The Shee-
phard shall endure for all the Sheepe which
was put to her charge,whiles shee dilligétly
prouideth for the giuing vpp of other Folks
accounts,shee shall also thereby bee made
more carefull of her owne ; and while by
her dilligent admonition , shee procureth
the amendment of others   , shee herselfe
is cleared and sett free from her owne.

Of the manner how to call and admit the sisters to Counsayle;

CHAPTER 3.

SOE often as any businesse of great importance falls out to bee done in the Monastary. lett the Abbesse call togeather the whole conuent and lett her giue them notice what is there to bee handled ; And hauing heard the aduise of her sisters lett her consider well there of with her selfe, and then lett her putt in execution that, which shee iudgeth to bee most expedient, wee therefore sayd that all should bee called to Counsayle . for that our lord often tymes reuealeth to the younger, that which may bee the best ; But the Sisters must soe giue their aduise, that it bee with all humilitie and submission, soe that they may not presume stiffly to stand to their owne opinion , but they may rather rely vppon the Abbesses Iudgment, that what soeuer shee shall Iudge to bee the more fitt , to that the rest may submitt themselues; but as it is conuenient the Schollers should obey their Mistris, soe againe it is thought meete that shee should prouidently and iustly dispose of all things, Therefore lett them all in all

thing

things follow the rule of their Miſtris, neither lett any bee soe bould as to ſwarue from it;in the Monaſtery none muſt follow her owne harts deſire,Neither lett any Dare to preſume arrogantly to contend with her Abbeſſe ; either with in or without ſhe Monaſtery,and if any ſhould happ n to bee ſoe preſumtious , lett her bee ſubmitted vnder reguler diſciplyne and Correction; Not with ſtanding lett the Abbeſſe doe all things with the feare of God;and according to the Rule,knowing that without all doubt ſhee is to yeald an accompt to God the moſt righteous Iudge of all her Iudgments, yet if any other things happen for the Commoditie of the Monaſtery which are of leſſe importance,ſhee may onely vſe the Counſayle of the Seniours , according to that which is written ; Doe all thy affayres with Counſayle, and after thou haſt done ſoe. it ſhall not repent thee.

Of the Inſtruments of good VVorkes.

CHAPTER 4

1. THE firſt Inſtrument is aboue all things to loue god whith all thy hart with all thy Soule,and with all thy Force
2.And

2. And thy Neighbour as thy selfe.
3. To doe noe murder;
4. To committ noe Adultery;
5. Not to steale;.
6. To haue noe vnlawfull desires;
7. To beare noe false VVitnesse;
8. To honour euery one,
9. Not to doe that to others which shee would not haue done to her selfe;
10. To deny her selfe that shee may the better follow Christ;
11. To Chastice the body;
12. To seeke after noe pleasures or delights.
13. To loue Fasting,
14. To helpe the poore,
15. To cloth the naked;
16. To Visitt the Sicke;
17. To bury the Dead;
18. To assist those that are in Tribulation
19. To Comfort those that are in greife or Desolation.
20. To with draw herselfe from the affayres and businesses of the VVorld.
21 To preferr nothing before the loue of Christ.
22. Not to worke her anger.
23. Not to watch for a tyme where in to execute and accomplish it;
24. To conceale noe guyle in her harte;

25. Not

25.　Not to make a fayned peace;

26.　Neither to leaue Charitie;

27.　Neither to sweare lest she for sweare

28.　To tell the Truth both in thought and word.

29.　Not to requite ill with ill againe;

30.　To doe iniury to none, but to suffer patiently, what soeuer iniury is offered her;

31.　To loue her Enemyes;

32.　Not to speake ill of those that speake ill of her, but rather to speake Well of them, and to pray for them;

33.　To endure persecution for Iustice sake

34.　Not to bee Proude;

35.　Not to bee a Dronkard;

36.　Not to bee an ouer greate eater;

37.　Not to bee giuen to sleepe and Idlenesse;

38.　To bee noe Murmurer;

39.　To bee noe Detracter;

40.　To repose all her hop in our God.

41.　If shee see any good in her selfe, to attribute it vnto god, and not vnto her selfe but what souer euill shee hath lett her know that it commeth from herselfe, and soe to impute it to herselfe;

42.　To dread the day of Iudgment;

43.　To haue a Feare of Hell;

44.　VVith all her force to desire the euerlasting life;

45. To

45. To haue allwayes her death before her eyes?

46. To haue a continuall eye to her Actions;

47. To know that shee is most certaynely in the sight of god;

48. To Crush quickly her euill Cogitations as they come with Remembrance of Christ, ãd to manifest them toher ghostly Father;

49. To keepe her Mouth from euill and in conuenient speaking;

50. Not to loue much talking;

51 To vse noe vayne words or which might moue to laughter;

52. To auoyde much ãd Dissolute laughter

53. To heare willingly Deuoute and holy lessons;

54. To giue her selfe much to prayer;

55. To confesse each day to god, in her prayers, her naughty life and offences, with Teares and Sorrow, and afterwards to amend her selfe of them;

56. Neuer to fullfill her sensuall and carnall desires?

57. To hate her owne will;

58. To bee obedient in all things to the Commaundements of the Abbesse al though shee, (which God forbidd) should doe otherwise then in duty shee

B 5   ought

ought to doe ; remembring what God commaundeth, doe that which your Superiours say, and not what they doe;

59.　Not to desire to bee esteemed good, before shee is soe, but lett her bee soe, that truly shee may bee accounted soe;

60.　To full fill effectually Gods Commaundements;

61.　To loue Chastitie.

62.　To hate none;

63.　To beare enuy and an euill mynde towards none;

64.　To loue noe manner of brabling and brawling;

65.　To fly vanting and bragging;

66.　To honour her Elders;

67.　To loue her Iuniours in Iesus Christ;

68.　To pray for her Enemyes;

69.　To retourne vnto peace and concord which those with whom shee hath disagreed and that before the Sunne goe downe;

70.　And neuer to mistrust the Mercyes of God.

Behould here the Instruments of the spirituall art, which if wee fullfill continually, Day, and night . hauing layed them vpp against the day of Iudgment; the Crowne which hee hath promised shalbee giuen vnto vs; The eye hath not seene, the eare

hath

hathnot heard, nor the hart conceaued, that which God hath prepared for those which loue him The shopp where wee may Dilligently exercise all these things is the Monastery and constant perseuerance in the Congregation;

Of the obedience of the sisters;

CHAPTER 5.

OBEDIENCE without delay is the first degree of humilitie, that which is most delightfull unto those vnto whom nothing is more deare then Iesus Christ, in respect of that holy seruice which they haue vowed vnto him, or for the feare of hell, or for the Glory of that life, which is euer to endure, soe soone as any thing is commaunded them by their Superiour, they can endure noe delay in accoplishing it; as though the Commaundement was made vnto them by God himselfe, of whom our lord sayth in the hearing of his eare hee hath obeyed mee, and hee sayth vnto Prelates, whoe soe heareth you heareth mee. Therefore all such persons, forsaking forth with that which liketh their owne Fancy and will, and leauing the workes of their hands, about which

they

they were occupyed vnfinished and vnper-
fited;lett them presently with the Foote of
obedience follow the voyce of the Comma-
under,and in one and the selfe some momét
lett the Action of the Scholler bee vnited
with the Commaundement of the Mistris in
all dilligence and in the Feare of God,which
twoe thinges are most comóly accóplished
by those that haue a desire to goe to the euer
during life,and therefore they take the narrow may which leadeth vnto life,to the end
they way not liue at their owne will ád pleasure,but to liue and walke after the Iudgmét
and cómaundement of another,liuing in a
Monastery,and desiring to haue an Abbesse
and Prelate ouer them; without all doubt
such persons as these , follow that sentence
of our lord where in hee sayth : I came not
to doe my owne will , but the will of him
that sent mee;Then shall this obedience bee
agreable vnto God, and delightfull vnto
men;if that which is commaunded bee accomplished not timorously slowly ,or with
murmuration , or with an answeare,as it
were of one who had noe mynde or will to
obey : for the obedience which is done to
Superiours ,is done to God; For heesayd
whoe soe heareth you heareth mee;and it is
necessary that the Schollers obey with a good
and a m erry Cheere , for God loueth the
                              merry

merry giuer; For if shee obey with a repining hart, al though shee murmur not whith her mouth, but onely in her hart, and yet fullfilleth that, which is commaunded, not withstanding it will not bee gratefull to God, which beholdeth the hart of the Murmurer; and by such an Action shee obtayneth noe Grace afall; but deserueth the scourge of such as are Murmurers, except shee Repent her and make due satisfaction by her amendment;

Of Silence.

CHAPTER. 6

LETT vs fullfill that which the Prophett sayth, I haue sayd I will keepe my wayes that I offend not with my Tong, I haue put a watch before my Mouth, I became speeth lesse, and humbled my selfe, and held my peace in those things, that where good; here the Prophett sheweth, that some tymes wee must not speake of good maters and that in regard of silence, how much more ought wee to keepe our Mouths from naughty and vayne talke, for feare of committing Sinne thereby, therefore the perfect Sister may rarely haue licence to talke, though otherwise of good and holy matters, in regard of

the

the great decency of silence; for it is written
in many words thou shalt not eschew sinne;
and in another place, life and death is in the
power of a Toung; for it belongeth to the
Mistris to speake and to instruct, and it
apportayneth to the Scholler to giue eare,
and keepe silence; And therefore if you haue
neede to demaunde any thing of the Abbesse
doe it with all humilitie submission, and
Reuerence. VVee vtterly condemne by this
perpetuall prohibition, in all places to vse
any scurrell speech, or idle words, giuing
cause to laughter, and wee doe not permitt
that the Sisters euer open their Mouth to any
such manner of talke.

Of the sundry and manifold Commenda-tions of Humilitie.

CHAPTER. 7

SIsters the holy Scripture cryeth out vnto
vs and sayth, hee which exalteth himselfe
shalbee humbled and hee which humbleth
himselfe shalbee exalted; and in soe saying
it declareth vnto vs that all exaltation is a
kinde of Pride, from which how dilligently
the Prophett, kept himselfe hee sheweth
when hee sayth; o lord my hart was not exalted,

ted, and my eyes were not borne aloft, neither haue I walked in marueylous things aboue my selfe, but what if I haue not thought humbly of my selfe, and if I haue exalted my Soule then lett mee bee rewarded in such sort, as the Child that is seperated frō his mothers breast, and therefore Sisters if wee will react to the topp of this soueraigne humilitie, lett vs by our Actions tending to heauen wards, reare vpp the ladder which appeared to Iacob in his sleepe, on which the Angells were seene to ascend and descend; this ascent and descent giueth vs to vnderstand nothing els but the exaltation which proceedeth of humblyng our selfes, and the deicent which is by exalting our selfes; And this ladder thus erected may bee sayd to bee our life in this world. the which by humilitie of hart, god lifteth vpp to heauen; and wee say our Soule and body are the sides of this ladder, where in his deuine Vocation hath sett diuers digrees of humilitie or discipline where by to ascend vpward.

Of the first degree of humilitie.

THE first degree is if shee haue the feare of God before her hyes, and that shee take heed that shee neuer for gett herselfe,

and

and that shee continually beare in memory
all which God hath commaunded, and how
those which contemne god shall endure the
paynes of Hell for their Sinnes and offences
and that shee haue allwayes her hart setled
on the euerlasting life, which is ordayned
for those that feare our lord, and that shee
keepe herselfe at all howers and moments
from Sinne, and Vice, either of the thought,
of the Toung, of the eyes, of the hande, of the
Feete, of her owne will, and that shee endeauour to roote out all fleshly desires, lett each
one consider that shee is continually in the
sight of God, which is in heauen, and to bee
seene with his deuyne eyes, and at all moments to bee presented before him, by holy
Angells; The Prophet sheweth this when
hee declareth that god is priuy to our very
cogitations, saying. God searcheth the harts
and Raynes; And againe hee sayth God knoweth the Cogitations of mē, and more ouer
thou vnderstandest my Cogitations a farr of;
and an other tyme, the thought of man shall
bewray it selfe to thee; therefore to the end
shee may bee carefull of her ill Cogitations
lett the humble Sister allwayes say in her
hart. I shall then bee pure and fayre in the
sight of God; when I shall keepe my selfe
from all Iniquitie; Wee are forbidd to doe
our owne Wills when the Scripture sayth
                                        vnto

vnto vs leaue your Wills, and wee say to god in our prayers, that his Will bee done in vs; Therefore wee are taught not to doe our owne Willes, when wee looke to that which the Scripture sayth, there are some wayes which seeme vnto men to bee right good, the end where of leadeth to the bottomelesse pitt of hell; and alsoe wee shall auoyde that which is sayd of the negligent, that they become Corrupt liuers, and abominable in their delights, lett vs sted fastly beleiue that God is still present to all our carnall desires, according to the Words of the Prophett spoken to god, before thee are all my desires; Therefore wee must esch ew all euill desires, for death standeth neere to the entry of delectation; And therefore the Scripture sayth, follow not thy Concupiscences; If therefore the eyes of God behold both good and badd, and if the god of heauen looke downe vppon the sonnes of men, to see if there bee any that attend and seeke after God, and if the Angells that are appoynted to keepe vs night and day shew our workes vnto our Creatour; wee must therefore good Sisters bee euer Watchfull to that which the Prophett sayth in his Psalme, that god see vs not at any tyme declyning vnto ill and becomming vnprofitable, ād thoughe hee pardon vs for the present becaufe hee is

C   me

mereifull, and expecteth that wee conuert
our selues to a better life, yet giue him not
occasion to say hereafter, thou hast committed these things and I held my peace and
sayd not a word;

Of the 2. Degree of Humilitie;

THE second degree is, if any not louing
her owne will, take noe pleasure to
worke her owne desires, but followeth in
her manner of liuing the voyce of our lord.
which sayth, I came not to doe my owne
will, but the will of him that sent mee; alsoe
the Scripture sayth, that the Will hath payne,
and necessity purchaseth the Crowne;

Of the third Degree of Humilitie;

THE third Degree is when shee ren-
dret hher selfe subiect in all obedience
to her Superiour, for the loue of God, inuita-
ting there in our lord of whom the Apostle
sayth, that hee was obediet euen vnto death.

Of

Of the fourth degre of Humilitie:

THE fourth degree is, if in obedience
exercised in hard, yea in Contrary
matters and in what soeuer iniuryes are
done her, shee inbrace patience in her Conscience with all Secrecy, and is not wea-
ryed of suffering and yealdeth not, the Scripture saying who soe shall perseuer vnto
the end shalbee saued ; and againe bee cou-
ragious of hart, and atted our lords pleasure;
And the Scripture (shewing vs that the
loyall Christian ought to endure all things
for gods sake though they bee neuer soe
contrary) sayth in the person of the patient
man; for the loue of thee, wee dy each day,
wee are esteemed as sheepe destinated to
the slaughter; and being by hope assured of
the reward at Gods hands, they say with
comfort that which followeth , But in all
these things wee ouercome by the healpe
of him which loueth vs all, soe the Scripture
sayth in another place; Thou hast suffred vs
to bee lett downe into the lake ; and hast
layd tribulation vppon our backs ; and for to
shew vs that wee ought to bee subiect to our
Superiours, it followeth , thou hast sett men
ouer our heads; fullfilling alsoe with patience the commaundements of God in

what

what soeuer aduersities and iniuryes may bee offered ; If being strooke on the one Cheeke they turne the other, and lett goe their Cloake to him that takes their Coate, when one forceth them to goe one mile lett them walke with them two; And enduring with S. Paul the Apostle the persecution of false brethren; blesse those that curse and speake euill of thee.

Of the 5. degree of Humilitie :

THE fift degree is, if shee hide not from her Superiours by humble confession all those naughty Cogitations which proceede from the hart, and the Sinne which shee hath committed in secrett; The Prophett exhorteth vs hereunto saying, Reueale thy wayes vnto God, ãd putt thy hope in him; and againe it is sayd, confesse your selfe to god for hee is good, and his mercy endureth for euer , and alloe the Prophett sayth, I haue manifested to thee my Sinne and I haue not Cloaked myn Iniustice , I haue determyned that I will pronounce against my selfe my Iniustice vnto God; and thou hast forgiuen mee the Sinne, of my hart.

Of

Of the 6. degree of Humilitie:

THE 6. Degree is if the Religious bee content which all basenesse and extremitie, and that shee iudge her selfe an ill labourer, and vnworthy of all those things which are enioyned her to doe, saying which the Prophett; I am brought to no thing and I know it not, I am like a brute beast towards thee, and I am allwayes with thee.

The 7. degree of Humilitie.

THE 7. Degree is, if shee not onely with the mouth confesse, but alsoe from her hart beleiue that shee is the least and the basest of all others; humbling her selfe and saying with the Prophett; I am a worme and not a man, and the scorne of men and the Refuse of the people, but being exalted, I haue beene humbled and confounded. Againe, It is good for mee that thou hast humbled mee, that I may learne to keepe thy Commaundements:

Of the 8. degree of Humilitie.

THE eight degree is, if the Religious doe nothing els, but as the common Rule of the Monaſtery , and the Examples of her Elders teacketh her ;

Of the 9. degree of Humilitie.

THE nynth Degree is if the Religious refraine her toung from ſpeaking , but keeping her ſilence ſpeake not before ſhee bee demaunded; for the Scripture ſheweth, much ſpeeck cannot bee without Synne and that hee which is full of Toung ſhall not well bee directed vppon earth.

Of the 10. degree of Humilitie.

THE tenth Degree is if the Religious bee not eaſy and prompt to laughter, for it is written, the foole laughing exalteth his voyce.

Of the 11. degree of Humilitie.

THE cleuenth degree is if the Religious vſe few words in her ſpeath and thoſe
very

veryreasonable, sweete without laughter
humble with grauitie, lett her not bee cla-
mourous in her voyce, as it is written, the
wiseman telleth his mynde in few words;

Of the 12. degree of Humilitie.

THE twelueth degree is if shee not
onely with her hart, but with her body,
alsoe shew allwayes humilitie, vnto those
which behould her, that is to say that in her
worke in the Church, Monastery or Garden
or in the way abroude in the Feilds, or in
what Place soeuer shee sitt, stand, or walke,
shee allwayes hould downe her head and
fix her eyes on the ground, euer calling to
mynde that shee is guilty, for her Synnes, ãd
offences, and that shee is already presented
before the dreadfull Iudgment Seate of
God, saying that with the Publican in the
Ghospell, lord I am not worthy to lift vpp
myne eyes to heauen, and againe with the
Prophett, I am pluckeddowne and humbled
on euery side; when therefore the Religious shall haue mounted ouer all these degrees of humilie, she shall come vnto that
Charitie which being perfect expelleth all
eare, and soe that which shee kept before
not without feare, shee shall begin to keepe

C 4   after-

afterwards vppon a Cuſtome , and in a naturall manner without labour;not for the feare ofeuell but for the loue of Chriſt, and by a good Cuſtome,and for the delight fullneſſeſhee ſhall finde in Vertue ; the which our lord will ſhew with his holy Spiritt in his laborer which is free from all Vice and Sin nefullneſſe ;

Of the deuyne Office in the night:

CHAPTER. 8.

IN the Winter tyme , that is from the Kalends or firſt day of Nouember vntill Eaſter according vnto reaſonable Conſideration they muſt riſe at the eight hower of the night, ſoe that they may reſt a litle more then halfe the night, and then riſe hauing well digeſted that which they haue eaten, but that tyme which remayneth after Mattins muſt bee employed in holy Meditations,(excepting thoſe Siſters which haue neede to learne any thing in their Pſalters) and reading;But from Eaſter vnto the affore ſayd Kalends of Nouember , lett ſoe the tyme of the watcking bee tempered that there may bee left ſome litle ſpace , wherein the Siſters may depart to doe that which
is

is needfull and neceſſary vnto nature, that they may incontinently beginn the laudes, which muſt bee ſayd as ſoone, as the day appeareth.

In what manner the deuyne Seruice is each day to bee accomplished;

CHAPTER 9

AS the Prophett ſayth ſeuen tymes a day I shewed forth thy prayſes, which holy number of ſeuen shall thus bee full-filled if wee pay the duty of our Seruice vnto him which the howers of mattins, Prime, Terce, Sixt, Nynth, Euenſong, and Complyne, for of theſe howers the Prophet meaneth, when hee ſayth ſeauen tymes each day I shewed forth thy prayſe; for of the Noďturne and Seruice in the night, the ſame Prophett ſayth, at Midnight I aroſe to giue prayſe to thee, therefore at thoſe tymes lett vs giue prayſe vnto our Creatour, vppő the Iudgments of his Iuſtice to witt at the howers of Mattins, Prime, Terce, Ninth, Euenſong, and Complyne, and lett vs riſe in the higheſt to doe honour and homage vnto him;

C 5   Of

Of the Difciplyne of finging the deuine Seruice;

CHAPTER 19.

WEE beleiue that God is prefent in euery place and that the eyes of our lord behouldeth both the good and the badd, yet notwithftanding lett vs beleiue this with out all doubt, efpecially when wee affift at the deuyne Seruice, beare therefore in mynde that which the Prophett fayth, ferue our lord with feare, and againe fing fauoroufly, that is with fpirituall taft and feeling: And in the fight and prefence of the Angells I will fing vnto thee; Therefore lett vs Confider how wee ought to behaue our felfes in his deuyne prefence, and before his holy Angells, and lett vs foe attend to our Song that our thoughts may accord with our voyces;

Of

Of the Reuerence which is to bee vsed in Prayer;

CHAPTER 11.

IF when wee deliuer any Supplication to men of account, wee dare not present our selfes before them but with lowly nesse and Reuerence ; therefore With much humilitie, Reuerence, and purity of Deuotion ought one to offer her prayers vnto God the lord of all things, and lett vs beleiue that our prayers are not herd for our babling, but for puritie of hart, and Compunction Ioyned with teares ; and therefore your prayers ought to bee breife and pure, except it bee prolonged by the inspiration of the grace of almightie God ; not with standing lett the tyme of Prayer bee short in the Couent, and after the Superiour hath giuen a Signe lett them all rise vpp;

Of the Deanes of the Monastery;

CHAPTER 12.

IF the Congregation shalbee great lett some Sisters of good Name, and holy Conuersa-

uersation bee chosen from the rest and appoynted deanes; whoe are to haue care of
ten other Sisters in all things according to
the Commaundemens of god and of their
Abbesse, the which deanes ought to bee ele-
ded in such sort as the Abbesse may securely part amongst them her burthē ād charge;
and lett them not bee elected according to
their order, but according to their life, and
deserts, and experience of their discretion,
for if any of them by chance being puffed
vpp with pride, should bee found worthy
of reprehension, being admonished for the
first, second, and third tyme.if shee amend
not, lett her bee throwne out of office, and
lett another succeede that shalbee found
more worthy of that place, and the like wee
doe appoynte to bee done as concerning
the Prioresse;

The manner how the Religious ought to Sleepe;

CHAPTER. 13.

LETT euery one sleepe alone in a beed
by her selfe, lett them receaue their bedding after the manner of their conuertion
                                                      at the

at the difposition and appoyntment of the
Abbeffe, lett them fleepe all in one place if
it may bee conueniently, but if the great-
neffe of their Company will not permitt it,
lett them take their repofe by tens and
twentyes togeather, with thofe ancients
which haue charge ouer them, let allways a
Candle burne in the dorture vntill it bee
morning, lett them fleepe in their Cloathes
girt with ropes, or other girdles, and whyle
they take their reft, lett them haue noe
kniues hanging by their fides, for feare of
hurting themfelues in their fleepe; and that
the Religious may allwayes bee in a readi-
neffe to rife forthwith as they fhall heare
the Signe, lett the make haft each one to bee
before the other at the worke of God,
which thing fee that they doe which great
modefty and grauitie; lett not the younger
fort haue their places one neere another,
but lett them allwayes haue fome of their
ancients betwixt them; when they rife vnto
the worke of god, lett each exhort the other
with modefty to make fpeede for the ex-
cufes of thofe that are drowfy and giuen to
fleepe;

Of

Of the Excommunication
of faults ;

CHAPTER 14.

IF any Sister should bee selfe willed, or
disobedient, or proude, or a murmurer,
or in any thing Repugnante to the holy Rule
and Precepts, if shee bee founde a Contemner of the ancients, lett this Sister bee admonished secretly for the first, and second
tyme by her Ancients, if shee amend not,
lett her bee reproued publickely before
others, but if shee will not amend for all
this, lett her bee excommunicated, if shee
vnderstand what kinde of punishment Excommunication is, but if shee bee shame-
lesse ãd past amendment, lett her bee Put to
bodyly, punisment † lett the Excommunication and punisment bee measured according to the qualitie of the fault, the which
qualitie shall bee iudged by the Iudgment
of the Abbesse; But if the Sister bee found
in some lesser faults, lett her bee depriued
from the participation of the Comon Table
with others; This is the order which must
bee obserued towards those that are depriued of the Company of the rest at Table,
that they beginn noe Psalme. or Antyme
in

in the Church nor reade any leſſon vntill
ſuch tyme as they haue made ſatisfaction,
lett her take her meate a lone after all the
other Siſters haue ended their refection, as
for Example , if the Siſters eate at the ſixt
hower, ſhee ſhall attend till the Nynth , and
if the Siſters eate at the Nynth ſhee ſhall
attend till the tyme of Euenſong , vntill by
dew ſatisfaction ſhee hath obtayned her
pardon;

Of the more greuious kinds of faults.

CHAPTER 15.

LET that Siſter that is guylty of the
more greiueous fault bee depriued from
the Church and refectory, lett her haue noe
conuerſation or Conference with any of the
Siſters, lett her liue all alone attending to
that worke which is enioyned her perſi-
ſting in the bitterneſſe of Pennance conſidering that terrible Sentence of the Apoſtle;
That ſuch a one is deliuered, to Sathan for
the deſtruction of the Fleſh that the Spirit
may bee ſaued in the day of our lord; lett
her take refection alone in ſuch quantitie
and

and at such tyme as the Abbesse shall thinke
good, neither lett her bee saluted or blessed
by any which passe by her, neither lett the
meates bee blessed that are giuen her
to eate;

Of those that Ioyne themselues wich such as are excommunicated.

CHAPTER 16.

IF any shall presume without the Abbesses lycence to ioyne her selfe in any
sort with the Sister that is excommunicated to speake to her, to send her any thing
let her incurr the punishment of the like
Excommunication;

In what manner the Abbesse ought to bee carefull of those that are Excommunicated;

CHAPTER 17.

LETT the Abbesse beare herselfe towards the Sisters that offend withall
carefulnesse, because the Phisition is not
needfull for those that are in health, but for
                 such

such as are sicke, and therefore shee ought
to vse all meanes of a wise Phisitian to send
to them secrett Comforters , that is to say
some of the Ancients, and some of the dis-
creter sort of the Religious, which may as
it were secretly comfort the troubled Sister, and incite her to humble satisfaction,
and might alsoe comfort her that shee bee
not wholly drowned and oppressed with
two much greife and discomfort; but that
as the Apostle sayth, Charitie may bee confirmed in her, and lett euery one pray for
her; for the Abbesse ought to bee right care
full, and to vse all prudence and dilligence,
that shee lose none of her Flocke, for shee
must vnderstand that shee hath taken the
charge of infirme and weake Soules, and not
any tyrannicall or cruell authoritie ouer
those that are Whole; And lett her feare the
threatning of the Prophett by whom our
lord sayth ; that which you saw to bee fatt
you tooke to your selues , and that which
was weake you cast away , And lett her
follow that Example of pitty of the good
Sheepherd whoe leauing nynety nyne
sheepe in the Monntaines , went to seeke
out one that had erred : vppon whose infirmitie hee had soe great compassion, that hee
vouthsafed to lay her vppon his sacred
Shoulders, and soe to bring her backe to his
fould againe ;   D   of

Of those that haue beene often corrected: and will not amend.

CHAPTER 18.

IF any Sister hath beene often corrected for any fault, and if shee will not amend though shee hath beene excommunicated; lett her haue more seuere correction, and then lett the Abbesse proceede euen to Chastisement by shrokes, and if for all that shee will not amend or els, (with God forbidd, puffed vpp with pride should mayntayne and defend her owne doings, lett the Abbesse doe that which the expert Phisitian vseth to doe, who when hee hath applyed the fomentations and oyntments of good exhortations, the Remedyes of holy Scriptures, and finally the burning and seering of Excommunication, to geather with the incision ãd launcing of bodyly Chastisement; if then shee see that her labour is in vayne, lett her vse (which is most effectuall) her owne Prayers and the prayers of all the Sisters for her; that our lord which is omnipotent would worke some cure vppon this infirme Sister, and if by this meanes shee shall not bee cured, then lett the Abbesse vse the knife of abscision, as the Apostle sayth; Take

the

the euill from amongst you , and againe if
the Infidell will depart lett her depart, lest
that one diseased sheepe should infect the
whole Flocke;

Of young Children and how they are to bee corrected.

CHAPTER 19.

EVERY one must bee measured according to their age and capacity , and the-
retore soe oft as the Children, or the younger sort, or such as doe not sufficiently
vnderstand how great a punishment Excommunication is, lett these when they
offend bee penanced or bee seuerely chasti-
sed with the road;

Of the ofice and duty of the Cellarier;

CHAPTER 20.

THE Cellarier of your Monastery ought
to bee such a one of your Congregaion
as is wise, gentle, and sober, not gluttenous,
proude, easy to bee in passion , iniurious,

sloug-

flouggish, or lauish, but which hath the
feare of God in her hart, and may bee as it
were a very Mother to the whole Congregation, and shee ought to haue the Care of
all things, and to doe nothing without the
Commaundement of the Abbiſſe, but ſtill
to accomplish that which is commaunded
her, and lett her not bee ouer greuous to
the Siſters, and if any should make to her
any vnreaſonable requeſt, lett her not for
all that by any contemptable vſage giue
them cauſe of diſguſt, but lett her in a meeke
ſort deny them, that with they doe not well
and reaſonably demaunde, lett her looke
well vnto her owne Soule : remembring
that which the Apoſtle ſayth, That they
which haue miniſtred well shall purchaſe
vnto them ſelues a good degree ; lett her
haue a moſt diligent care of the ſicke Children, of the gueſtes, and of the poore : knowing that without all doubt shee shall
render an accompt for al theſe att the day of
Iudgment, lett her haue the Cuſtody of all
the Veſſells, neceſſaryes, and Subſtance of
the Monaſtery, and lett her looke vnto them
as shee would vnto thoſe things that are
conſecrated vnto Gods Altar, and lett her
not thinke that any thing is to bee negligently regarded ; lett her neither bee too
ſparing, or a waſter of the Subſtance of the
                                    Mona-

Monastery, but lett her doe all things with moderation, according to the Commandements of the Abbesse, before all things lett her conserue her selfe in humilitie, and when shee hath nothing to giue vnto her which requireth any thing of her, at lest wise giue good wordes, for good words are much better then a good gift, lett her haue a care ād Custody of those things, which the Abbesse shall appoynte her to haue in charge, and shee shall not presume to intermeddle her selfe with any thing that shall bee forbidden her, lett her giue the Portions ordayned for the Sisters without all deceipt and delay to the end that none bee scandalized, being mynde full what they deserue according to the words of God, whoe scandalyze any of these litle ones, If the Congregation bee great lett her haue the assistance of some Sisters, by whose ayde shee may ioyfully accomplish her duty and charge; That which is to bee giuen or distributed must bee done at competent and fitt tymes, and that which is to bee requested of her lett it bee requested in a due season that none may bee troubled or molested in in the house of God;

Of

Of the Iron Tooles and other things belongnig to the Monaſtery;

CHAPTER 21.

AS concerning the Subſtance of the Mónaſtery, the Iron Iuſtruments, the Apparell, or what els ſoeuer, lett the Abbeſſe prouide ſuch Siſters of whoſe life and good behauiour ſhee may bee ſecure, to whom ſhee may deliuer certayne things, as ſhee ſhall thing good to bee by them kept or amaſſed ād gathered togeather, of which things the Abbeſſe muſt keepe an Inuétory, that when the Siſters come to demaund any thing ſhee may know what ſhee receaueth and what ſhee giueth out. If any vſe thoſe things which belong to the Monaſtery negligently or ſluttiſhly lett her bee puniſhed, and if ſhee doe not amend lett her bee put to regular diſcipline;

VVether the Religious ſhould haue any thing proper to themſelues or noe;

CHAPTER 22.

THIS Vice of propriety much bee wholly plucked vpp by the Rootes

out

out of the Monastery that none presume to
giue or Receaue any thing what soeuer proper to themselues: not soe much as a booke
or writting Tables or any Instrument to
write withall, yea nothing at all; for they
ought to haue neither bodyes nor wills at
their owne disposing; They must receaue
all their necessaryes from their Abbesse
neither shall it bee lawfull for them to haue
any thing, but that which the Abbesse shall
giue them, or appoynte them to haue; lett
euery thing bee common to euery one as it
is written; neither lett any presume to say
that any thing is her owne, If soe bee that
any shalbee found to take delight in this
pernitions Vice, lett her bee once or twice
admonished, and if shee amend not lett her
bee punished;

VVhether euery one ought to receaue all necessaryes equally.

CHAPTER 23.

IT is written that to euery one was distributed according to their necessity; Wee
say not that their should bee any distinction
of Persons (god for bidd) but rather that
Consideration bee had of euery ones infirmity,

D 4

mity, foe that shee which hath leffe neede
bee thankefull to god therefore, and noe
way greiued in her mynde ; but shee that
hath more neede muft bee more humble
in refpect of her Infirmitie, and not puffed
vpp with pride for the mercy which is vfed
towards her , and thus euery member shalbee in peace and quietneffe; Wee giue you
this fpeciall Caueat to bee ware that the
Sinne of Murmuration may not for any
occafion appeare either in Worde or in any
externall figne what foeuer, and if any bee
taken in this fault , lett her bee putt vnto
feuere punifment.

Of the hebdomadaries or weekely Of-
fices in the kitching ;

CHAPTER 24.

LETT the Sifters ferue each othersand
none muft bee excufed from feruing in
the kitching, except shee bee hindred by
fickneffe , or in refpect of fome greater
Commoditie, for here by the more Charitie
and merritt is gayned ; lett the weaker fort
haue fome folace , that they may not doe it
male con tent but lett them haue fome affiftance, according to the State of the Con-
gre-

gregation , and situation of the place ; If the
Conhregation bee great the Cellarier shalbee excused from the kitchin ; or whosoeuer is hindred with businesse of greater importance , as wee haue sayd , but let all the
rest serue each other with all Charitie ;
being at the weekes end to goe out of office
lett her on Saterday make all things cleane;
lett her wash the clothes where with the
Sisters wipe their hands and Feete ; Both
shee that is to enter , and shee that is to depart must wash the Feete of all the rest; Lett
her resigne all the Vessell belonging to her
office neate and whole vnto the Cellarier,
the which Cellarier must deliuer the againe
vnto her that entreth into that Office , that
shee may know what shee deliuereth and
what shee receaueth ; The Hebdomadaryes
must take some peece of bread, ãd a draught
of drincke ouer and aboue their ordinary
Portion , one hower before the rest of the
Couent take their Refection , soe that at the
hower of Refection they may serue their
Sisters without murmuring for their ouer
much labour; vppon Solemne Feasts they
must abstayne till Masse bee ended ; Euery
Sunday the hebdomadaryes wich enter and
goe out of office shall kneele them Downe
before euery one requesting their Prayers;
They that goe out of office must say this
D 5   verse

verse Benedictus es Domine Deus qui adiu-
uisti me, & consolatus es me; blessed bee
thou o lord god wich hast holpen mee and
comforted mee, which Verse being three
tymes repeated, lett her that entreth into
the Office follow and say, Deus in adiutoriū
meum intende, Domine ad adiuuandū me
festina. and this being in like manner thrice
repeated of all hauing receaued the Benediction lett her enter into her office.

Of the infirme and ßcke Sisters;

CHAPTER. 25.

BEFORE and aboue all things care
must bee had of the sicke, soe that Seruice bee done vnto them as to Christ himselfe; for hee hath sayed, I was infirme and
sicke, and you visited mee; ād that which you
haue done to one of my litle ones, you haue
done it to my selfe; yea lett the infirme Consider with themselues, that all this Seruice
is done them for the honour of God, and
lett them not bee trouble some to the Sisters
which serue them, by ouer much superflui-
ty Not withstanding they are much to bee
borne withall; for by such as they are the
greater; merritt is obtayned, therefore lett
the

the Abbesse bee carefull that they endure
nothing, vppon the negligence of others,
Vnto the sicke a place must bee appoynted,
and some to serue them that haue the feare
of God, and are carefull and dilligent; lett
the infirme haue the vse of the Bath soe ofté
as it shalbee expedient, but lett it bee rarely
granted to those that are whole especially
to the younger sort, ye lett t hose that are all
togeather weake eate flesh for their Recouery; but when they are recouered lett them
abstaine from flesh as they were wont to
doe; lett the Abbesse haue especiall care that
the sicke bee not neglected, either by the
Cellarier, or by those that serue them, for it
is imputed vnto her fault how soeuer her
Scollers err and offend;

Of those that are old and very younge;

CHAPTER 26.

A'L though that man of his owne nature
is easely, drawne to pitty the ould and
young, yet notwithstanding lett them bee
prouided for by the authoritie of your Rule;
lett allwayes consideration bee had of their
Weaknesse, and vse not in any wise the

strick-

ftrickneffe of the Rule as concerning their
dyett,but allwayes lett them bee confidered
with pitty, and lett them preuent the ordinary tymes of eating;

Of the hebdomary Reader

CHAPTER 27

THE Sifters muft neuer bee without
reading at meales, yet lett not euery
one prefume to reade as by chance shee
shall take the booke in hand, but lett her
beginn vppon Sunday that is to read all the
weake following, whoe entring into the
office muft requeft the Prayers of the reft
ymmediately after Maffe and Communion
that God would deliuer her from the Spirritt of Pride, and lett this Verfe bee recited
thrice of all them in the Church, Domine
labia mea aperies & os meum annuntiabit
laudem tuam, and foe lett her beginn to
reade hauing firft receaued her benediction;
let foueraigne filence bee obferued at meate
neither whifpering or other noyfe be there
herd but onely of the Reader, and lett all
that is neceffary both for meate and drinke
bee foe deliuered to the Sifters, that none
may haue neede to demaunde any thing;
Not-

Notwithstanding if any thing shalbee wanting, lett it rather bee demaunded by the sound of some Signe, then by their voyces; neither may any of them presume to speake either of that wich is reade or of any thing els, that noe occasion may bee giuen to your ghostly enemy; except peraduenture the Superiour will say some what breifely for their edification; lett the Reader take some litle pittance in bread and drinke before shee beginn to reade, lest peraduenture her fasting night bee ouer greuious to her, and afterwards lett her take Refection with those of the kitchin and the other Seruants; The Sisters must not read according to their order but onely those that can best edify others by their reading;

Of the quantitie of their meate

CHAPTER. 28.

WEE beleiue that two boyled pittances may serue for their dayly Refection, in euery Month of the yeare both one the day when the Fast, and when there is noe Fast, and in respect of the infirmities which may bee incident to diuers of their Complexions, that those which cannot eate

of

of the one , may make their repaſt of the other ; therfore lett two boyled pulmentaryes or pittances ſuffice for all the Siſters, and if there bee any Apples or new Fruytes then make them a third dish of the ſame, one pound of bread muſt bee their dayly allowance , whether they make onely dinner or both dinner and Supper, and if they are to receaue their Supper lett the third parte of their pound bee reſerued by the Cellarier for their Supper , if their labour happen to bee greater, then shall it bee in the Abbeſſes will and power to augment it as shee shall thinke good , hauing eſpecially care that all exceſſe and ſurfeting bee eſchewed, that the Religious might neuer bee troubled with indigeſture ; For nothing is more contrary to a Chriſtian then gluttony; As our lord himſelfe ſayeth ; ſee that your harts bee not ouer charged with ſurfeiting and dronkenneſſe, lett not the ſame quantity bee obſerued , to the younger ſort, but rather leſſe then thoſe that are greater ; obſeruing frugalitie in all things ; lett all abſtaine preciſely from eating flesh of foure footed beaſts except thoſe that are ſicke and Feeble ;

of

Of the measure of their drincke.

CHAPTER 29.

EVERY one hath a proper gift from God, one after this manner, and another after that ād therefore the measure of other Folks dyett, is appoynted by vs with a certayne kinde of scruple and perplexitie, not with standing considering the weaknesse of those that are sicke, wee beleiue that a pynte of wine may suffice for euery one a day, lett them vnderstand that they shall haue a peculier reward vppon whom our lord shall bestow the gift of abstinence; But if either the necessitie of the place or their trauyll or the heates of the Summer shall require more; lett that bee remitted to the arbitrement of the Superiour, who must alwayes duely consider, that it bee done without saciety and dronckennesse; Althoughe wee reade that wine is noe drincke for those that lead a Monasticall life, yet because wee cannot soe perswade these of our tyme at lest wise in this sort lett vs yeald there vnto, that wee neuer drinke our fill but moderately, for wine maketh euen the wise to become Apostataes, where the necessitie of the place soe requireth that the afore sayd

cam-

measure may not bee had, but either much
leſſe, or none at all; lett thē which dwell in
thoſe places bleſſe our lord and beware of
Murmuration, allwayes warning you in the
ſpecialleſt ſort wee cann, that the Siſters
euer liue free from all Murmuration;

At what howers the Siſters muſt take their refection;

CHAPTER 30.

FROM Eaſter to whitſontide the Siſters
muſt take their dinner at the fixt hower,
and their Supper at night, But frō whitſontide forward through the whole Summer
let them faſt wedneſday, vntill the Nynth
hower, except they labour much, or that the
exceſſiue heates doe much moleſt them, but
vppon other dayes they dyne at the ſixt hower, the which tyme of dynning, at ſixt may
bee contynued either when they labour or
when the heats of the Sommer are exceſſiue great, and lett all theſe things remayne
in the prouidence and diſcretion of the Abbeſſe, who muſt ſoe wiſely temper and diſpoſe all things, that the Soules of her Siſters
may bee ſaued, and that they may doe their
dutyes without murmuring; But from the
                                              Ides

Ides of September vntill the beginning of
lent, the Sisters must dine at the Nynth; In
lent vntill Easter they must take their Refe-
ctiõ at Eueningwhich Euening must bee soe
considered that those wich eate may not
onely neede Candle light, but moreouer
that all thinges may bee finished within the
day light, and at all Seasons of the yeare the
hower of Supper and of their refection
must bee soe contynued that by the light of
the day all things may bee wel dispatche d̃

Of Silence in the night.

CHAPTER 31.

AL wayes the Sisters must haue care
to keepe silence, but especially in the
seasen of the night and therefore at all tymes whether fasting or dining if it bee a
tyme to dyne in ymmediately after they
haue risen from Supper lett them litt downe togeather all in one place, and lett one
reade the Colations or liues of the holy Fathers, or some what els that may edefy the
hearers, but lett them not reade at that tyme
the fiue bookes of Moyses, or the bookes of
the kings for it wilbee litle profitable for
those that are of smale Capacitie at that
E tyme

tyme to heare that parte of Scripture but
rather lett them reade it at other tymes, But
if it bee fasting day, a litle after Euensonglett
them goe to the lecture of the sayde, collatiõs
as wee haue said and after foure or fiue leaues
haue beene read, or as the hower will permit
all mee tingtogeather by the space of the sayd
lecture, if any bee occupyed about any busi-
nee enioyned her by the Superiour, lett
her then come alsoe, and when all are assē-
bled lett them make an end and goe to complyne, and after none may speake vnto any
about any thing, for if any bee found to
breake this Rule of silence, let her bee seuerely punished, except it bee vppon the arri-
uall of some guesse, or that the Abbesse,
should commaund any thing to bee done
which notwith standing must bee done
with all decency and moderation;

*Of those that come late to the Seruice
of God, and to the Table.*

CHAPTER 32.

LETT euery one runnwith all speede
leauing what soeuer worke is in her
hads, soe soone as shee shall heare the
Signe to bee giuen vnto the deuine Seruice,
yet

yet with grauity, that scurrilitie may finde
noe entertaynment among you; Therefore
beware that nothing bee preferred before
the Seruice of God, for if any come not to
Mattines before the Gloria of the 94 Psalme
bee sayd (with Psalme for this cause wee
will haue sayd in a long ād leisurely māner)
lett her nott stand in her owne order, but
either the last of all or in some other place,
which the Abbesse shall appoynte for such
negligent Sluggerds, that soe shee may bee
seene of the Superiour, and of all the rest
vntill shee hath done true pennance and
pyblike satisfaction at the end of Gods Seruice; and for this cause wee iudge it meete
that they should remayne in the last place
or els in a place seperated from the rest, that
being noted from all the rest, they may bee
amended for the very shame it selfe; for if
shee should remayne out of the Church, per
aduenture there would bee some, which
would either lay them downe to sleepe
againe, or would sitt without and prate with
others, and thereby giue occasion to the
ghostly enemy, but lett her enter in, that she
lose not all, and that shee might doe Pennāce
for the other parte; At the howers of the day
shee that shall not come to the deuine Office after the Verse at the Gloria of the first
Psalme which is sayd after the verse, lett
her

E 2

her remayne in the laſt place according to
the rule affore ſayd , and lett her not preſume to put her ſelfe in Company with
thoſe that Sing in the Quier, except the Abbeſſe ſhall permitt her ſoe to doe , and vppō
this Condition that shee doe afterwards
ſatisfaction for her fault; but at the hower of
refection shee that shall not come before
the Verſe that all may ſay the Verſe, Prayer,
and all at once come to the table togeather,
shee that through her fault and negligence
shall not be preſent, lett her for thrice beere-
buked for her fault , and if afterwards shee
amend not, lett her not bee permitted to ſitt
at the Table with the reſt , but ſeperated
from their follow shipp ; let her take refection alone with drawing from her , her
Portion of wine , vntill shee hath made
amendment and ſatisfaction ; alſoe let her
bee puniſhed in like ſort which shall not
bee preſent at the Verſe which is ſayd after
meate, and lett none preſume to take either
meate or drinke before or after the hower
appoynted for their Refection; Moreouer if
the Superiour offer any thing to any of thē
and ifshee refuſe to receaue it then , and afterwards shee haue a deſire to that , which
shee refuſed or to any thing els lett her in
noe caſe receaue it , vntill shee hath made
due amendment ;

Of

Of those that are excommunicated and what satisfaction they must make.

CHAPTER 33.

SHEE that for her greuious offences shalbee excommunicated from the Church, and Refectory: lett her ly prostrate before the entrance into the Church at the hower that the deuine Seruice is celebrated in the Church, and lett her say nothing but lay her head vppon the earth prostrate all along before the Feete of all, as they come from the Church, and lett her continew doing this soe long vntill the Abbesse shall thinke shee hath duly satisfyed; who being called by the Abbesse lett her cast herselfe at the Abbesses Feete, and afterwards before the Feete of all the Sisters that they will pray for her, and then if the Abbesse shall soe appoynte it, lett her bee receaued into the Quire, but in the Order that the Abbesse shall thinke good, soe that shee presume not to intone either Psalme, lesson, or any thing els in the Church except vppon the Commaundement of the Abbesse, and at euery hower at the end of the deuine office, lett her cast her selfe to the ground in the place where shee remayneth vntill such tyme as

E 3   the

the Abbeſſe ſhall commaunde her to ceaſe
from that kinde of ſatisfaction , but thoſe
that for ſome ſmall fault, are excommunicated from the Table, lett them ſatisfy in the
Church ſoe long as the Abbeſſe ſhall pleaſe
to commaund them , and in ſuch ſort lett
them ſtill continew vntill ſhee giueth them
her bleſſing and ſay it ſufficeth.

Of thoſe that committ any Errour
in the Church;

CHAPTER 34.

IF any Siſter committ any Errour in the
Church in the deuine office , when ſhee
pronounceth any Pſalme, Reſponſary , Anthym, or leſſon if in the way of ſatisfaction
ſhee humble not her ſelfe before the reſt,
let her bee ſeuerely puniſhed for the ſame,
becauſe ſhee would not amend that with
humilitie, which ſhee committed through
her negligence; But the Children for ſuch
a fault muſt bee whipped;

Of those that offend in any other thing;

CHAPTER. 35.

IF any while shee laboureth in the kit-chin, Seller or other Office, Bakehouse, Garden, or in any Art, where in shee is oc-cupyed, or in what Place soeuer shee hath offended, or hath broken or lost any thing, or hath committed any excesse and doth not presently come before the Abbesse or Con-gregation and offer herselfe to doe satisfa-ction, and shall not bewray her owne fault lett her bee more seuerely punished, if by any other it come to their knowledge; But if it bee a secrett Sinne of the Soule lett her manifest it to her Abbesse or ghostly Father who knowes how to cure and heale their owne and other folkes wounds, and not to detect and publish them;

Of the manner how to signify the hower of Gods seruice.

CHAPTER 36.

LETT the Abbesse haue the care to make knowne both by day and night
E 4   the

the hower of Gods seruice, and either see
shee doe it her selfe, or enioyne it to some
other dilligent and carefull, that all things
may bee a complished in their proper and
competent tymes and seasons, lett those that
are commaunded intone the Psalmes or
An hymes still in their order after the Abbesse, but lett none presume to sing or read
but those that can well execute the office,
that the hearers may bee edifyed, the which,
shee shall doe with all humilitie, grauitie,
and Reuerence who herevnto by the Abbesse shalbee commaunded;

Of the workes of their hands.

CHAPTER 37.

IDlenesse is an Enemy to the Soule, and
therefore the Sisters ought to bee occupyed, at certayne tymes with the labour of
their hands, and at other tyms in reading
spirituall and deuynes things, and therefore
wee thinke that according to this manner
both tymes may bee well disposed of, that
from Easter vntill the Kalends of October
going from Prime in the morning they
should labour vntill the fourth hower, in
that which shalbee neede full, and from the
fourth

fourth hower vntill the sixt , they should
attend to reading;after the sixt rising from
the Table , they shall rest in their bedes
with all silence , and shee that will read
vnto her selfe may reade soe that shee bee
not trouble some vnto others,and they shall
say the Ninth hower somewhat sooner,
neere vnto the eight hower,and then againe
they shall proceede to doe that,that is to bee
done vnto the Eueninge, But if the necessity
of the Place or their pouerty should require
that they themselues should reape and gather their Corne, lett them not bee greiued
there at , for then they shew themselues
truly Religious,yf they liue by the labour of
their hands , as our Fore fathers , and the
Apostles werewont to doe;yett lett all thing
bee done with diseretion , and with Compassion towards those that are weake harted,and cannot endure much labour , From
the Kalends of October vntill the beginning of lent, lett them attend to their reading vntill the second hower bee expired;
at the second hower say the Third, and then
lett euery one attend to that worke which
is enioyned her vntill the Nynth , when the
signe is giuen to the Nynth, lett euery one
lay away the worke and bee in a readi-
nesse at the second Signe ; After Refection
lett them attend to reading spirituall bookes

E 5   or

or the Pſalmes, vppon thoſe dayes that come
in lent , lett them attend to their reading
vnto the third hower full out , and then lett
them worke , that which is commaunded
them vnto the tenth hower , vppon which
dayes lett euery one take her a booke out of
the library , the which shee muſt reade
through out, and theſe bookes muſt bee deliuered to them at the beginning of lent; See
that one or two aucient be appoynted to
goe through the Monaſtery, at ſuch tymes
as the Siſters apply their bookes, and ſee that
noe Siſters bee found Idle or prating with
others, and not occupyed in reading , and
there by is not onely vnprofitable vnto her
ſelfe, but troble ſome vnto others, if ſuch an
one (as god forbidd) should bee found in
this ſort , lett her bee rebuked for the firſt
and ſecond tyme, and if shee amend not lett
her bee put to regular Correction , in ſuch
ſort as others may bee kept in feare ãd awe,
neither lett one Siſter bee found with another at vnfitt howers , and ſeaſons ; vppon
Sundayes lett all apply their reading except
ſuch as are deputed to other offices; If any
shalbee found ſoe negligent , and ſlothfull,
that shee either will not or cannot meditate
or reade, lett her haue ſome other worke
enioyned her that shee may not bee idle
and vnoccupyed; lett ſuch workes an arts
bee

bee enioyned to thofe Sifters that are weake
and delicate, that neither they may bee Idle
or oppreffed with the violence of their labour, that thereby they should feeke to
shunn it, and foe their weakneffe is of the
Abbeffe duly to bee confidered;

Of the manner of the obferuation of lent;

CHAPTER 38

AL though the life of the Religious
should bee a perpetuall lent, yet becaufe this vertue is found in very few, there
fore wee admonish you, that in the tyme of
lent you lead your life, in all purity, that is to
wipe away all the negligences of former
tymes by the good obferuation of thefe facred dayes, which is then worthyly performed if wee abftaine from all Vice and
attend to our prayers with compunction of
hart, lett vs therefore on thefe dayes add
fome what to the ordinary tafke of our
Seruice, as abftinence both in meate and
drinke, and fome peculier prayers, lett euery
one offer freely with Ioy of the holy Ghoft
fome what vnto God, aboue all that which
is appoynted her, that is that shee with
                                        draw

draw from her body some what of her meat drinke, sleepe, talke scurrilitie expecting the sacred Feast of Easter with ioy in all spirituall and ghostly comfort; notwithstading whatsoeuer it is that euery one doth offer, lett her signify it to her Abbesse that it may bee done with her good will and benediction, for what soeuer is done with out her permission and of the ghostly Father is to bee accounted persumption and vayne glory and in noe wise meritorious; Therefore all things are to bee done with the good liking of the Abbesse;

Of the Oratory of the Monastery;

CHAPTER 39

LETT the Oratory bee that which the name there of doth imparte, neither lett any other thing bee there done or disposed; after the worke of God is ended lett euery one depart with silence and with reuerence done to God, that that Sister that can bee able to pray perticulerly may not bee hindred by the misrule and importunity of others; but if it bee soe that any other will make there her prayers, lett her enter in with all simplicitie and pray not with a

loude

loude and clamorous voyce, but with teares
and deuotion of hart, s heet herefore, that
doth not this may not bee permitted after
the seruice to stay in the place of Prayer, lest
(as I haue sayd) another suffer an impediment thereby;

How it is vnlawfull for the Sisters to giue or receaue any letters or Presents;

CHAPTER 40.

IT is altogeather vn lawfull for the Sisters
to receaue or giue letters bookes of deuotion, or what other present how litle soeuer,
either to their kinsfolkes or to any other
person, or one to another without the com-
maundemét of the Abbes; And if any thing
should bee sent them from any of their
kinsfolkes, let them not presume to receaue
it before it bee shewed to the Abbesse, and
if shee commaund them to receaue it, then
shall it bee in her power to giue it to her,
vnto whom shee shall commaund to giue
the same; And lett not that Sister to whom it
was sent bee sorry if it bee giuen to another
to the end noe occasion may bee suffred for
the deuill to enter amongst you, and if shee
presu-

preſume to doe the contrary lett her bee
ſubmitted vnto reguler diſcypline and Correction;

Of the Cloathes of the Religious;

CHAPTER 41.

LET the Siſters haue their cloathes giuen them according to the qualitie of
of the place, where they dwell and diſpoſition of the ayre; for there is neede of more
in colder Countryes, and in hotter of leſſe;
therefore lett this conſideration pertayne to
the Abbeſſe, notwithſtanding wee beleiue
that in temperate places, it may ſuffice the
ſiſters to haue acuculua ãd anin warde coate
They muſt haue a Cuculua in the winter
and that ſome what groſſe and hayry, and
in the Sommer more ſynd and well worne,
and a Scapular to labour, and as concerning
their Feete they ſhall haue hoſe and Shoes,
but as concerning the Colour or groſeneſſe
of thẽ, the Siſters maynot inany wiſe diſpute
but let it bee ſuch as may bee found in the
Prouince where they dwell, or that which
may bee bought the beſt cheape, let the Abbeſſe looke to the meaſure there of, that the
cloathes bee not two ſhort for thoſe that
weare them, but of a Competent greatneſſe;
                                    when

when they receaue any new thing, see that presently they giue vpp their ould to bee referued in the Guardroabe for the poore; it sufficeth that eath Sister haue two Coates, and two Cuculuers both for the nights and for to wash them, and that which shalbee ouer and aboue this shalbee superfluous, and must bee cutt of, and as concerning their shooes and what ould thing soeuer, see they render it vpp when they receaue any new; as for their bedding lett it suffice they haue a Mattresse, a Couering ouer that, and another to couer them, and a boulster; which bedds must bee often searched by the Abbesse for feare of propriety, that there it may not bee found, and in whom soeuer it shalbee found, to haue any thing that shee receaued not from the Abbesse, lett her bee most seuerely punished; and that this Vice of propriety may bee wholly rooted out, lett all things that are necessary bee giuen them by the Abbesse, that is their Cuculua a Coate, shoes, hose, a muffe, a knife, penn and Inckhorne, needles, handchatchers, ād some litle Tables; that all excuse of necessity may bee remoued; Notwithstanding the sentēce in the Acts of the Apostles is duly to bee considered of the Abbesse, that to euery one was giuen as they had neede, euen soe lett the Abbesse consider the Infirmity of those,

that

that are in want, and not the euill difpofed mynds of the enuious, yet in all her Iudgments lett her thinke vppon the Retribution of Almighty God;

Of thofe Sifters that are shillfull in any art ;

CHAPTER 42.

IF there bee any fifters in the Monaftery that are cunnig in any Art lett them exercife them felues in thofe Arts, foe that the Abbeffe shall commaund them there vnto: but if any should wax proude of her cunning, becaufe shee efteemes herfelfe profitable to the Monaftery, lett her bee put from her Art, and lett her not vfe it againe vntill the Abbeffe after her humiliation shall commaund her thereunto ; if any of the workes of thofe skilfull religious are to bee fould lett them looke vnto it through whofe hands they are to paffe, that they prefume not to committ any fraude and lett them bee allwayes myndefull of Ananias and Saphyra left peraduenture all thofe that haue committed any fraude in thes affayres of the Monaftery incurre that death in their foules which thefe incurred in their bodyes ; as
tou-

touching the prices of those wor'estake
heede that noe auarice creepe in but lett
them bee giuen better cheape of you then
they would bee o other secular people, that
in all your Actions Gods glory may bee exalted;

Of the manner of receauing of Nouices;

CHAPTER 43.

VVHEN any cometh newly to
conuert herselfe to god from the
World, permitt her not to haue easy entrance amongh you; But as the Apostle sayth
proue the Spirritts whether they bee ofgod,
if therefore shee that commeth shall perseuer in knocking, and shalbee seene to beare patiently for foure or fiue dayes iniuryes
that are offered her and the difficulty that is
made her of her admitting, then graunt her
entrance and lett her remayne for some
fewdayes in the guesse lodging, afterwards
lett her liue in the Cell or the Nouices, and
there let her meditate eate, and sleepe, and
lett some ancient bee appoynted ouer her,
as it is fitt to gayne Soules, who must bee
very curious and carefull in considering

F   whe

whether shee seeke god in very deede, and
is dilligent in his seruice, in obedience, in
reading and in enduring of iniuryes: let her
haue declared vnto her the hardnesse; and
asperity; by which shee must labour to come
to God, and if shee shall promise perseuerance of her continuance, then after two
Monethes are expired, lett the rule all in
order bee reade to her, and lett it bee sayd
vnto her: behould here is the law vnder
which thou desirest to fight, if thou art able
to obserue, enter, but if thou canst not, depart
with all liberty and Freedome; If shee still
continew then lett her bee brought to the
affore sayd Cell of the Nouices, and there
lett her patience bee throughly proued, and
after the space of six monethes lett the rule
by reade againe vnto her, that shee may
know what shee taketh in hand, and if shee
as yet perseuereth after foure Monethes, lett
the same rule bee reade againe and if after
shee hath throughly deliberated with her
selfe that shee will promise to obserue all,
and to fullfill al things that shalbee commaunded her, then lett her bee admitted
and receaued vnto your Congregation,
knowing that by the vigor of the Rule it is
decreed; that from that day afterward shee
may neuer depart from the Monastery, nor
may withdraw her neeke from the yoake
                                          of

of the Rule, that which shee might haue refused hauing foe long and mature deliberation;

Of the manner of their Profeſſion;

CHAPTER 44.

SHEE that is to bee admitted muſt make promiſe publikely before all in the Church b fore God and his Saints of her ſtability, change of manners and obedience, that if peraduenture shee should doe otherwiſe afterwards shee may know that shee shall receaue the ſentence of damnation of Allmighty God whō shee hath mock d, of the which promiſe by her made lett her make a petitiō in the name of thoſe Saints whoſe Reliques are in that place and of the Abbeſſe there preſent, The which petition muſt bee ſubſcribed with her owne hand, if shee cannot write, let another write it at her requeſt, and then lett her make a Signe there vppon, and afterward lay it vppon he Altar with her owne hand, which after she hath there layed, lett her preſently beginn this verſe; Suſcipe me domine ſecundum eloquium tuum, & viuam, & non confundas me ab expectatione mea, that is to ſay; receaue mee a lord according to thy holy

F 2   word

word, and I shall liue, and confound mee not in my expection, the which verse the whole Congregation anſweareth three tymes, adding Gloria Patri &c. to the laſt; Then lett the new Siſter proſtrate herſelfe before the Feete of euery one that they will pray for her, and ſoe from that day lett her bee accounted one of the Congregation, if ſhee hath any thing lett her either diſtribute it to the poore, or lett her make a ſolemne donation thereof to the Monaſtery, retayning nothing at all vnto herſelf, for ſhee is to vnderſtand that from that tyme forwarde ſhee hath noe authoritie or challenge not ſoe much as to her owne body; Therefore lett her fortwith in the Church bee ſpoyld of all her owne where with ſhee was cloathed, and lett her put on the habitt of the Monaſtery; but lett thoſe Cloathes which ſhee hath put of bee layed a ſide, and bee kept in the guardroabe that if at any time ſhee ſhould coſet to the deuill to leaue the Monaſtery (which God forbidd) that then being ſpoyled of her Monaſticall habitt ſhee may bee caſt and expelled thence. But lett her not receaue the writting which the Abbeſſe tooke from the Altar, but lett it bee reſerued and kept in the Monaſtery;

of

Of the manner of receauing the daughters of Noblemen, gentlemen, Ritchmen, or pooremen ;

CHAPTER 45.

IF any Nobleman or gentleman offereth his daughter to God in your Monastery, if the child shalbee very young, lett her parents make the foresayd petition for her, and with their oblation lett them wrapp the fore sayd petition, and the hand of the child in the Towell of the Altar, ād foe they may offer her; but as concerning her goods, lett them promise vnder their oath in the present petition, that they will neuer by themselues or by any other person, or any way besides giue her any thing, or at any tyme offer her occasion to haue any thing, or if they will not doe this, but that they will giue any thing in Almes to the Monastery for their Merritt; lett them make a donation of those things which they will giue to the Monastery, retayning to themselues (if foe they pleafe) the vfe and proffitt of the fame, and foe lett euery thing bee shut vpp and concluded, that noe fufpition may rest in the Childs heade, whereby shee may bee deceaued and (as god forbidd) may

F 3   perish,

perish, as wee haue seene by experience in others; In like sort lett them doe that are of poore Condition; but lett them that haue nothing onely make their petition and with oblation lett them offer their daughter in the presence of some Witnesses;

How externe and foraigne Religious should bee receaued;

CHAPTER 46

IF any strange Religious women shall come vnto you from some farr Prouince, if shee will dwell as a guest in your Monastery, and wilbee content with the Custome of the place which shee shall finde there, and will not bee trouble some to the Monastery with her superfluyty, but will bee simply content with that which shee therefindeth lett her bee receaued for soe long a tyme as shee desireth, but if shee reprehend any thing reasonably and with humilitie lett the Abbesse deale with her prudently, fort at perhapps shee was sent thither euen for this purpose from god himselfe, but if afterwards shee haue a desire to make their her aboade, lett not her request bee refused; especially seing that in the tyme of her
being

being a Guesse her life might bee well and
throughly discouered ; But if in that tyme
shee shalbee found vitious and giuen to su-
perfluytie, shee must not onely not bee ioyned with the Corps of the Monastery, but
lett her haue honest warning giuen her to
depart, lest by her miserable behauiour
others may bee corrupted ; But if shee bee
such a one as deserueth not to bee dimissed,
lett her not onely bee admitted into your
Congregation if shee request it, but perswade her to remayne that others may bee edifyed by her good Example, and becausse in
all places one lord is serued, if the Abbesse finde her to bee such a one as shee
may bee, shee may promote her to some
higher degree ; and soe the Abbesse may
appoynte her Religious to higher degrees
and preheminences without regard of the
tyme and of their Entrances, if shee finde
their life to bee accordingly; yet lett the Abbesse beware that shee admitt not any Sisters of another Monastery knowne vnto
her to abide and dwell amongst them with
out the licence and letters of their Abbesse;
for it is written doe not that to another that
thou wouldest not haue done vnto thy selfe;

of

Of the Order of the Congregation

CHAPTER 47.

LETT them obserue such Order in the Monastery as by the merritt of the tyme of their conuersion shalbee determyned, or as the Abbesse shall appoynte, the which Abbesse must not bee troublesome to the flocke committed to her charge, neither may shee vniustly dispose of any thing, vsing her free power ad authoritie, but lett her thinke shee must yeald an account to Almighty God of her Workes and Iudgments; Therefore according to that Order which shee shall appoynte, or which the Sisters shall haue, they shall come to receaue the Pax Communion, to intone the Psalmes, or to stand in the Quier, and see that in all places their ages make noe differece in their order, nor bee preiudiciall vnto them, for because both Samuell and Dauid being young children iudged the Elders; therefore lett euery one keepe that Order as they were conuerted, excepting onely those (as wee haue sayd) whom the Abbesse shall promote vppon some secrett reason, or shall degrade for some certayne Causes, as for Example shee that came to the Monastery at the second

cond hower must hold herselfe to bee Iunior vnto her, who came at the first, though
shee bee otherwise of what soeuer age or
dignitie; yett lett all vse good disciplyne towards Children, and in all things;therefore
the Iuniours must honour their betters and
Elders, and those againe must loue their Iuniors and youngers; euen in the very naming of each other it shall not bee lawfull
for one to call another simply by her name,
but the Ancients shall call the Iuniours
Sisters,and Iuniours shall call their Anciēts
mothers,by which name they must vnderstand the motherly kinde of Reuerēce they
must beare vnto them; But the Abbesse because shee is thought to beare the person of
Christ must bee called Lady and Abbesse,
not for any presumption of her owne, but in
regard of the honour and loue of Christ; But
shee must well consider with her selfe, and
soe to behaue herselfe, that shee may bee
worthy of soe great an honour; wheresoeuer the Sisters meete one another, lett the
Iuniour request her benediction of her elder
and when soeuer the elder passeth by, the
younger must rise vpp and giue her place to
sitt downe, neither, may the Iunior presume
to sitt downe with her except her Ancient
doe cōmaūde her, that that may bee fullfilled which is writtē; with honour preuēting

F 5   one

one another ; lett the Children or youth
keepe their Order both in the Churches and
at the Table with all good difciplyne , but
out of thofe places , in what place foeuer
fee you obferue good watch and difciplyne
ouer them, vntill they come to yeares of difcretion and vnderftanding ;

Of the Manner and order how to elect
and choofe the Abbeffe ;

CHAPTER 48.

IN the ordination of the Abbeffe lett there
bee vfed fuch Confideration that shee
may bee appoynted whom the whole Congregation with the feare of god , or apart
though otherwife small elect ; let her that is
to bee ordayned bee elected for the merritt
of her good life and wife dome al though
shee should bee the lowest of all the congregation ; But if the whole Congregation
should by vniuerfall confent , choofe fuch a
perfon , as might yeald vnto their Vices
(which god forbidd) and that their Vices
bee in fome fort knowne vnto the Bifhopp
in whofe dioceffe the place is fituated , or
shalbee euidently knowne to the Abbotts
or Chriftian people dwelling neere abouts,
                                    lett

lett them for bidd that the Congregation of
the wicked take place , and lett them
appoynte a worthy dispensatrix Steward
ouer the house of God , knowing that for
soe doing they shall receaue a good reward;
doing it vppon a pure intention and for the
Zeale they beare to gods cause , as on the
Contrary part they shall fall into Sinne if
they neglect it. Lett her that is ordaynedfor
Abbesse allwayes consider what a burthen
shee hath taken vppon her,and to whom
shee must render an accompt of herSteward
shipp; And shee is to vnderstand thatshee
must rather seeke to proffitt her flocke then
to haue preheminence and the first place
amongst them;shee must bee skillfull in the
law of god , that shee may know to bring
forth of her Treasure new things and ould;
shee must bee chast and sober , pittyfull and
humble,with mercy surpassing the Rigor of
Iustice , that shee may for her owne selfe
deserue mercy at the hands of God , shee
must hate all manner of Vice,loue her sisters
and in her Correction shee must behaue her
selfe discretely that shee persecute nothing
ouer much, for feare lest whyle shee indea-
uoreth to scoure away the rust she breake
the Vessell in peeces ,and lett her allwayes
stand in suspition of her owne Fraylty , and
lett her Remember that the broken Reede
is not

is not vtterly to bee crushed in peeces, and
herein wee say not that shee suffer vice to
bee nourished but that shee seeke with prudence and Charitie to Roote it out , as shee
shall finde it most expedient for euery one
as already wee haue sayd, and lett her endeauour to bee rather loued then feared ; lett
her not bee troublesome, sadd. superfluous,
and obstinate in her owne opinion, not to
iealous or ouer superstitious , for then shee
will neuer bee quiett, lett her bee prouident
and carefull in her commaundements whe
ther they concerne god or the World , lett
her discretely weigh and moderate all those
workes which shee shall enioyne vnto
others , with considering the discretion of
holy Iacob saying, if I shall make my Flocke
to ouer labor themselues in walking tey
will all dye in one day, hauing this and such
like examples of discretion the mother of all
vertue , lett her soe moderate all things that
those that haue a good desire , may bee still
strong and able to accomplis it; and those
that are infirme and weake may not seeke to
shunn and auoyde it, and especially that they
intyrely obserue this present Rule, that whe
shee hath administred all things shee may
heare of our lord that which the good Seruant herd that distributed his Corne to his
fellow Seruants in dew seafon, Amen I say
vnto

ṽnto you (sayth our lord) I promote him ouer all my goods;

Of the Prioreſſe of the Monaſtery;

CHAPTER 49.

IT hath often tymes fallen out, that by the Ordination of the Prioreſſe many great ſcandalles haue riſen in Monaſteryes whyle there are ſome that being puffed vpp with the accurſed Spirrit of Pride thinking them ſelues to bee ſecond Abbeſſes take vppon them to tyraniſe ouer others, foſtèr ſchãdalls and rayſe diſſentions in the congregation, and eſpecially in thoſe places where the Prioreſſe is ordayned of the ſame Biſhop or of the ſame Abbotts that ordayned the Abbeſſe, which thiñg how abſurd it is may eaſely bee perceaued, for that euē from the beginning of her ordination ſhee hath matter of Pride offred vnto her, whilſt it reſorteth vnto her thoughts and Cogitations how ſhe is freed from all power of her Abbeſſe becauſe ſhee is ordayned of thoſe by whom the Abbeſſe herſelfe is ordayned; herevppon Enuye, Anger braules, detractions, diſſentions, and diſcords are rayſed; for whilſt the Abbeſſe and the Prioreſſe are of contrary opi-

opinions it is necessary that their owne
Soules stand in much danger by this dissen-
tion, and those that are vnder their charge
and gouernment whyle they flatter each
party perish vtterly ; The fault of which
danger falleth vppon their heads who were
the cause of such an Ordination, Therefore
wee foresee it to bee expedient for the Conseruation of peace and Charitie that the or-
dering of the Monastery depend onely
vppon the Abbesses Iudgment and aucto-
ritie; And if it may bee done lett all the Commoditie of the Monastery be ordered(as wee
haue sayd) at the Abbesses disposition by the
deanes, that whyle the charge is committed
to many, noe one may bacome insolent and
proude; But if the place soe require it, or the
Congregation shall request it vppon reasonable Causes with humilitie, and the Abbesse
shall iudge it expedient whomsoeuer shee
shall choose with the aduise of her Sisters
that hath the feare of God lett her ordayne
her for Prioresse, which Prioresse, notwithstanding must execute those things with Reuerence which shalbee inioyned her by her
Abbesse, doing nothing againit the Abbesses
Will or Order, for by how much shee is
preferred before the rest, by soe much the
more carefully ought shee to keepe the commaundements of the Rule ; And if the Prio-
                                            resse

reſſe shalbee found vitious or deceaued by
the haughtineſſe of pride, or shalbee proued
to bee a Contemner of the Rule, lett her bee
admonished with words for ſome foure or
fiue tymes and if ſoe bee, that ſhee will not
amend her ſelfe, then lett her bee caſt from
her degree of Prioreſſe, and another put in
her place, that shall bee foūd wortly there of
But if afterwards shee behaue not her ſelfe
quietly and obediently in the Congregation
lett her bee expelled out of the Monaſtery,
yet lett the Abbeſſe Conſider that shee muſt
render an account of all her Iudgments to
god, leſt shee with the Flame of enuy and
Rancour of mynde should ſett on fyre her
owne Soule;

Of the Portreſſe of the Monaſtery;

CHAPTER 50.

LETT ſome ancient and wiſe Religious
bee appoynted to keepe the Porte of the
Monaſtery, which knoweth well both to
receaue and render an anſweare, whoſe
grauitie will not permitt her to bee ranging
and wandring vpp and downe; The
which Portreſſe ought to haue her Cell
neere

neere vnto the Gate that those which come may allwayes finde her present, from whom they may receaue their answeare, and fortwith soe soone, as they shall knocke, or any poore person shall call vnto her, lett her answeare, Deo gratias, or blesse me, and with all meeknesse in the feare of God lett her retourne them an answeare with all speede possible, and with all feruour of Charitie; which Portresse if shee need any other for Comfort lett her haue some younger Sister; The Monastery ought soe to bee buylt, if it bee possible that it may contayne within it all things that are necessary for it, as Water, a Mill, a garden a Bakehouse, or soe that diuers arts may well bee exercised within the Monastery, that there might bee noe necessitie for the Religious to runn abroade, because it is not in any wise expedient for their Soules; Our Will is that this Rule bee often reade in the congregation, that none of the Sisters for their excuse may pretend Ignorance;

Of

Of the Sisters that are sent abroade;

CHAPTER 51.

VVHEN any of the Sisters are sent abroade, let them commend themselues to the prayers of all their Sisters, and of the Abbesse, and allwayes at the last Prayer of the deuyne Seruice; lett a Commemoration bee made for all those that are absent; But when the Sisters are retourned, the very day of their Retourne, let them ly prostrate vppon the ground in the Church through out all the Canonicall howers whyle the Seruice of God is a doing, and lett them request the Prayers of all the rest for their excesses, lest peraduenture some euill thing either in sight, hearing, or Idle words might haue happened to them in the way; neither may any presume to relate vnto others, the things that they haue seene or heard out of the Monastery, because it is an exceeding disedification; which thing, if any shall presume to doe, lett her bee put to the seuere Chastisement of the Rule; as in like manner, those that shall presume to goe out of the Inclosure to any place what soeuer, or to doe any thing thoughe neuer soe litle without the Commaudemét of the Abbesse;

G   Of

Of those that haue any thing enioyned
them that is impossible ;

CHAPTER 52.

IF peraduenture some Sister should haue
any thing enioyned her that is impossible
to bee done, lett her receaue the Commaundement of her that commaunded her
with all sweetenesse and obedience, and if
shee see that the weight of the burthen doth
altogeather exceede the compasse of her
force, then lett her at some fitt tyme , and
with all patience declare vnto the Superior
the cause of the Impossibilitie thereof, without all pride, Resistance, or Contradiction;
And if after her suggestion, the Commaundement of the Superiour , continew in the
former Rigour; let the Inferiour then vnderstand , that it is expedient for her that it
should bee soe, and soe lett her obey with
all loue and Charitie reposing her trust in
the helpe of God;

How

How one may not defend another in the Monastery;

CHAPTER 53.

YOV must take good heede that one Sister presume not to defend or beare out another in the Monastery for what cause soeuer, though they bee neuer soe familiar and neere in bloode; and in noe sort lett this bee presumed by the Sisters, for thereby great occasion of schādall may arise; And if any transgresse this Rule, let her bee seuerely punished;

That one may not presume to stricke another;

CHAPTER 54

TO the end that all manner of presūption may bee excluded out of the Monastery, wee ordayne and appoynte that it bee not lawfull for any to excommunicate or stricke the Sisters, excepting her onely to whom this authoritie is giuen by the Abbesse, Butt lett those that offēd bee reprehended before the rest, that others thereby may

G 2   bee

bee kept in more awe; But lett Chaſtiſement
or ſharpe correction bee giuen vnto Childrē
by the Siſters, vntill they come to ſixteene
yeares of age, and lett good watch bee held
ouer them, yet with that regard and diſcretion that it paſſe not the bounds and meaſure
of reaſon, for whoe ſhall preſume to ſtricke
them when they ſhall come to riper yeares,
without the commaundement of the Abbeſſe, or to worke her paſſion indeſcretely
vppon ſoe much as the very Children, lett
her bee ſubmitted to the puniſhment of the
Rule. for it is written, that whichthou woul-
deſt not haue done to thy ſelfe, ſee thou doe
it not to another;

That the Siſters muſt obey one another;

CHAPTER 55.

THE Vertue of obedience ought to bee
performed of euery one, not onely to
the Abbeſſe, but alſoe the Siſters muſt obey
one another, knowing that by this way of
obedience, they ſhall goe to our lord; Therefore after the Commaundement of the Abbeſſe, and of the ancients put in office by her
(before whoſe cōmaūdemēts wee permitt
that noe perticuler perſons commaundements

ments should take place) lett those that are
younger obey those that are their Ancients,
with all loue and dilligence, ãd if any should
bee found to bee a Comtemner of her Ancients, lett her bee punished; likewise if any
Sister bee in any sort reprehended by her
Abbesse or any of her Ancients for any cause
how litle soeuer, or if shee perceaue that the
Countenance of her Ancient be: neuer
soe litle changed with anger against her (I
say howlitle soeuer it bee)lett her forth with
cast herselfe vppon the ground, and there ly
prostrate before her feete doing her satisfaction soe long, vntill that motion bee cured
with some benediction, and if any should
contemne to doe it, let her bee put to some
corporall punishment, and if shee continew
still hardned in her opinion then let her bee
thrust out of the Monastery;

Of the good Zeale and Charitie the Sisters
ought to haue one towards another;

CHAPTER 56.

AS there is an euill and bitter Zeale and
hatred, that seperateth from God and
leadeth vnto hell; euen soe there is a good
Zeale that seperateth from Vice and leadeth

G 3   **vnto**

vnto God, and vnto his euerlasting life; Therefore lett the Sisters exercise one towards another this good Zeale with a most feruent loue and affection, that is to say lett them preuent one another with honour, bearing patiently each others infirmities, whether they bee of body, or of their behauiour, and let them striue to obey one another with all their power and abilitie; let none follow that which, to her owne Iudgment seemeth good and profitable, but rather that which shall seeme good to another shewing all sisterly Charitie in a most pure and chast loue, see they feare God, loue their Abbesse, with a sincere and humble affection, and preferr nothing before our Sauiour Iesus Christ who of his goodnesse bring vs all to that life that neuer shall haue end; Amen.

How that the obseruation of all Iustice is not contayned in this Rule;

CHAPTER 57.

VVEE haue sett downe this Rule, that by the obseruing it in the Monastery, wee may shew vnto others, that we haue in some honest kinde good behauour and the beginning of a holy Conuersation

fation ; But for thofe that fpeede forward in
the perfection of holy Conuerfation , there
are the good leffons of holy Fathers , the obferuation where of bringeth a man to the
topp of perfection , what Page or what
Word of the diuine Authoritie is not a moft
right Rule of mans life , or what booke of
the holy Catholike Fathers, doth not found
out this, that by a direct Courfe wee may
come to our Creator ; Alfoe the Collations
of holy Fathers , and the Rule of our holy
Father S. Bafill, what other thing are they, but
the Examples of good life , and of obedient
and good people , and the very Inftruments
of Vertues, but to vs fluggish, ill, ãd negligent
people they, are a shame and confufion ; therefore whofoeuer thou art, that makeft haft
to that heauenly Country , fullfill by the
ayde of our Sauiour Chrift this litle Rule
written for young beginners , and then afterwards by the protection of God thou
shalt come to thofe more greater perfectiõs
of doctrine, and vertuous life, where of wee
haue already made mention. Soe bee it

F I N I S

STATVTES
COMPYLED FOR THE
BETTER OBSERVATION
OF
THE HOLY RVLE OF
THE MOST GLORIOVS FATHER
AND
PATRIARCH S. BENEDICT

Confirmed by the ordinary Authoritie of the right honorable ād Reuer. Father in Chr. the Lo. MATTHIAS
HOVIVS Archbishop of Macklin and Primate of
the Netherlands &c. as alſoe by authority from the
Pope his Holyneſſe delegated to him, and by him
deliuered to the English Religious VVoemen
of the Monaſtery of our bleſſed Lady the
perpetuall Virgin Mary in Bruxelles and
to all their Succeſſours ;

*Quis eſt homo qui timet Dominum ; legem ſtatuet
ei in via quam elegit. Pſal. 24.*

*VVhat a kinde of perſon is that, who ſeareth our lord
bee will conſtitute him a law, for that State of life
where of hee hath made choyce ;*

Printed att Gant by Ioos Dooms.

THE FIRST PARTE

OF THE STATVTES

OF THOSE THINGS THAT

Appertayne to common Disciplyne

AND ARE TO BEE

OBSERVED OF ALL

CHAPTER I.

Of Piety.

1. WHERE as the cheifest scope and end of Euery Religious Order is to aduance the Professours there of to the Saluation and spirituall perfection of their Soules, therefore all that enter this Congregation, must dilligently apply themselues, that by meete and conuenient, meanes, they may attayne to the proposed end of their Vocation : the cheife meanes where of are, the exercises of true piety, and deuotion, as often prayer, me-

A 2   ditation,

ditation, confeſſion of their Sinnes , the holy
Communion, and the Mortification of themſelues ;

2.   Beſides the tyme appoynted for the
accompliſhing of the deuyne Office , and
reading of ſpirituall bookes, euery one ſhall
each day imploy one whole hower in mentall prayer. the which tyme that they may
fruytefully ſpend, to the comfort of their
Soules; the Abbeſſe ſhall endeauour that thy
may bee inſtructed by ſuch ſpirituall men , as
are well experienced in that godly exerciſe
that they may not onely ſtirr vpp in themſelues , ſuch affections as may further them
to vertue, but that they may alſoe the better
diſcouer the illuſions of the Ghoſtly Enemy
and know how to auoyde them ;

3.   If any of the Religious bee found vn
apt for this kinde of exerciſe , lett her beſtow
the afforeſayd tyme, either in vocall prayer,
or in ſome other deuoute imployment , according to the Iudgment of the Ghoſtly
Father ;

4.   They ſhall confeſſe and Communicate once euery weeke, the which they ſhall
doe alſoe vppon the cheifeſte Feaſts of the
Church, and the Order ; except the ghoſtly
Father ſhall iudge ſome tymes otherwiſe,
for ſome in perticuler , and more then this
they may bee permitted ; as the Abbeſſe
with

with the approbation of the Ghoſtly Father ſhall thinke good ;

5. When they haue made their vowes and profeſſion. for three dayes they ſhall receaue the holy Euchariſt; that they conſidering the greatneſſe of the benefitt which they haue receaued, they may become more gratefull to the king of heauen to whom they are eſpowſed.

6. Out of the tyme of Confeſſion none ſhall ſpeake with her ghoſtly Father vppon any pretence whatſoeuer, but in ſuch manner and tyme as to the Abbeſſe , and Superiour ſhall ſeeme meeteſt , and then leaue ſhalbee graunted to conferr with him ſoe oft, as the Abbeſſe or Superior ſhall perceaue that it will bee for her good , that requeſteth licence: which licence the Prioreſſe, Miſtris of the nouices, ãd Cellarier may grante to thoſe that are vnder their ſeuerall Charges : ſoe that firſt they know the ghoſtly Father his opinion whether, and in what manner hee ſhall thinke it profitable for them;

7. The Lady Abbeſſe muſt ſett downe a certayne tyme for their confeſſions, and ſhee muſt ſee that all goe to one ghoſtly Father (whom the Biſhopp ſhall appoynte them for that purpoſe) if the number will permitt it, otherwiſe ſhee with her Conuent ſhall

chooſe

choose another approued by the Ordinary,
vnto whom that parte of the Conuent shall
confesse . which the Abbesse shall thinke
good to appoynte ;

8.   None of the Religious shall presume
to censure her Confessor , either in the way
of praysing or discommending him before
others, neither by Comparison to prefer the
one a boue the other , or to manifest their defects , but onely to the Abbesse ; and if hee
haue giuen Counsayle or aduise to any of
them, lett her not discouer it in any such sort,
that any hurt or detrimēt may ensue thereof;

9.   They shall all confesse to their Ordinary Ghostly Father, and to noe other, except
the Abbesse giue them leaue , and all shall
confesse twice or thrice euery yeare to that
Preist that the most Reuerend lord Bishopp
in speciall manner for that purpose shall
appoynte; alsoe the Lady Abbesse shall prouide some three or fower Preists (according
to the number of the Couent) vnto whom,
by her leaue they may confesse , as often as
shee shall deeme fitting for their spirituall
good, hauing notwithstanding still good regard, that shee disturbe not the good order
of her Monastery hereby; And this conformable to the decree of Clement the V I I I.
made for Superiours of Monasteryes in the
yeare of our lord 1594.

Let

10. Let the Abbesse appoynte them a certayne tyme for the dayly examination of their Consciences, that thereby they may the better Consider of the state of their Soules, and what fruyte they reape by their holy Exercises;

11. If the Abbesse perceaue that some doe not soe much attend to their spirituall proffitt, as they should, and thereby giue her lesse satisfactió, let her in a motherlike manner exhort them to vse more dilligence for the tyme to come, and therefore it will much proffitt them, that at lest once a yeare all the Religious liue retyred from the rest (but not all at one tyme) that they may the better Recollect and confirme themselues in Spirit, but this wilbee most expedient for them, that make lesse progresse and aduancement in vertue and Religious life;

12. None shall seeke for any spirituall aduise or receaue any such directions, but from those which the Abbesse shall approue neither shall shee receaue any Instructions for that purpose without the expresse consent of her sayd Superiour;

13. Lett the Abbesse haue especiall care that noe bookes that sauour not of a Religious Spirit, or which doe not helpe there vnto, bee at any tyme brought into the Monastery; And lett the Catoloque of all the

bookes

bookes of the Monaſtery bee examined of
ſome learned diſcreete man, whoe may dif-
cerne whether they are profitable for Religious Spirits or, noe, and lett her allow but
ſome few for euery one, commaunding the
reſt to bee kept by one of the Religious, to
bee communicated vnto others as neede
ſhall require;

14. None without the leaue of the Superiour ſhall vſe vppon herſelfe any Corporall auſteritie, ouer and aboue that which
the rule and Statutes doe appoynte, or which
the ghoſtly Father ſhall not approue; yet the
Lady Abbeſſe may not onely permitt, but
alſoe enioyne ſome auſteritie to her Religious Subiects, when ſhee ſhall Iudge it
meete for their ſpirituall good;

15. If the Abbeſſe ſee any one of her
Religious giuen to more auſteritie then the
reſt, and to bee more feruent in her good
Exerciſes, ſhee muſt endeauour to aduance
and helpe her in her good deſires, yet ſoe
that all bee done within the limitts, of prudence and diſcretion; And all the Religious
of this Congregation are to vnderſtand that
there is nothing appoynted in any other
Religious Order, which may helpe for the
increaſe of Gods holy Spiritt, which ſhall
not alſoe bee moſt willingly permitted to
them of this holy Congregation, if ſoe bee
it

it shall bee thought expedient for them;

16. They that are permitted to vſe vppon themſelues any bodyly affliction, or mortifi-cation, muſt ſoe endeauour to conceale the ſame, that (as farr as lyeth in them) it may not bee knowne to the reſt, except the Ab-beſſe for ſome other good reſpects ſhall otherwiſe appoynte

17 Once euery weeke each one ſhall make a diſciplyne for ſoe long a tyme as the Ab-beſſe ſhall thinke good, and it is to bee done on Friday at night, except the Abbeſſe ſome tyme ſhall appoynte ſome other day;

18. Although the Abbeſſe may apply the prayers and deuotions of her Religious, for the obtayning of gods aſſiſtance and grace, or for ſome other benefitt from his deuine goodneſſe, yet ſhall ſhee bring in noe new obligations, but with great moderation, or with very great Conſideration;

19. They ſhall ſay or ſing their howers, and the deuyne office, according to the Ro-mane vſe, they ſhall ſay the litle Office of our bleſſed lady, the Office of the deade, the Graduall Pſalmes, the ſeuen penetentiall Pſalmes, and Litanies, in ſuch ſort as is ap-poynted in the breuiary of Rome;

20. They ſhall ſing the Mattines, laudes ãd the reſt of the howers vppõ the princi-palleſt Feaſts of the yeare, kept either by the

A 5   pre-

precept of the Church; or vppon Cuſtome, vppon the Feaſts of their Patrones ; and Patroneſſes, both of their Order and of their perticuler Churches, and of the Feaſt of the dedication of the ſame, alſoe they are to ſing euery day their conuentuall Maſſe, except the Abbeſſe for iuſt cauſes for a tyme ordayne otherwayes, both in theſe latter, as alſoe in the former Solemnities; Once euery weeke a Maſſe of the holy Ghoſt is to bee ſung, or ſayd, and as often as the Office of the bleſſed Virgin is ſayd on the Saturdayes, ſoe often a Maſſe is to bee celebrated of our bleſſed Lady, for this end that the Conuent may obtayne of our lord ſpirituall progreſſe and aduancement

22. Whyle they ſing, or ſay the deuyne Office, lett them obſerue due grauitie and Modeſty, and decent compoſition of their cariage, neither may they poſt ouer their ſeruice, but they muſt pronounce each worde with moderate leiſure, diſtinctly, and truly, and with ſoe loude a voyce, that they may bee well herd and vnderſtoode by thoſe that are out of the Quire ;

23. None may intreate or labour to haue leaue to intone or reade any thing, but as it ſhall bee appoynted her, neither may ſhee any wiſe refuſe any thing that ſhee is willed to ſing or reade, except ſhee firſt make know
her

her impediment to the Superiour ; to whofe Commaundement shee is wholly to submitt her selfe ;

24. They may some tymes vse Musicke
in the deuyne office , yet it must bee with
great Moderation, togeather with the good
edification of the hearers , and only such
Songs they are to sing as are truly graue and
modest ;

25. If vppon iust hindrance any shalbee
absent from the other Canonicall howers,
yett all must bee present at Complyne , except some vrgent Cause shall excuse them,
or that the Abbesse shall iudge some other
businesse to bee more necessary and important ;

CHAPTER 2.

Of Pouertie;

I. **A**LL such as make their profession
of Religion in this Congregation,
must vnderstand that they can haue nothing
in propriety, euen as the Rule hath enacted;
what soeuer therefore is giuen them by ther
frends;and kinsfolkes , is to bee applyed to
the vse of the Conuent and Communitie;
But if the Abbesse will permitt any to haue
any

any thing of smale price as a memory of
their Frends, it may not bee any thing that
is made of gould or Siluer, and much lesse of
pretious stones, sett either in gould or Siluer;

2. Goulden or Siluer Vessells may not bee
vsed in this Congregation, except for the
Church or Infirmary, and for this latter in
meane and smale quantitie and number;
Neither may the Abbesse vse such Vessell
in her Cell, or in the Refectory, but this may
bee permitted for the intertaynment of
Guestes, (when it shalbee thought expedient to vse any such entertaynment) yet
with this moderation, that in them all vanitie and secular pompe is to bee eschewed;

3. They must auoyde all notable singularitie and curiositie in their apparell, Images,
and all other Furniture of their Cells, and
they are to haue only those things, whichbe-
fitt religious decency, and are for their health, and they must willingly imbrace what
soeuer appertayneth to their diett and Apparell according to true Religious pouertie;

4. There woolen or linnen apparell may
not bee made of any fine Costly Cloath, yea
though itt bee giuen them, or bee by their
parents bestowed vppon them, but they are
to weare those things, that are of a moderate
price, and are lasting;

5. They shall not giue or receaue one of
another

another any thing, without the lady Abbeſſe or the Superiours licence, ye the Prioreſſe, Miſtreſſe of the Nouices, and Celarier may ſome tyme giue leaue to thoſe that are vnder their charge, to giue or take one of another, ſome matter of litle moment or value;

6. Let none begg any thing of her frēds or Parents, for her proper vſe, but if her frēds or Parents will giue any thing, lett it bee ſoe done that it may bee applyed to the Communitie, or left to the will and diſpoſition of the Abbeſſe, that ſhee may beſtow it vppon them as ſhee ſhall thinke good ;

7. It may not bee lawfull to lend or grāt any thing appertayning to the Monaſtery to any abroade, without leaue from the Abbeſſe;

8. Each Religious ſhall once euery yeare (to witt before the firſt Sunday in lent) goe to the lady Abbeſſe and with due humilitie and reuerence declare vnto her, that what ſoeuer they haue, they willingly offer it vnto her, leauing it to her Will, whether ſhee will ſuffer them to retayne, reſtore, or otherwiſe diſpoſe ther of in the beſt ſort, as in our lord, ſhee ſhall thinke moſt meete, and if the Abbeſſe will take a vew of each thing in perticuler, they ſhall bring them all vnto her, in all Fidelitie, neither may they haue any thing loc
ked

ked vpp in Cheftes or Coffers, without the
leaue and knowledge ofthe Abbeffe;

9. And to the end euery one may ftricktly
and carefully keepe their vow of pouerty, it
is enacted, that if any after her death (which
God forbidd)should bee found a Proprietary
and to haue any thing of notable value for
her vfe, or in the Cuftody of any other, without the Abbeffes knowledge, shee shalbee
infallably depriued of Chriftian Buriall;

CHAPTER 3.

Of Chaftitie;

IT is very fitt the Spoufes of Chrift imitate
all Angelicall puritie, which may con-
ferue in them the integritie of their bodyes
and myndes; therefore they muft fly all fuch
things which may any wayes caufe any im-
preffion in their myndes, contrary to puritie

2. They shall conceale noe greiueous
temptation, which they shall not manifeft
to their ghoftly Father yea and to their im-
mediate Superiour, or to the Abbeffe, if they
thinke they may receaue from them any
comfort or helpe; lett them shew all modefty and humilitie in their wordes, Countenances, geftures, and Actions, and lett them
behaue

behaue themselues each to others with due
respect, and Religious grauitie , and euery
one is to behould as it were Chrift himfelfe
in her Sifter;

CHAPTER   4.

Of Obedience;

I.   AS the Religious haue vowed to
God and to their Superiours them
felues , and w at foeuer els they haue, foe
muft they suffer themfelues to bee guyded
and gouerned by their Abbeffe, and Superiour, as the Interpretours of Gods holy will;
therefore let them wholy giue themfelues
to perfect holy obedience , and let them labour to bee excellent in the fame, not onely
willingly and promptly, performing thofe
things that are enioyned them , but fullfilling them in fuch forte and fashion, as they
thinke to bee moft conformable to the Superiours Will;

2. Euery one muft bee ready to vndergoe
all bafe Offices and exercifes , what foeuer
the Abbeffe shall thinke good to impofe
vppon them, neither may they thinke themfelues exempt from this by any office, degree
or Qualitie, nor may they expect any priuiledge

ledge, but in cafe of Neceſſitie onely , but euery one is to know. that all are to liue equally vnder one and the felfe fame Rule of Obedience, without exception of any perſons or perſon;

3.　When the Superiour commaundeth any thing,that may bee hurtfull to their health, or an hindrance of a greater good, or that it cannot bee performed within the tyme allotted them , then let them ſoe manifeſt the difficultie to her , that yet withall, they leaue all to her Iudgment and diſcretion,and ſoe obey , if it may bee done without manifeſt Sinne;

4.　If any should requeſt any thingof her Superiour which shee thinketh needefull for the health of her body or Soule , or for the performance of any duty and charge enioyned her , lett her firſt commend the matter to God, and with a reſigned mynde lett her open the cafe to the Superiour , and after it hath beene ſome two or three tymes denyed her,lett her neuer mention the matter more, except shee verely thinke , her Superiour hath for gott it,and that shee will take it well , that shee bee put in mynde there of ;

5.　They shall not onely obey the lady Abbeſſe,but alſoe all others of the Conuent, whether they bee of the Quire or Conuerſe)

whoe

whoe from her receaue power and Authoritie, otherwise none may commaund, or reprehend another, without expresse leaue from the Abbesse, and of her, shee is to vnderstand how farr she may proceede in commaunding, or in her reprehension.

6. If any bee commaunded any thing by the subordinate Superiour, which is different from that which the chiefe Superiour or Abbesse did commaunde or apoynte, let the Inferiour manifest to the Subordinate her Superiours Will, and Order, and lett her without further Contradiction reuerently obey, if shee see her persist and continew in her commaunde, but let the subordinate afterwards informe her Superiour of the Case if any error or fault happen thereby.

7. If at any tyme happyly the subordinate Superiours, commaunde diuersly any one, in things appertayning to their charges, lett them represent their difficulties, each one to the other, without contention: and if the case soe require it, with externall and mutuall shew of Reuerence, lett them remitt it to the arbitrement of the Abbesse, or Superiour laying barely open the Case without further dispute, and soe lett them thinke that to bee best which the Abbesse or Superiour, sufficiently informed, shall iudge to bee soe;

B   S. What

8. Whatſoeuer is denyed by any ſubordinate Snperiour, ſhee may not aske the ſame of the Abbeſſe, except alſoe ſhee declare vnto her, that the Subordinate Superiour did deny it, togeather ith the reaſon of her ſayd deniall, ſoe far as ſhee knoweth or can gueſſe;

9. They are to obey her that commaundeth any thing in the lady Abbeſſes name, al though in very deede ſhee haue noe ſuch authoritie ſoe to commaunde, and ordinary ly in th ir Commaundements, they are rather to vſe the Abbeſſes name, then their owne, except onely the mother Prioreſſe, Miſtreſſe of the Nouices, and Cellarier, towards thoſe of their charge;

CHAPTER 5.

Of the Incloſure;

1. THey muſt haue a ſpeciall care of keeping their Incloſure, ſoe much commended and (with vehement words expreſſing the neceſſitie thereof) commaunded by the ſacred Counſell of Trent: moreouer ſeing they haue bound themſelues by vow to the obſeruation thereof, they muſt hold it neceſſary to bee kept;

2. Their

2. Their Inclofure muft bee enuyroned with high Walls, which may contayne that parte of the Church, to witt the Quyre allotted to their proper vfe, togeather with the Cloyfter dormitory Refectory, and all the Offices and buyldings, which are appertayning to the proper vfe of the profeffed Religious; togeather with the Gardens, Orchards, and fuch like, foe that none from abroade may enter into this Inclofure, by any Stayres, or Gates, but onely by one dore or Gate, if it may bee any wife fo contriued commodioufly;

3. Noe profeffed Religious may goe out of this Inclofure, but vppon conftraynte of Fyre, extreme famyne, Warr, ruyne of the buyldings, and fuch like greueous dangerous cafes, and for other Cafes approued vppon vrgent neceffitie, or commaunded by the lord Bifhopp, or the Vifitor; yet when the Schollers of Religion are to receaue their Religious habitt, or the Nouices are to make their Profeffion, the Abbeffe with fome few of her Religious, may goe out of the Quier, and enter into the outward parte of the Church, that they may affift them in that folemne Action; which is alfoe permitted to the Abbeffe newly chofen, that with a decent Company of her Religious, shee may alfoe enter the fame, to receaue the

B 2　　　　Bir-

Bishopps Benediction : for which , and
for some other necessary Causes and vses,
there may bee a Conuenient passage betwixt the Quier and the outward Church. ·

4. All that are not Religious or not of the
Conuent of what sex, age , or Condition soeuer they bee, may not enter into the Inclosure but vppon necessary Causes , approued
and licenced by the Bishopp in writing,
without which licence according to the
decree of the Counsayle of Trent , both the
person that entreath , and the person that
admitteth him, incurreth the payne of Excommunication ;

5.   Other Religious weomen of the same
Order liuing vnder these Statutes, being sent
by their Superiours to some other place, may
in their passage be receaued in to any Monastery of this Congregation, and therein they
may stay for two or three dayes , or longer ,
as according to prudence and Charitie it
shalbee thought conuenient ;

6. The Visitours accompanyed with certayne modest and graue Clergy men may
enter in, to performe their Visitation, or for
any other necessary businesse ;

7. When the ghostly Father entreth into
the Monastery to visite the sicke, or for some
other necessary matter , one or two Religious appoynted by the Abbesse for that pur
pose

pose shall allwayes bee present with him, and if any Religious bee to bee buryed, soe many from abroade may bee present at that Office, as shalbee thought needefull.

8. The Phisition, Surgeon, Workemen, Gardiners, Porters, Carters, Masons, and all such as haue any necessary imployments within the Monastery may bee suffred to enter ; they must keepe accompt in what number they enter, that in the same number they may departe, and those that enter must bee accompanyed by two or three of the Religious to those places where they are to bee ymployed, none of the Religious may approach to those that are entred without the expresse licence of the Abbesse, the which not withstanding shee may not graunt to any one alone.

9. When the people from abroade haue leaue to speake with the Religious, lett it bee done at a Grate when neede shall require. within the Grate lett a Curtayne hang which may soe hang shutt, or bee drawne to lett the Religious bee seene, or not to bee seene, as the Abbesse shall thinke best expedient.

10. In the place where the Religious make their Confessions, lett a Gloth bee soe drawne and fastned, that the penitent may

not seethe Ghostly Father, nor yet bee seen by him; All that the Religious are to receaue into the Inclosure, lett them receaue it by a Turne, except it bee of that kinde, that by the Turne they cannot receaue it ; the Turne with in must bee locked and made fast, in such sort that it may not bee tourned about, but at such tymes as any thing is to bee receaued in thereby;

CHAPTER 6.

Of Silence;

1. IN such places and tymes as soueraigne silence is to bee kept ; (to witt, in the dormitory , Refectory, Chapter house, Quier, and Cloyster, and in the howers assigned for silence , as are to bee seene afterwards in the twelueth Chapter, and in the 7. 8. and 9. Numbers , and after Complyne vntill Prime ended , none may speake but vppon vrgent necessitie , and that by noe other meanes shee can expresse her meaning , and make her selfe vnderstoode, for then shee may speake , but yett with a low voyce and with all breuitie;

2. At what tyme they worke togeather in the Common workehouse they may speake, but yett onely of things necessary

and

and with a low voyce;

3 . If any should seeke for another, lett her goe and seeke her , but without noyse, ãd shee may not call her with a loude voyce, and if shee finde her with others . lett her deliuer vnto her the Superiours commaundement , that others may not vnderstand it, and shee that is called for to another place, lett her giue notice thereof to the Superiour of that place to the end shee may know whe ther shee goeth;

4 . Soe often as they speake togeather, they must haue good care that they may not bee heard out of the place where they are at that present; In their Recreations (when they are permitted them) lett them bee soe myndefull of modesty and Religious decency, that one push and thrust not another, noe nor soe much as touch her , soe farr as lyeth in her; In their speeches and Conuersation lett them auoyde and fly all shew of contempt and litle esteeme of others , all kinde of mocking , and scoffings , and all other things what soeuer, whereby either throughe their wordes or actions , any kinde of occasion of brabble or displeasure may arise;

5 . And for as much as here mention is made of the Recreations of the Religious; it is prohibited that within the Inclosure

any

any kinde of beasts bee kept or fedd, but for the vse of the Communitie, and not for the priuate Recreation of any one alone neither vppon any coulor or pretext what soeuer may they permitt any dwarfes, Idiores, or young Infants to bee nourished or brought vpp within the Inclosure.

6. Their mutuall conuersation must bee vsed for their health, and Conseruation of Charitie, and therefore it must bee vsed in publike, and not in Corners, or in their Cells nether may the Religious vse any speech of such matters, which they haue heard or secular people abroade, except they bee of such, which may yeald Edification, and spirituall Comfort and proffitt to the hearers.

7. In their Conuersation lett the so shew loue and Charitie to euery one, that withall they take good regard that they shew not themselues mare singularely affected to one then to another, and lett them doe reuerence to euery one, according as tneir State shall require, neither may they shunn the speech and Conuersation of any whoe soeuer.

8. They must bee very carefull that they talke not of their Stocke, and Nobilitie of their kindred, nor of plightes, Controuersies and debates, among their Parents, kindred, and Families, or dispute of them, yea they may

may not admitt any talke among themselues
(but with great warynesse) of the Iarrs or
enmities that one Prouince or Country hath
with another.

9. None may speake of the imperfection
of any other, but onely to the Abbesse, or
Superiour, or to those from whom they may
expect helpe and redresse;and if any damma-
ge or hindrance by any ones defect, may bee
thought to fall vnto the Monastery, and that
by noe other way it can bee remedied, all
shalbee bound to informe the Abbesse there
of, that in good tyme both the hurt that may
be fall vnto any person in perticuler, or the
mischeife that may happen to the whole
Conuent in generall may bee hindred.

10. None shall heare any thing of any
Religious vppon Bond of secrecy, and vppō
that Condition that the Abbesse may not
know it, yea rather they ought to hould it a
thing right grate full and pleasing to them,
that shee should bee informed of all matters
that may any wayes aduance, and sett forward the good gouernment of the Monastery.

11. None may enter into the Office or
Cell of another, without leaue, or vppon
commaundement of the Superiour, and nether may they then enter, before they haue
giuen a signe by knocking at the doare and

B 5   haue

haue receaued an anſweare to enter, lett the
dore ſtand open ſoe long, as they talke and
bee togeather within, except the Superiour
doe expreſſely appoynte it otherwiſe;

12.   Whyle they ſpeake one to another,
or of another, they may not call them by
their bare names, but the Abbeſſe, Prioreſſe,
Miſtris of the Nouices, and Celarier
ſhall call their Subiects Siſters, the profeſſed
of the Quier ſhall call alſoe the Conuerſe.
Siſters; but the profeſſed of the Quier, muſt
call them dames ſpeaking of others that are
profeſſed of the Quier, the Prioreſſe muſt bee
called of all Mother; the Miſtriſſe, of her Nouices muſt bee called Miſtriſſe, the Cellarier
is alſoe to bee called Mother of thoſe that
are vnder her charge; But the Abbeſſe of all
is to bee named lady: that by theſe names
due honour and Reuerence may bee yealded
each one in that Vocatiõ, ãd degree in which
ſhee is placed by our lord ãd Sauiour Chriſt;

13.   As they meete one with another
lett them doe Reuerence each one to the
other by an Inclination and bending of
their bodyes, and lett each one endeauour to
preuent the other with honour according
to due Religious modeſty; and all thoughe
the Iuniour profeſſed ought principally to
vſe this preuention to her elders, and more
Ancient in Religion by honoring and Reue-
rencing

rencing them, yet none but Superiours may exact it of them;

14. In speaking lett none vnmannerly interrupt anothers speech , or in twight her Sister of Errours: but in there Conuersation lett them bee myndfull to vse all due modesty, and decent cariage, with all Ciuilitie auoyding both in their Words and behauiour, all Rudenesse, sowernesse, or lightnesse, as alsoe all secular vanity and affectation : which noe wayes standeth with the grauitie, which appertoyneth, vnto Religious persons; let alsoe their speech bee very sparing, and for the most part lett it bee about spirituall matters, or at lestwise about such matters as may sauour of spiritt, and nourish the same;

15. In their going and shutting of the doores, lett them make noe noyse, as much as lyeth in thê, but this they must beware of in tyme of soueraigne Sylence, and whê the Religious are at their reading ãd meditaion;

16. When any (hauing obtayned leaue) visitt the Sicke, lett her soe behaue herselfe, that shee may recreate and ease them ; and to the end shee may not bee trouble some vnto them, shee must first learne of the Infirmare by what meanes shee may best Côfort them, and auoyde to bee greiuous to thê

17. When secular people come, and (by
the

the Superiours permiſſion) ſpeake with the
Religious at the Grate, lett them ſignify vnto
the Abbeſſe either by themſelues or by ſuch
as are appoynted to accompany them, thoſe
things whereof they had talke as the matter
ſhall require ; And then let them auoyde
long conference, if it may bee done without
offence, or except the matter bee of that moment and conſequence, that longer ſpeach
may bee permitted.

18.   Whyle they ſpeake with ſecular
people, and thoſe that come vnto them from
abroade ; if the Prefect of the Turne, or her
Companion cannot bee preſent, let them
haue another appoynted by the Superiour,
who may heare and ſee all that is ſpoken
and done, who may neuer departe or leaue
them alone till the ſpeech bee fully ended.

19.   Although nothing ordinarely ought
to bee ſayd which they would not haue herd
and vnderſtoode, yet when the caſe requireth Secrecy, and that the Religious cannot
goe commodiouſly to the Abbeſſe, lett her
requeſt leaue by the Thourere to ſpeake in
ſecrett, and by her lett her deliuer the cauſes
for which ſhee requireth ſuch ſecrett conference, and of her ſhee is to expect an anſweare how ſhee muſt proceede.

20.   If any Religious bee not permitted
to ſpeake with any at the Greate, none may
tell

tell her that shee was called for by any abroade, and that shee was denyed to speake with them.

21. None may speake with people abroade of the domesticall affayres of the Monastery, except they bee such matters as every one may well vnderstand them, or which they know the Superiour will not bee vnwilling they should bee made knowne vnto them : and if any Externe should request the assistance of any of the Religious in any affayre, yet lett her not take vppon her to doe or write any thing without the lycence the Abbesse;

22. Whyle the Religious are in the speaking place, lett them speake with soe low a voyce, that they may bee onely heard of their Companions, and of the persons with whó they speake; Moreouer lett them endeauour to behaue them selues there with all edification, and to apply some parte at lest of their talke to a spirituall end, neither lett them show that in such Conuersation they seeke for their omne priuate solace and Comfort, but rather for the Comfort of those that come to Visitt them, finally lett them soe bestow that tyme vppon others, that at the first peale they depart to the Quiar, from which none may bee absent, without the expresse licence of the Abbesse or Superiour;

23. In

23. In lent and intyme of Aduent this accesse of externes may not bee permitted, as neither vppon the dayes of Confession and Communion, and then the Religious may not bee seene of them, if vppon any occasion they bee permitted to speake with them except some important great reason shall require the contrary;

CHAPTER 7.

Of the Fasts, and the Common diett ;

I. IN Aduent they must fast except the Sundayes, on which they obserue abstinence, and from Quinquagesima Sunday, included vntill Easter (excepting all Sundayes) they shall Fast , and abstayne from white meates; except the approued Custome of the Country, and the dearth of lenten meates doe perswade otherwise ;

2. From Septuagesima included vntill Quinquagesima they shall abstayne from all flesh , in which tyme vppon Mundayes, Vednesdayes ãd fridays they shall fast, except some double Feasts fall on those days; Alsoe fró the Feast of the Ascention of our lord excluded, vntill the Vigill of Penticost they shall keepe Abstinence;

3. From

3. From the Feasts of the Natiuity of our blessed lady excluded, vntill Easter they shall Fast euery wednesday and from the Kalends of Nouember excluded, they shall fast alsoe Mundayes, except vppon those ferias (out of lent) a double Feast bee celebrated;

4. From the Feast of the Resurrection of our Sauiour Christ, till the Feast of the Natiuity of our blessed Virgin Mary included they may receaue twoe Refections euery day excepting Notwithstanding Fridayes, on which they shall obserue the approued Custome of the Prouince where in they liue, or els they shall fast; *(We fast)*

5. They must appoynte the howers of their Meales according to the Differences of the tymes of the yeare, or according to the deuine Seruice, and the holy Office of the Masse, as is sett downe in the Roman Missal

6. In the Fasts and abstinences of the Rule and Statutes, the Abbesse may dispence with such as are weake, and aged, and whesoeuer any perticuler reason may perswade her there vnto, soe that Flesh bee not eaten in the Refectory, and that the grant passe not into a *{ Vnlett att a table apart.}* custome: but vppon those dayes that are forbidden by the Church, their approbation is to bee required who haue authoritie therein, according to the Custome of each Country;

7. Vppon

7. Vppon due Confideration of the paynes and labours that are to bee fuftayned in this Congregation, as alfoe of the Sex, but efpecially of the weake Complextions, and educations of very many which are admitted into this order thofe things that appertayne to their dyett, are fo to bee moderated and tempered, that the Religious may with more ftrength goe forward in the performance of the deuine Seruices, and bur thens of their Inftitute, and with more alacrity perfeuer and continue in the fame; therfore ordinaryly vppon Sundayes,Tuefdayes,and Thurfdays through out the yeare, as alfoe vppon Chrifmaffe day falling vppon a friday,or Saturday,they may eate flesh, excepting hereafter according to the Rule they fhall altogeather abftaine from flesh.

8. The meafure of their meate and drinke fhall depend vppon the Iudgment of the Abbeffe, and as fhee is not to permitt them any fuperfluyty in their dyett, foe is fhee alfoe to haue care that nothing bee Wanting according to Religious decency, and each perfons neceffity,as on the cótrary fhee is to haue a fpeciall regard, that whilft fhee endeauoreth to priuide for euery one in their Neceffaryes,fhee permitt not fuperfluyty to enter and take place amongft them

yet

yet ordinarely when they eate flesh , shee
may giue to each one an Antipaſt , or ſallet, a
pittance of fleſh of halfe a pound, and a poſt
paſt in fruyte, or ſome what els in ſleade of
fruyte, when thy faſt, beſides the afforeſayde
(if they may bee had) lett her endeauour or
giue vnto the Conuent what may bee gotten, or may well ſerue for their neceſſitie.
If beſides this the Phiſition thinke any thing
more , and aboue to bee giuen to any
or that their neceſſitie or infirmity doe require any thing in perticuler , lett her endeauour to performe it towards them , with
all pitty, charitie, and alacritie, ſoe that it bee
not done in the Common Refectory , but either at the Superiours *or infirme table* or in the
Infirmary ;

9. Out of tymes of Refection they may
not eate or drinke any thing , without the
leaue of the Superiour, neither may they refuſe thoſe things that are appoynted them
by their Superiour for their health and comfort, yet in theſe things the Prioreſſe , Miſtreſſe of the Nouices , and Cellareir may
giue leaue vnto thoſe that are vnder their
ſeuerall Charges ;

10. If by experience it bee found, that the
Comon dyett is not wholeſome for ſome
lett that bee made knowne to the Abbeſſe,
who ſhall prouide therefore, as in our lord

C   ſhe

shee shall thinke good, and shee shall euery
yeare declare vnto the Visitor what forme
and manner shee obserueth in these things
and withall lett her not suffer any to keepe
any sweet meates,conserues,or Confections
in their Cells, except the Phisition thinke
that they must haue often vse thereof;

CHAPTER 8.

Of the Apparell of the Religious and of those things that appertaine to their bedding;

I.　FOR their apparell they may vse
that which the Abbesse (hauing regard of tymes and places) shall approue ;

2.　Besides the vpper or greate habitt
they may haue two vnder Coates whereof
the one or both in Winter may bee lyned
with Furr ;

3.　The greate habitt must bee longer then
their other Garments, which must reach to
the ground, yet it may not bee soe long that
it may hinder them in going, or bee dragged
on the ground, and soe worne ; and soe it
must bee made , that the sleeues must bee
three foote large, and what soeuer couereth
the

the body must bee loose;

4.   This greate habitt must bee blacke, and soe must the Scapular, and inward coate next to the Scapulare, if they vse any other coates or garments, it shall litle importe of what colour they bee, soe they bee either white, or blake or some other brownish or darke Colour;

5. Their Cloathes which are vnder their scapulare must bee open from the shoulders downe to the gird le and soe clasped, and for their sleeues they must not bee two wide, nor yet soe straight that they may not put their hands easaly into each sleeue, neither in any of their garments, may they vse any buttons or any silke;

6. They must not haue or weare any linnē next their bodyes, without leaue from the Abbesse or Superiour, or except their necessitie, or health should otherwise require;

7. The habitts of the Conuerse Sisters must bee like that of the Quiar: excepting onely that the sleeues of their greate habitt must bee straighter by the halfe and when they weare their greate habitt they must gird them to their bodyes;

8. All must put on their greate habitt when they goe to the Quier, Refectory, Chapter house, and speaking place, in such sort and soe oftē as in their Ceremonyes is expressed

          9. Euery

9. Euery one must haue a note of all their Cloathes, where of the Guardroabe must haue a Coppy, that they may bee able to render an accompt of them, when it shall-bee demaunded; they may not sett any letters of their names on their Vayles or Garments which they are to weare, but rather certayne numbers or other Carecters, they must not bee two carefull of hauing new Cloathes, but lett them permitt themselues to bee prouided for herein, by the Abbesse, as in other matters;

10.   At what tyme soeuer they shal chance to haue a new Garment, they must giue vpp their old, neither must they bee desirous to haue more then may bee serui-ceable for their health, and necessitie and what soeuer cloathes they receaue, lett them haue regard to keepe them carefully, and clenly as those things that appertayne to the poore of Christ;

11.   In the night they are to take their rest in their Cloathes, hauing on their Scapulars, and stokens that they may bee the readyer to rise vnto mattins; The professed must weare their white and blake Veyles, but the Nouices must sleepe in their white : yet when the heates are greate, or when they are sicke, they may leaue of their Cloathes and stokens and lay their Scapulars on their bedds, yet

may

may they not then bee without their Veyles, and they are dilligently to keepe, and obserue all other things what soeuer is appoynted and set downe in the holy Rule;

12. Euery one must sleepe apart vppon a straw and a Wollen Matrice : for their Couerletts and Curtaynes they must stand there in to the Iudgment of the Abbesse in what sort they are to haue them : they must ly in Wollen, except through the Indisposition of their Corporall health , the Abbesse shall thinke otherwise;

13. Those that are in health may not haue the vse of Feathers but in their pillowes, which may bee couered with linnen Pillow beeres, and they may admitt nothing in their Cloathing or bedding, which hath any shew of singularitie : but onely they may haue such things as are af a meane price, and best indureth !

CHAPTER 9.

Of letters and Messages.

1. NOe Religious may receaue any letters writings or tokens , either for her selfe or for any other, for that is the Office onely of the keeper of the Parlow; what soeuer is deliuered, the Abbesse or

by

by her permiſſion the Prioreſſe ſhall ſee, and they ſhall deliuer or retayne it as they ſhall thinke good : neither may any tell that ſuch letters or tokẽs were brought to any, except the Abbeſſe or Prioreſſe (by the conſent of the Abbeſſe) ſhall iudge otherwiſe!

2 When they write to their frends, lett them ſtudy to write thoſe things which bee ſeeme their ſtate and profeſſion, and lett them doe it diſcreetly and prudently, that the ir frends may receaue Edification, and ſpirituall proffitt from them.

3. They muſt not bee very eaſy to write often to their frends, or parentes, except vppon neceſſitie, or for ſome ſpirituall good that may ſeeme to enſue thereof, yea a Religious perſon ought to bee very ſparing in that kinde, as benig one dead to the world, and that deſyreth one ly to liue to Chriſt alone.

4. They may not write to their frends or parents be fore they haue leaue, ne ither may they prepare for them any to kens, without the knowledge of the Abbeſſe, and without her conſent; It is alſoe forbidden all of them, to beſtow any Newyeares gift vppon any; yet the Abbeſſe may ſend ſomewhat to the Common Frends of the Monaſtery or beſtow ſome whatt vppon others inway of gratitude!

What

5. What writings letters, or Tokens
soeuer they are to send lett them de liuer to
the Abbesse and lett them leaue it to her
iudgment, whether shee wll send them or
noe; neither aftherwards may they curiously
inquire in what sort shee disposed of them!

6. None may carry any Messages or Salu-
tatious from people abroade to any of the
Monastery wthout the Abbesse commaunde
them soto doe!

CHAPTER 10.

Of the Chapter ;

1. The Chapters were instituted and appoynted for the exercise of humilitie, Conseryation of Monasticall disciplyne, and for the aduancement of the Common good of the Conuent : There fore
very great heede must bee taken that the
peace tranquillitie, and due subordination
(whereby increase of spiritt, and due order is wont to bee gotten and conser ved)
may not thereby bee disturbed!

2. Once enery weeke Chapter is to bee
kept, and that vppon friday, except some
solemne Feaste fall vppon that day, for
then it must bee kept vppon Manday, or
Wednesday not hindred with the like

Feaſt except ſome of the enſuing Vigils
come that weeke, or ſome other iuſt occaſion hinder it;

3. They are to meete in Chapter vppon
the Vigils of Chriſtmaſſe, and Eaſter and the
Aſſention of our lord, and on the Vigi-
les of Penticoſt of the Aſſumption of our
bleſſed lady, and of the Patrone of their Order, and of their Church, and ſo often like
wiſe as the Abbeſſe ſhall thinke good wherein they are to performe the things that
are ſett downe in their Ceremonyes, both
for the manifeſting of their deſects, and for
the Correction thereof, as alſoe for the or-
dering buſineſſes, and affayres as may occurr!

4. In the Chapter the Religious are to
accuſe them ſelues of the breach of their Rule, or Statuts, or of their negligences or defects, which when they doe, lett them doe it
in ſuch ſorte, that thoſe that heare and ſee
them, may bee edefyed by the Exemple of
their humilitie! if it may bee doubted whether they may bee rather offended then edifyed, lett them not accuſe themſelues in pu-
blik thereof, vntill they haue conſulted with
the Superiour about the ſame!

5. Ordinarely they are to accuſe them
ſelues of thoſe things that they committed in
publike, or which they thinke in tyme will
come to the notice of others; therefore lett
them

them no publish their secrett faults, and defects, except the matter bee of smale moment, or for their greater mortification, or which they thinke may proue of great edification vnto others, which notwith standing they shall first declare vnto the Superiour, that from her they may haue leaue to doe the same!

6. It properly apper tayneth to the Prioresse, Mistris of the Nouices, and Cellarier to informe the Abbesse of those persons that are subiect vnto them, and to accuse them in the Chapter, although others of the Religious alsoe may, and must in forme the Abbesse a bout them, when they see any tking committed domageable for the spirituall good of any or contrary to the common good, or reputation of the Conuent, or th it they perceaue that these things are not marked by o thers, or to bee neglected by them!

7. If any bee commanded to accuse another lett her doe it with due modesty, moderation laying aside all bitternesse of mynde, and exageration of Wordes, but rather see they doe it with great shew of Charitie, and beneuolence!

8. In the Chapter none may bee accused of any fault, which is onely knowne to the accuser her selfe, or which cannot bee proued by the Testimony of two at the least,

C 5   yet

yet all may tell the Abbesse or Superiour of the Faults of any, though neuer soe secrett, except perhapps priuate admonition, may more proffitt the offendors, and there fore may wel suffice, whereby it may bee Iudged to bee preferred and first to bee vsed ! yea euery one is to know that it is most seuerely prohibited them to accuse any, or blame them to the Superious, without sufficient ground and knowledge of the matter !

9. None may either by worde or deede tax any Sister, or gird at them for any fault, or defect, whereof they haue beene admonished by the Abbesse, or Superiour or for which they coiecture or suspect that they haue bee ne reprehended, or punished ! for they are to thinke that that admonition, reprehension, or Correction proceeded of Charitie, togeather with an intention to vphold good discipline and Order ; and that it was alsoe receaued of the party offendent, with full purpose to amend and reforme her selfe thereof, for the tyme to come!

10. The Sister accused may not refute the saying of her that accuseth her, except the Superiour commaund her to declare the State of the matter; neither may they contend, or presume after wards to brabble amongst the selues vnder punishment of a great Pennance, which the Superiour is to impose on
them;

them; which thing is alſoe to bee obſerued, when any may chance to bee accuſed out of the Chapter, As the faults where of they are accuſed, ſome are greater, then other ſome; in like manner for the better auoyding and redreſſing of them, greater and ſmaler penances are to bee enioyned, which is left for the moſt parte to the Diſcretion of the Superior, to enioyne ſuch penances for euery offence which may bee thought conuenient who is to haue regard ſhee ſeeke notto afflict or trouble any but rather to endeauor thei amendment, for the greater honour of God, and her Charges proffitt, None muſt thinke them ſelues exempt from theſe Penances, but as all are tyed to the ſame Rule and Statutes, ſoe muſt they thinke them ſelues ſubiect to the ſame Penances, for their negligences in obſeruation of diſciplyne, or exerciſeing vertue : and there fore the Abbeſſe may not in theſe things bee more indulgent or fauoureable to one, then to another, but ſhee is to beare an euen hand ouer all, ſeeking for the ſpirituall good and proffitt of all!

12. For as much as Penances are not one-by to bee giuen for the correction of faultes, but for the exerciſe of Vertues, and mortification of their Paſſions (as hath bee ne ſayd) there fore whoeſeouer ſhalbee reprehended

ded at any tyme by the Abbesse or Superiour,
or shall by them receaue any Pennance
for any Fault, for which the Rule or Statutes
haue sett downe nothing expressely, lett
her giue noe shew of impatience, soe farr
fort as lyeth in her, nether lett her frame
answeares, or excuses for her selfe except
perhapps the reasons of those things for
which shee is reprehēded and punished; bee
demanded of her, or that somewhat bee to
bee revealed which was not knowne, but let
her endure all without murmuration, and
with as great peace of mynde as shee may
much lesse it may bee lawfull for any to excuse her that is reprehended, and (esperially
in her presence) seeke to extenuate her fault,
although shee may after wards certify the
Abbesse of all that hath passed; if soe bee that
it may seeme soe expedient; And to the end
all occasion of murmuring may bee taken
away none may complayne to any of the Religious, or to any other person, but onely
to her from whom shee may expect redresse,
and if any feele any disgust for any matter,
lett her make her recourse to the lady Abbesse, or to the Superiour, who shall with
Compassion giue eare to her Playntes, and
performe that towards her which shalbee
iudged to bee according to Iustice!

13. If shee that is penanced, or any other
for

for her at some tyme, will not confer about
her with the Superiour or Abbesse, for that
they may thinke that they cannot deale with
them in such free manner as were necessary,
then may they goe to the Assistants, or to some one of them, and make knowne to them
those things, whereof they would haue their
Abbesse or Superior to bee informed

14. For smaller faults such penances as
these following may bee enioyned by the
Abbesse or Superiour vnto the offenders as
the sayd Superiours shall thinke good: to
witt certayne prayers, knee ling on the ground, and eating on the same, to serue in the
Refectory or Kitchin, to abstaine from some
parte of their meate, and such like And if
any committ often any error, or through
Custome or contempt fall into greater tres-
passes, shee may bee punished with fasting,
with publick or priuate disciplynes, and
with other such like Chastisements yet noe
Religious may giue a discipline to an other,
but the offendor is to in flict it vppon her selfe, except the Abbesse for some great cause doe otherwise appoynte l

15. For most greweous faults let those
things bee done, which are appoynted in ano
ther place for the correction of such faults,
without exception or re gard had to any degree, or Office what soeuer, although wee
hope

hope that (throughe the grace of God) this Congregation wilbee allwayes cleere and free from all such faults!

16. When in the Chapter they are to conferr about the affayres of the Monastery, lett euery one deliuer their opinions with all Religious simplicie and sinceritie, as god shall put in their myndes, and shee that hath once finished her speech, may not speake againe except shee haue new leaue granted her, neither may any presume to argue or dispute aguinst the saying of any other Sisters!

17. The professed of the Quier haue voyces in the Chapter, and their they sitt each one according to the order of their Professions, except the lady Abbesse, the mother Prioresse, the deames, and the Mistris of the Nouices, who take their places, both here and in all places where the Conuent meeteth, in that order as here they haue beene named; for the most part the Iuniors or younger professed speake first, that with greater liberty they may vtter their opinions concerning those affayres, that are then in deliberation;

18. In matters of great moment the Abbesse shall fore warne the Chapter of them some two or three dayes be fore, if the matter will suffer soe long delay; But in those maters where in the Religious may conferr
among

among them felues, they may take their light and information onely from the Abbeffe, Prioreffe, Affiftents, or the Officers, if the matters to bee deliberated vppon, appertayne to their Charges and Iurifdictions;

19. what by the Chapter is approued or denyed, the fame the Abbeffe is to approue or deny, except in fome cafes hereafter fpecified;

20. That both the Abbeffe, and alfoe the whole Conuent may procede in their Confultations, and determinations with more fweetineffe, light, and affurdeneffe; it is expedient that they haue fome one prudent and vertuons man, but efpecialy well practifed in regular life and difcipline, with whom they may conferr and confult in matters of greater difficulty and wight; And this Man muft bee fuch an one, as may bee according to the liking and Iudgment of the Religious, and by their fuffrages hee is to bee elected;

21. If it foe happen that the Religious difagree in their opinions about fome matter; lett the fayd difficultie bee propounded either in Worde or writing to the chofen perfon in the prefence of the Abbeffe, of the Affiftents, and of fome other two of the Chapter, vnto whom the faye Chapter fhall committ this affayre, and all fhall bee bound to follow that Order and Refolution, which hee

shall

hee shal iudge expediēt, vntill the right Re-
uerēd lord Bishopp or the Visitor shall other
wayes ordayne;But hee shall deliuer in writing to the Conuent his sayd Iudgment, that
afterwards to the Bishopp or Visitor it may
better appeare how and in what termes the
whole businesse passed ;

22. If the Abbesse would appoynte any
thing which the Conuent doth not like of,
or would not doe,that which the Conuent
would haue done, and if shee would proceede in some cases cōtrary to the Iugdment of
all her Assistēts, or will not assemble thē to
geat her(for some secrett Cause which shee
thinketh good not to communicate with
them) if the matter bee of great momente
shee must cōsult with the afore saydehosen
person, and shee may proceede according
to his Counsayle deliuered her in writing;

23. Out of Chapter none may seeke to dis-
proue the saying of any vttered in Chapter,
neither may any manifest vnto any that was
absēt from the Chapter,that which was sayd
or done by her selfe,or any other,which may
any wayes touch her or any other whoe soeuer ; They are to bee absent from the Chapter, about whom there is any question to
bee propounded in Chapter, or any thing to
bee handled about them : as, all those (if the
Chapter thinke it meete) whoe are neere in
                                    bloode

bloode or kindred to them; and the Superiours are to warne and commaunde such persons, as are to bee soe absent, that curioustly they doe not enquire what was any way handled concerning them selues;

CHAPTER 11.

Of the sicke and infirme Sisters.

1. When any feeleth her selfe more greiued in her bodely health then accustomed, lett her warne the Superiour and Gouernour of the the Infirmary thereof, and when shee hath fully informed her of her State, with due humilitie and quietnesse of mynde, lett her suffer hir selfe to bee disposed of by them, as they shall thinke goode;

2. Lett none refuse any thing ordayned them by the Phisitions, but hauing made knowne her difficulty to the Abbesse, shee must leaue it to her what shee will determyne of her case, and soe shee must bee obedient to her, with all patience and shew of religious resignation;

3. See that shee bee not greivous to the Infirmere and others that haue care of her, neither may shee bee over importune in crauing of those things which by the shee shall vnderstand not to bee expedient for her;

D   4. Whyle

Whyle shee vseth corporall remedyes for the recouery of her health, let her not forgett her spirituall good, which allwayes is to bee more prised; therefore shee must haue regard to arme and shengthen her selfe inwardly with the holy Sacraments of Confession, and of the blessed Eucharist; and if shee perceaue, that the force of her Disease with perill to grow vppon her lett her endeauour to call for the Sacrament of Extreme Vnction, and for the holy Viaticum, according as the Abbesse, and Confessarius shall thnike best for her;

5. Shee must take noe medicine which the Phisition or Superiour shall not approue, nether may any of the Religious Councell her to receaue any medicine, nor may the sicke her selfe aske the Counsayle or advise of any other, without the Superiours knowledge; yea noe Religious may bee soe presumptuous, as to finde fault with the vsage of the sicke person in her hearing.

6. As it is expedient that the sicke vse such dispensations as by the Superiour are granted them whyle they are infirme and weake, yet they must beware that they bee not ouer care full of them selues; yet all may vse a discreete and prudent liberty, vntill they bee sufficiently recouered, and restored to their former strength, and such as

are

are in their Recouery(if they bee many)muſt
ſitt togeather with modeſty at one Table,
and in the beginning of their meales ſome
ſpirituall thing muſt bee read vnto them;

CHAPTER 12.

Of the diſtribution of their Tyme and howers;

1.   TO the end they may proceede in
the Seruice of God with greater
alacritye, and that their ſpirituall Exerciſes
doe not ouerpaſſe their bodely ſtrength and
health, it is thought meete and conuenient,
that euery one haue granted her ſeuen whole howers to take her reſt, and ſleepe, and
that from eight of the Cloke at night, vntill
three in the morning *or from ten till fiue* except hereafter it bee thought more ſitt ãd expedient, that thy riſe to Mattins at midnight;

2.   Therefore they ſhall riſe to Mattins at
three, *vnleſſe the ſayd ouer night*, and when they
haue ended the ſayd Mattins with the laude
euery one muſt repayre to their Celles in
good and ſitt tyme(ãd as the Abbeſſe ſhall appoynte) they ſhall beſtow an hower in Me-
ditatiõ or mentall prayer, after which hower
ended they muſt cõtinue in their Celles vntill

nen in foueraigne filence.

3. At feuen of the Clocke they beginne
Prime after wich hower ended ordinaryly
they keepe Chapter when it is to bee kept, al
thoughe the Abbeffe may call a Chapter at
any other hower, when neede shall require.

4. After Prime, or the Thirde, a Maffe is
to bee fayd, at which all are to bee prefent,
excepte fome Officer vppon neceffitie bee
excufed.

5. After nyne of the Clocke (when they
doe not faft) they muft recite their third:
after their Third, their Conuentuall Maffe
is to bee fung, or fayde; after Maffe the Sixt
is fung or fayd: after that hower is ended
they goe to the Refectory; But when they
Faft according to their Rule, or according
to the Commaundment of the Church the
Prime, or the Third being fung, or fayd after
feuen of the Clocke a Maffe is to bee celebrated, if there bee a Preift to celebrate at that
tyme; after ten of the Clocke they muft fing
or fay their Sixt, their Conuentuall Maffe and
Nynth; In lent after their Sixt, Nynth and
Conuentuall Maffe, the Cuenfong is to bee
fong or fayd.

6. Lett them foe end their Maffe and howers before noone, that when they faft not,
they may dine at the halfe hower before
a eleuen; but when they faft according to the
Rule,

Rule, they may dine at a eleuen; but when it is a fast of the Church according to the Custome of the Country, they dine at the halfe hower before twelue: but in lent they are to dine at twelue: and Whyle they are at the Table their must bee allwayes reading; Therefore at the first Table whether it bee at dinner or Supper, the Benediction, and afterwards Grace, must bee allwayes sunge or sayde; But at the second Table euery Religious shall performe this by her selfe; But the reading both at the first and second Tables must bee performed after the same manner and altogeather with the same obseruation of silence and then they are to reade whom the lady Abbesse, or Superior, or shee who shall haue the Charge shall appoynte.

7. After dinner an hower is permitted the for Recreation, and afterwards at Noone or somewhat after, they sing or say the Nynth, but soe that vppon those dayes in which they fast not, they may bee all in silence about one of the Clocke after Noone, that their for the space of an hower they may recollect themselues. or occupy themselues in prayer, or in the reading of some spirituall bookes: But vppon fasting dayes this hower of silence is put of vntill foure of the Clocke.

8. Out of lent they are to sing or say their

D 3   Euen-

Euenſong at three of the Clocke after noone, which ended , they may ſpend the reſt
of their tyme till ſupper or Collation according to their diſcretion, or deuotion; yet
allwayes in ſilence except the Abbeſſe ſhall
thinke good to vſe their helpes and aſſiſtancein ſome buſineſſe or Office: but if they faſt
then they keepe their ſilence from foure till
fiue, as hath beene ſayde.

9. When it is not faſting day they goe to
Supper halfe an hower before fiue , but
when it is a Faſt they receaue their Colation
at fiue which being ended an hower of recreation is permitted them; halfe an hower
after ſix they muſt all goe to Complyne, frō
which time they are to keepe ſoueraigne ſilence vntill the end of Prime the next day;
as alſoe the ſayd ſilence is to bee kept , from
the firſt Peale to all the howers and Eueſong
vntill they bee ended, except for ſome very
great reaſons the contrary bee thought ſome
tymes requiſit.

10. They are to haue allowed them a quartir
of an hower after Complyne for the examination of their Conſciences, ymmediately
after they are to reade or heare the matter
of their meditation for the next day. When
they haue ended that they muſt for ⎰ *vn leſſe*
thwith depart to their dormitory ⎱ *they ſay*
and ſoeapply the Remnant of their ⎰ *matins.*

                              tyme

tyme in their neceffary affayres, as at eight the may bee in bede.

11. Wee haue thus breifly comprifed thefe matters in this place which are more amply and perticulerly fett downe in their Ceremonies, what tyme foeuer shall bee Vacant and free from the deuine Office, from Silence, and from their other affore faide Obferuances, the Religious muft imployin fuch labours and Workes as by the Abbeffe and Superior shalbee appointed foe that they worke no curious vayne, and feculer things for wordly vfes, as are purfes, Bandes handcbercheifes and the like.

12. When they come to the Worke houfe the Mother Prioreffe, or the more ancient deane in her abfence beginneth the Prayer Actiones noftras &c. after which followeth fome short Leffon or reading in fome Spirituall booke, from the hearing where of none may bee abfent without leaue This ended euery one is to bee difmiffed or licenced to their workes, labours, or Offices as it shalbee appointed them, all they muft indeauor to accomplish with due filence, except per happs neede require that they fpeake fome what breifely, and by the way of fuch matters as appartayne to their Offices and bufineffes, Finally when they leaue of their worke the prayer *Sufcipe Clementiffime Deus*, being

fayd, they are in all peace to depart to their other Obediences.

CHAPTER 13.

Of such prayers as by Obligation are to bee sayd for the liuing and the dead.

ONce euery Month a Masse is to bee sung or sayd for your Benefactors that are aliue, and soe often euery Religious shall say for them one Rosary, or the third parte of the Psalter of our blessed Lady, contayning fiue Pater nosters and fifety Aues with a Greede.

2. When the Abbesse hath rendred her Soule to her Creator, euery Religious in fitt tyme when they shall haue opportunitie shall say fifeteene Rosaryes in manner before specified, and the Conuent shall take care to procure that therty Masses bee sayd for her.

3. Thirely in their Church after the whole Office of the dead a solemne Masse must bee sung for the Abbesse deceased: like wise

se a solemne Masse (without the Office of the dead) is to bee sung on the third, seuenth, and thirtith dayes after her decease, or vppon some other dayes more fitt.

4. Alsoe euery yeare vppon the Friday of the first weeke of Aduent, not hindred with a Feast, other wise vppon some other day in like manner not hindred, they shall sing the Euensong and the Nocturne, with the Laudes, and a solemne Masse for all the Abbesse of ther monastery departed this life.

5. When any professed Religious dyeth, in her Monastery, at the first opportunity the whole Office of the dead, and a solemne Masse is to bee sung, and the like is to bee performed for her vppon the Third, Seuenth, and Thirtith dayes (but without the Office of the dead) or soe many Masses shalbee sung for her vppon some other dayes more fitt for the performance there of, and other seuen Masses are to bee sayd for the some, Moreouer euery one of the Conuent shall say fiue Rosaryes for her, and euery day after Mattines and Euensong for the space of a moneth they shall say de profundis with the Prayer Absolue, both for the Abbesse as alsoe for the Soules of their Sisters deceased.

6. Vppon the Friday after the first Sunday in Lent, not hindred with a double Feast.

Feaſt, otherwiſe vppon another fitt day next
following, a ſolemne Maſſe ſhalbee ſung
for them that haue dyed in the Monaſtery
as alſoe the Euenſong of the dead with
one Noƈturne and the Laudes ſhalbee ſung
or ſayd for them, the which may bee performed the day before the afforeſayd ſolemne Maſſe bee celebrated.

7. One ſolemne Maſſe, with the whole
Office of the dead, ſhalbee ſung for thoſe
Nouices, who in their Nouiſhipp ſhall
depart out of this life, after they haue receaued the habitt of holy Religion.

6. Such Scollers as haue entred in to the
Monaſtery with intention to goe forward
in Religion, ſhall haue granted them after
the Euenſong and whole Office of the dead,
a ſolemne Maſſe to bee offered and celebrated for them.

9. Once euery yeare in Aduent after the
Maſſe celebrated for the Abbeſſes (as hath
beene ſayd) another ſhalbee ſung in due
tyme for the Soules departed, of ſuch Religious of other Monaſteryes as are of your
Congregation, and liue vnder the ſame
Rule and Statutes with you.

10. For the founder departed this life, all
thoſe things are to bee performed which
are appointed for an Abbeſſe deceaſed, and
for a perpetuall memory they ſhall ſing his
                                    Anniuer-

Anniuersary Office with a solemne Masse and both aliue and dead hee is made pertaker of all the Merritts of the whole Congregation.

11. When the Father or Mother of any professed Religious departeth this life, a Masse must bee sung for euery one of them.

12. For the right Reuerend Bishopp in whose dioceffe they reside they shall sing the whole Office of the dead, and vppon the Third, Seuenth, and Thirtith dayes, or some other three more fitt dayes, they shall sing three other Masses, and euery one shall say a Rosary for his Soule: all which must bee performed for their Ghostly Father, who hath much laboured and taken paynes in aduancing the good of the Monastery, and hee may bee made pertaker of the mirritts of the Conuent, if soe to the Conuent it shall seeme expedient. Other Benefactors and frends when they dy, besides this Offices and Masses which the Conuent may grant them in perticuler they shall alsoe bee made pertakers of all those Masses which (according to the Miffall of Rome) are sayd or sung euery Munday by your Chaplaine.

13. If any thing be thought expedient to bee further granted to any of the afforesayd, lett it bee done vppon deuotion, and according

ding to their deferts, with this prouifo, that
noe burthen bee impofed vppon the Conuent for any long fpace.

14. The Abbeffe and Conuent shall found
noe Maffe for any perfon in perticuler: yet
they may mayntayne a Chaplaine whoe may
fay Maffe for fuch perfons deceafed, as appertayne to the Monaftery, yet foe, that the
Fundation may not bee thought to bee made for any one in perticuler.

15. Let a Regifter bee made, where in
the names of all the Benefactors both liuing
and dead who haue notably aduanced the
temporall good of the Monaftery may bee
fett downe, In the fame al foe are to bee
fett downe all the names of fuch Religious as in the Monaftery departed this life,
and in the fame alfo is to bee written if
any thing of noate hapned to them, either
in their life or at their death that it may
ferue for an Example to Pofteritie, and lett
thefe things bee reade the day before their
yeares yndes, or Annyuerfaryes, that
peculiar care and memory may bee had
of them.

16. And for as much as after holy deuoute Prayers, Almes deeds doe much helpe for the extinguishing of the Paynes in
Purgatory, it is here ordayned that in that
monaftery, where in any of the profeffed
Religious

Religious passeth out of this life, all such meate and drincke as is giuen to the rest of the Religious, bee dayly sett on the Table in the Refectory, in the same place where the fore sayd Religious was wont to sitt, as if shee ware yet liuing; all which or as much as the Lady Abbesse or Superior shall appoynte, afterwards is to bee giuen in Almes to some one poore person or to diuers, for the space of thirty dayes and that for the benefitt of the Soule departed, Neither may any other sitt in that place, but it being left voyde, lett a litle Crosse bee placed on the Table couered with a blacke Cloth, and another blacke Cloath bee made fast to the Wall in the vacant place in Remembrance of the dead Religious Sister, that the rest may bee moued to due Compunction by the memory of death, and bee the more excited to pray with greater seruour for her that is dead, and finally may there by bee stirred vpp to lead their liues more carefully and perfectly for the tyme to come,

THE
SECOND
PARTE OF THE
STATVTES.

OF THE OFFICERS OF
the Conuent, and of certayne
other persones belonging to
the Monastery.

AT GANT.

Printed by Ioes Dooms. 1632.

CHAP: THE FIRST.

Of the chousing of the Abbesse.

I. **A**LL Order of good disciplyne, and almost the whole good and Conseruation of the Monastery dependeth vppon the prudent gouernement of the Abbesse, therefore it appertayneth to euery one, for the good desire they beare to the good aduancemēt of the Conuent, to bee very carefull in this poynte, that they chouse such an one for the Gouernesse of all, whoe is likest to prouide for the peace and tranquillitie of all, and especially for the setting forth of God his honor in all things; Therefore such Religious as are professed for the Quier, (for such onely haue actiue and passiue Voyces in the chusing of the Abbesse, and cheifest Officers) shalbee bound as in a matter of soe great moment and weight, to make election of her whom in their Consciences they thinke most fitt for that Office.

A 2   2. None

2. None may bee chofen for Abbeſſe that is vnder fourty yeares of age, and who hath not liued laudably for eight yeares, after their expreſſe Profeſſion, as the holy Councell of Trent hath decreed; except in Caſe ſuch a one cannot bee found in the Monaſtery, then by grant of the ſame Counſell, another fitt perſon may bee chofen whoe is aboue thirty yeares ould, and that hath beene profeſſed for the ſpace of fiue yeares, and hath all requiſitt Conditions for this dignitie, ſoe that with all the Biſhopp doe yeald his conſent there vnto.

3. They ſhall obſerue that Order in deliuering their Voyces that is ſett downe in that Counſell, which is, that they are to deliuer them at the Grate, and moreouer the Elect muſt haue two parts of three of the Voyces, according to the Bull of Gregory the 13. ſett forth the 7. of Aprill. in the yeare of our Lord 1574.

4. The Abeſſe (beſides thoſe Conditions where of mention is made in the ſecond, and ſixty foure Chapters of the Rule) muſt bee ſuch a one, as of whom their hath beene had noe ſiniſter opinion, either ſince her comming to the Conuent, or before whyle ſhee hiued in the World, that ſhee bee endewed with the Giſtes of body and mind
as

as may beſt reṭayne Authority, that ſhee
be in eſpeciall manner free from all inordinate Paſſions, and finally that ſhee bee
ſuch a one, that ſhee may bee Iudged ſitt
and able to gouerne, and adminiſter well
the Temporalities and Spiritualities of her
Monaſtery.

5. Albeit it may ſoe fall out that ſhee
which is vnlawfully be gotten, may bee
admitted into this Congregation; yet is not
expedient to promote any ſuch to the gouernement of the Manaſtery; Wherefore
ſhee ſhall not haue paſſiue Voyce to this
dignitie, except very great Reaſons doe vrge
the contrary: and when it ſhall ſeene re-
quiſite to procede otherwiſe, ſhee muſt haue
for her election, three partes of all the
Voyces of the Chooſers, as in like manner
that Religious whoe is within three degrees
of Conſanguinitie to the next precedent
Abbeſſe, muſt haue the ſame number of
ſuffrages for her Eliction.

6. Noe perticuler Religious may haue
a double Voyce for the Election of the Abbeſſe, or of any other Officer of the Monaſtery, as neither ſhee that is abſent out
of the monaſtery hath any Voyce to chouſe
al though the ſayd abſent Religious may
haue paſſiue Voyce. But the Religious that
A 3   is ſoe

is foe ficke that shee cannot bee prefent at the Scrutiny muft deliuer vpp her Suffrage and Voyce by thofe Scrutatrices, that for that tyme shall bee chofen by the Conuent.

7. None of what dignitie, Nobilitie, or degree foeuer befides the Religious of the fame Monaftery profeffed for the Quier may haue any Voyce to elect. If therefore any other perfon either by word or writing shall commend any one to bee elected by the Conuent they muft all take good heede that they deliuer not their Voyces in regard of that Commendation : as alfoe shee may not fucceede the deceafed Abbeffe, for whom the faide Abbeffe did in her life tyme folicite the Conuent, except shee bee chofen in fuch fort as before hath beene declared.

8. The Prioreffe when the Abbeffe is wanting muft gouerne the Monaftery, vntill an other Abbeffe bee elected. Shee shall certify the right Reuerende Lord Bishopp of the death of her Superior, whom shee shall dilligently haften to the election of her that is to fuccede, the which ought to bee done with in a Moneth, at the moft, if the Bishopp cann bee prefent or conueniently appoynte an other, whoe in his place may
                                                        affift

assist as the Election.

9. The Prioresse shall certify the Conuent what answeare shee hath receaued from the right Reuerende the Lord Bishopp, and if shee receaue from him any letters lett her carefully see they bee read to the Conuent, as alsoe all such Statutes cōceruing the Electiō, neither may any aske any Counsayle of any person for the Election of any but onely of the ghostly Father, to the End shee may bee the better directed in her Conscience yet soe that the Religious consult not one with another about the promoting or putting downe of any, if they shall doe otherwise, they shall not onely euer bee depriued of actiue and passiue Voyce, but shee shall endure all whatsoeuer other Censures the Prioresse and Conuent shall in flict vppon her.

10. It shall not bee lawfull for the Prioresse or any other Religious to speake with Externes except some most important cause perswade the Contrary; and how often soeuer they are then to speake with them two of the Deanes shalbee present who together with the Prioresse shall heare, and see whatsoeuer is sayd or done; and what soeuer of speciall moment hapneth after the Abbesses decease, shee shall diligently

A 4 declare

declare to the Bishopp or to his Vicegerent.

11. For as much as they incurr priuation of Actiue and passiue Voyce, as alsoe other penalties who haue sollicited to gett the Voyce of another to the promotion of any, soe all shalbee obliged to reueale all such practises. vnder the same penaltye; and it shall belong to the Bishopp. to discerne and determyne what words and procedings are to bee held for direct or indirect solliciting.

12. Althoughe they may haue an Eye to the Nobilitie, and honor of the kindred of any that is to bee elected, yet the Conuent must bee very carefull, that they doe not neglect the spirituall good of their Monastery, whyle they regard the temporall commodity.

13. To the End the election may the better proceede, and that they may procure for them selues God his holy assistance in that which soe much maketh for their common good, after the Funeralls of the deceased Abbesse the Conuent shall apply all their prayers and Exercises for this End.

14. When they are to deliure their suffrages they shall abstayne from mutuall Conuersation for the space of three dayes, neither shall they come to geather but to the celebrating of deuine seruice, to the reading,
and

and to the Refectory; and vppon the very day of the election, after they haue song a Masse of the holy Ghost, they shall retyre themselues to their Cells, vntill they bee called to giue their Voyces.

15. To the end noe Error happen in deliuering their Suffrages, the Prioresse shall deliuer the names of all the professed in writing that haue any Voyces, either to the Bishopp or to him whoe supplyeth his place and in the sayd writing shee shall sett downe ther age, the yeares and tyme of their proffession, togeather with all such Exceptions or Canonicall impediments, as the Statutes haue sett downe against their Election.

16. Two or three mature graue and Religious men are to bee chosen by the Chapter, whoe for the more honor of that Action may bee present with the Lord Bishopp at the Election, and the Bishopp or hee, who (at the Bishopps appoyntement) shall preside at the Election hauing obserued all that is sett downe in the Statutes, shall declare at the Grate the person elected; But if in it the first two Scrutinyes sufficient suffrages doe not agree, then lett those three which had the most suffrages in the last Scrutiny bee proposed to the Conuent, and in the third shee that by balloting or by Boules

A 5   shall

shall haue sufficient Voyces, is to bee held for Elect. And if againe in all the sayd three Scrutinyes they haue equall, or not sufficient suffrages. then the more Ancient proffessed among them is to bee preferred and to bee denounced Abbesse.

17. The election ended, and declared by him that presided, all the Religious are to retyre themselues into the Chapter: where (after the Elect hath according to the manner accused herselfe in generall of all her defects) shee must according and to the tenor and forme of that writing that is sett downe in the booke of Ceremonyes, promise that shee will neuer suffer any further libertie to bee brought into the Congregation, then the holy Rule and Statuts doe permitt; but that shee will endeauor togeather with the grace and assistance of God that the Congregation bee conserued in Spirritt, and aduanced in the same, and if shee shall espy that it fayleth in any thing other wise then it ought, that shee will labour (calling those to counsell by whose prudence and authority shee may best worke reformation) to reduce and restore it to the former good estate, and to all this shee is to signe and subscribe, After this protestation made, lett the Rules and Statutes bee
reade

reade which concerne the Abbeſſe, and then by the Prioreſſe, or (if the Prioreſſe be thoſen) by the ancienteſt deane lett her bee placed in her Seate, and aftherwards eath one in perticuler shall doe her that Reuerence, and in ſuch manner as is declared in the booke of Ceremonyes, and from that tyme euer afterwards, shall yeald dutifull Obedience to all hir Commandements; and all the Officers shall in publike reſigne to her their Offices, leauing it to her Freedome, either to confirme them in their Officers, or according to the Statutes by ſuffrages to appoynte new Officers, euen as in our Lord shee shall thinke moſt expedient.

18. The Elect is abſolutely forbid and prohibited to inquire of any whether shee gaue her ſuffrage for her Election, neither may shee either directly or indirectly ſifte what paſſed by her Subiects in the matter of her Election, neither may any tell to any of the Religious, or to the Abbeſſe, or to any other, either directly or indirectly vppon whom shee beſtowed her Voyce; If the Abbeſſe shall offend herein, shee is to vnderſtand that there by shee hath loſt all Iuriſdiction, but if others ſignify ſoe much either to the Abbeſſe or to any others, in ſoe doing they looſe both actiue and paſſiue

Voyce

Voyce for euer ;

19. The Elect, before her benediction, for the space of some dayes shall liue seperate from the rest, that well and dilligently shee may examyne her owne defects and that shee may imploy that tyme in Contemplation of spirituall matters, where by being illuminated by thy spiritt of Gods light, shee may the better imploy her selfe in those things that appertayne to her Office : and principally to obtayne of him the guift of Wisedome, and humilitie, and a fervent and burning zeale of his deuine honour, and that shee may endeauour to Correct and reforme her owne defects, or any such perticuler abuses, as shee shall note to haue crept into the Congregation.

20. In fitt tyme (when the Lord Bishopp shalbee at leisure) lett the accustomed Benedictió bee parformed, either in theChurch of her owne Monastery, or in some other as hee shall appointe : at which some foure professed Religious (at the left) elected by the Conuent shalbee present, and those Expences (by consent of the Chapter with regatd had of Religious pouerty) are to bee made, as may seeme fitt and seemely for such an Action.

21. The Abbesse of this Congregation must bee

bee perpetuall, except through age, notable Infirmity, or (which god forbied) for some greuious Fault, (as here after is sett downe) shee shalbee iudged by the Voyces of two parts of three of the Conuent, togeather with the Verdict of the Ordinary to bee vnfitt for gouernment.

22. It may not bee lawfull for the Abbesse or Elect (that is accused of any fault for which shee may bee brought into danger of deposition (either by her selfe or others, to seeke out who gaue their Voyces against her. If shee shall doe otherwise euen thereby shee shalbee depriued of her dignity, and they whoe either directly or indirectly discouered what others haue done there in conceruing her, shall loose both actiue and passiue Voyce for euer after.

23. If the Abbesse would resigne her Office because shee findeth her selfe much broken in age, and in her strenght, or that shee might the better attend to her owne spirituall good, shee may not obtayne leaue to doe it, except two of three parts of the Conuent, togeather with the consent of the Ordinary do yeald there vnto.

24. If the Abbesse shall obtayne leaue to resigne, shee shall make her sayd Resignation in the presence of the right Reuerend
Lord

Lord Bishopp, or of him whom hee shall substitute in his place, And because it is presumed, that shee hath done this for the common good of the Couent, the Abbesse that shall succede, must vse her as a perpetuall Assistant about her, and to bee subiect to none but to her selfe onely; and in her diett all such allowance must bee giuen to her as is accustomed to the other Abbesse, and the rest are to vse the sayde Reuerences to her, as they are accustomed to their other Abbesses, and when shee dyeth shee is to enioy all those priuiledges which they enioy that dy in their Offices, and shee is to haue a double Voyce in the Election of her Successor, (but for her owne Resignation shee shall haue noe voyce) as alsoe shee must haue a double Voyce in the election of all the other Officers, which by the Conuents Voyces are to bee chosen.

25. If the Abbesse espy any Error committed by her predecessor, lett her soe handle the matter, that shee seeke still to conserue her Reputation, and as often as shee maketh mention of her deceased Predecessor, shee must neuer name her but in honorable manner, as shee must likewise haue care that all her Subiects doe the same.

THE

THE II. CHAPTER.

Of the chosing of the other Officers.

1. NOe Religious may haue passiue Voyce for the principall Officers, except shee haue liued laudably foure yeares at the least in Religion, after her Profession; and bee fiue and twentie yeares ould compleate, except vrgent necessitie bee to the contrary.

2. The principall Officers, to witt the Prioresse, deanes Mistresse of the Nouices, Assistants, depositary Cellarier, Sacristane, Chantresse, Portresse, Thourier, Infirmare, and Guardrobe, must bee chosen by more then halfe the Voyces of the Conuent, their Voyces must bee sett downe in writing, and the sayd writings must bee perused by the Abbesse, and the Scrutatrices, and they are to bee publickly reade in the hearing of all either by the Abbesse or by one of the Scrutatrices, whom shee will appoynte, and the sayd writings are all to bee burned before they departe out of the Chapter.

3. If any difficulty arise about the deliuering of their Suffrages, and that it happen

that

that sufficient Voyces doe not agree, lett
that Order bee taken as before was sett
downe in the Election of the Abbesse, when
the like case doth fall out.

4. Shee that shall endeauour to procure for
her selfe, or for any other, by any meanes
the Voyce of any for any of the afforesayd
Offices, shee shalbee depriued of all actiue
and passiue Voyce whyle she liueth; which
punishment shee shall alsoe incurr, that by
vn iust perswasions and complayntes shall
labour to hinder any from any Office, except shee make her complaynts onely to the
Lady Abbesse.

5. These before named Officers are to
bee chosen euery third yeare, and therefore
at a tyme for this appoynted (to witt vppon
the first Munday in Lent not hindred by a
Feast, otherwise vppon the next day following) they shall all resigne their Offices
in the Chapter house, and the Conuent must
chouse others in their places; Yet it is permitted that the Conuent may onely once
confirme the selfe same person in her Office; where in notwithstanding shee shall
not continue more then for six yeares; But
if any one is able to fullfill and well accomplish diuers Offices, it is left to the Conuents libertie to constitute fewer.

                                    6. The

6. The terme of three yeares is limited onely for thofe Officers as haue well performed their Offices: but if any bee found not fufficiently fitt for her Office, shee may bee difcharged of her Office whenfoeuer the Abbeffe and Conuent thinke fitt.

7. The Sifter of the Lady Abbeffe may not bee chofen for Prioreffe, deane, Affiftant, depofitary, Cellarier, Thourier, or Portreffe, whyle the Abbeffe liueth, except shee hath the third parte, of foure of the Voyces of the Conuent.

8. The Inferior Officers, whoe are not fett downe among the afforenamed principall Officers, and are appoynted for diuers Functions in the Conuent, may bee chofen for fuch offices by the Abbeffe her felfe alone, and whereas they may bee often changed, as the reft, yet if any haue laudably behaued her felfe in her charge shee may the longer bee contynued in the fame, yet foe, that this bee done rather vppon neceffitie, then vppon any priuate and perticuler affection.

9. None may confer with any about the fetting vpp or taking away of any Office, but with the Abbeffe alone, or in publike Chapter, and if she proceede otherwife, she is to bee punished at the difcretion of the

B   Abbeffe

Abbeſſe and Conuent.

18. All the Officers are to reade or heare once euery moneth all ſuch Rules, directions, and Statutes as appertayne to their Offices: and the Inferior Officers are to haue them written, and ſett vpp in ſome place in their Offices.

THE III. CHAPTER.

Of the Office of the Abbeſſe.

1. FOr aſmuch as the Abbeſſe is by almightie God appoynted Gouerneſſe ouer the Spowſes of Ieſus-Chriſt, to direct and confirme them in the way of his holy Commandements and of a perfect Religious life, there fore shee ought to excell all her Subiects in Charity, Fayth, Chaſtitie, Wiſedome, and notable humilitie, that shee may aduance and ſett them fowards to the due keeping and obſeruance of their holy Rule and Conſtitutions and to the topp of all perfection noe leſſe by her exemplar life, and behauiour then by the authoritie and dignitie of her Office, Where vppon shee muſt carry to all a motherly harte and affection, and endeauour to make them familier and tyed in loue

in loue towards her selfe , that with greater confidence they may make their recourse vnto her , as to their common mother
and there by submitt themselues to all her
Commandements, and Councells, and performe all things , drawne rather by the
spiritt of loue, then by feare and force of
Constraynt;

2. Euery day in perticuler manner shee
ought to imploy some tyme where in shee
may seriously consider with her selfe , by
what manner and meanes , shee may best
sett forward the Common good and proffitt of her charge. And shee ought to endeauour (soe farr forth as the sundry bur thens
and businessesfo the Monastery will permitt)
to assist with the rest and bee present in
the Quier and other places of Obseruances,
and to obserue all those things vnto which
the rest are tyed.

3. Shee must haue a care of the spirituall and Corporall good of all, yea and of
euery one in perticuler , shee must suffer
each of them to haue a free accesse vnto
her , soe often as they shall requestit, or
as shee shall know or vnderstand it wilbee
profitable vnto them , and that shee her
selfe may well and fittly attend thereunto.

4. Shee

4. Shee must receaue and intertayne such as come vnto her with all suauity and gentlenesse; and shee must bee very wary that by her Countenance, or vehemency of her words, or manner of carriage and proceeding shee doe not at any tyme feare them, that with freedome and Confidence they may not discouer and lay open their difficulties vnto her.

5. Lett her shew a motherly affection to such as any way offend, that they may see that heir fault and not their person is displeasing to her, and lett her carry her selfe, that shee may not bee noted to bee disgusted with any one; finally in giuing of Penances lett her haue an Eye to the spirituall good of euery one, and that noe wayes shee seeke their trouble and vexation, allwayes diligently and maturely thinking and casting with her selfe, by what meanes the pennances which shee enioyneth, may helpe to aduance their spirituall good.

6. In such things as touch the Common disciplyne, lett her shew her selfe firme and constante, and lett her not at any tyme suffer any thing to bee violated and infringed; where vnto they are bound by Rule or Statute. But in those things that are held lesse essentiall lett her not bee to hard, and difficill

ficill in difpenfing, and foe lett her mayntay
ne good Order and difciplyne, that shee
may difcretely and prudently apply her
penfations to the folace of her Subiects,
and the more feruice of almighty God.

7. Lett her often enquire of the Prioreffe and conferr with her, concerning the
State of the Conuent, and alfoe of the Miftreffe of the Nouices, depofitayre, and Cellarier, concerning all fuch matters as belong to their Charge; and shee muft commaunde them to repayre to her fo often as
neede shall require.

8. Shee shall once euery moneth, either
by her felfe or by fome others, whom shee
shall appoynte, (efpecially the deanes) vifit
all the Offices of the Monaftery but efpecially of the depofitayre, Cellarier, Sacriftane,
Guarderoabe and Infirmair; alfoe once euery moneth shee shall vifitt by her felfe, or by
her fayd affignes the Cells of all the Reli-
gions, and the peculiar offices of all vnder
Officers, that shee may fee how in all
things Religious decency, cleanlyneffe, and
order bee kept, and obferued;

9. Lett her bee vigilant that all the Officers execute and performe their Offices
with great fweet neffe, Charity and humility, and lett fuch bee put from their Offi-

B 3   ces,

ces that behaue them selues trouble somely therein; and are found harsh and greuious to other ; yet lett her not giue easy eare to Inferiours against their Superiours, and what shee heareth lett her maturely and dilligently wayghe and examyne , and without very reasonnable cause Inferiours are not to haue accesse vnto her, for those matters , which the subordinate Officers can sufficient ly per forme by them selues, and would doe soe if the sayd Inferiours would come vnto them.

10. Althoughe shee ought much to confide vppon her Officers, yett lett her beware that nothing bee permitted to their inordinate Passions, and if at any tyme any Contention or dispute should happen among them, whereby auersion of mynds and indignation may bee feared , lett her carefully seeke to hinder this Inconuenience, by making peace among them, and by procureing that they allwayes shew such signes of humilitie , and Charitie each to other, as may nourish and increase religious affection, and loue among them.

11. Shee must haue a speciall care of such as are sicke and infirme, and those shee must often visitt, and endeauour to confort, and in all things (as much as lyeth in her power)

lett

lett her haue care of peruerty, but yett foe
that Religious decency bee ftill mayntai-
ned.

12. Lett her frequent the common Refectory with the reft, foe often as by her health,
or her other great affayres shee may, and at
Table lett her haue fome meate aboue, and
different from the reft, whereof shee may
imparte to thofe whom shee shall thinke to
bee moft infirme and weake, and when shee
is abfent from the Refectory, lett her by turnes inuite fuch Religious, as by this way shee
shall thinke their weakeneffe and infirmitie
may bee holpen or conforted.

THE IV. CHAPTER.

Of the Office of the Prioreffe.

1. THE Prioreffe is chofen to eafe
the Abbeffe of a great parte of
her burthen, shee, in her fpeach efpecially,
and in her conuerfation, ought to ftudy how
to edify euery one, whoe as shee is a guide to
others, foe much shee bee a Rule of all good
Vertuous life and behauiour, not making
any shew of affected Superioritie or permit-
ting the fame to any other, that the Inferiours being conioyned with Elders and Su-

B 4   periours

periours may ſerue each other in ſincere humilitie; and therefore albeit ſhee bee the
mother of the reſt, yet according to her Office is ſhee to labour to ſerue the reſt;

2.   When the Abbeſſe by reaſon of her
other hindrances cannot execute thoſe
things that appertayne to her Office, then it
belongeth to the Prioreſſe, to doe all thoſe
things which the Abbeſſe her ſelfe ſhould
haue done, if ſhee had bee ne preſent, as to
giue the Benedictions in the Quiar, to grant
leaue to ſpeake with Externes, to receaue
and giue preſents, and ſuch like; where of
afterwards ſhee is to certify the Abbeſſe in
ſitt tyme, yea commonly ſhee may doe
all thoſe things, which in theſe Statutes are
ſaide, and ſett downe, that by the Superiour
they may bee done; eſpecially then when
they cannot haue acceſſe to the Abbeſſe her
ſelfe.

3.   In the Abſence of the Abbeſſe ſhee is
to commaund according as matters occurr in
the Quiar, Chapter houſe, Refectory, dorture, and Worke houſe, yea and in all other
places, where the Conuent is in any tyme
aſſembled; In theſe places ſhee is allwayes
to bee preſent with the Conuent, or if ſhee
cannot bee preſent, ſhee ſhall haue care that
ſome one of the deanes may ſupply her place
                                                        4. In

4. In her Wordes and externall behauiour lett her demeane her selfe with all sweetenesse, and lett her take diligent care that in the Chapter house (where in the absence of the Abbesse shee is to reside as hath beene sayd) nothing bee done either by her selfe or others, that may giue iust occasion of offence, but lett her endeauour to induce her Sisters with all suauitie, and externall shew of loue to the accomplishing of those things which are expedient, and lett her offer her selfe ready to yeald them all comfort and satisfaction, making herselfe familiar vnto them yet retayning her due grauitie, that by those meanes all may reuerence her and with their dutifull cariage acknowledge her for their Superiour.

5. Once euery moneth shee shall goe to the Abbesse to acquainte her with those things, which shalbee thought requisitt shee should vnderstand.

6. Lett her not thrust her selfe in to meddle whith those Offices, whose care and Charge, are by the Abbesse and Conuent committed to others, neither lett her offer to dispose of the Conuerse Sisters.

7. She must not suffer such as haue Offices to dispose of themselues without her knowledge, yet may shee not hinder them in

B 5   their

their Functions, and Offices ; that soe all
matters may bee performed in the best Order, and without Confusion.

8. Shee must not permitt that any thing
bee infringed or innouated, and when shee
perceaueth or feareth any great inconuenience to ensue, lett her acquaint the Abbesse therewith, that according to her appoyntement some remedy may bee prouided
for the same.

9. Although shee may reprehend and
correct her Subiects for lesser faults, as the
Mistresse of the Nouices may the Nouices
and Schollers, and the Cellarier the Conuerse Sisters, yet if any faults bee doubtfull
or more greiueous then ordinary, or of that
Consideration that they may seene worthy
of more seuere Chastisement. then shee (as
alsoe those two others) shall make them
knowne to the Abbesse, that it may bee prouided for according to her Iudgement, and
by her authoritie.

10. Lett her dilligently put in Execution
what soeuer is appoynted and ordayned by
the Abbesse , and in her proceedings and
Actions lett her wholly submitt her Iudgment and opinion to hers, persuading all
others to doe the same, not contradicting
or improuing her Ordinances; if shee doe
other

other wise, besides due Correction (vnto which shee is subiect) shee must vnderstand that shee may bee deposed from her Office as vnworthy thereof.

11.   Lett her not permitt any to bee in the Cloyster, or Garden without leaue, nor in the Garden without a Companion; in tyme of Recreation lett her haue care that all meete togeather, that shee may see what soeuer passeth; finally at night when they goe to bedd, either by her selfe or by some other, shee is to visitt all their Cells.

12.   Shee shalbee exempt from seruing in the kitchin, and Refectory, except the Abbesse for the increase of her humilitie, shall otherwise ordayne or permitt.

THE V. CHAPTER.

Of the Deanes.

1.   THE Deanes haue noe other Office in the Monastery, then prudently to obserue, if there happen any thing in the behauiour, or procedings of the professed Religious, that may neede correction or amendement, yet may they reprehend none, but that which belongeth to their Office, is this, to helpe all by their Counsayle, and

and their mature Iudgment if foe bee that
they may thinke they bee able to helpe them
with their frendly admonition; but if by that
way they finde that they doe them litle or
noe good, then lett them make it knowne to
the Abbeſſe, or Prioreſſe, or Cellarier that
they may apply more forcible and necef-
ſary Remedyes to the ſpirituall diſeaſe.

2. Alſoe of theſe deanes the Aſſiſtentes
are choſen, and if all the deanes cannot bee
Aſſiſtentes (becauſe the number of the deanes may bee greater then the number of the
Aſſiſtents, which may bee but foure) then
they that are the more ancient profeſſed,
mnſt bee preferred before the reſt. If the
deanes are fewer then the Aſſiſtants, then
x thoſe Religious who haue noe other Office
in the Monaſtery may bee elected to make
vpp the number of the Aſſiſtants.

The lady Abbeſſe is to appoynte ten Religious, or thereabouts to the care of theſe deanes: ſoe that all the profeſſed (onely the lady
Abbeſſe and Prioreſſe excepted) muſt bee
vnder their charge; euery one of the profeſſed vnto theſe deanes (as all the Religious to
the lady Abbeſſe, and Prioreſſe : and the
Conuerſe Siſters to the Cellarier; and the Nouices to their Miſtreſſe) muſt doe that Reue-
x other fit persons are to be elected rence
ed to make up the number of Con-
sultresses —

rence and shew that respect, which the holy Rule in the seuentie one Chapter commandeth to bee done to their Ancients, and in that case, these onely are to bee esteemed their Ancients.

4. The deanes in the absence of the Lady Abbesse and Prioresse, are to preside in all places of obseruances, and to beare the place of their Superiour; which euery one of them are to performe, according to the antiquitie of her profession; as alsoe in the absence of the deanes the more ancient professed must beare the same Office, except the Abbesse or Prioresse shall appoynte otherwise.

THE VI. CHAPTER.

Of the Mistresse of the Nouices.

1. ALL singuler shew of Vertue, togeather with a great Zeale, and desire of perfection must appeare, and brightly shyne, in the life and behauiour of the Mistresse of the Nouices, that by her good Example shee may the better excite and stirr vpp those, that are vnder her charge, vnto all those things which their state of life requireth of them; In her cariage lett her
all-

allwayes giue shew of sweetenesse, and loue, and in her words, lett her haue a speciall care to auoyde all bitter contumelious, and disgracefull language, and lett her accommodate her commandements to tymes, persons, and places, well considering with her selfe what euery one is able to doe, and not onely what they ought, or should doe, seing they come to Religió, that desire to bee there in perfected, and are not as yet perfect.

2. As euery one commeth to the Monastery, let her soe dispose of her as the Abbesse shall appoynte, and shee shall haue care that such as haue entred doe examyne and discusse their life past very dilligently and soe make their generall Confession, as soone as they can possibly. *

3. Whatsoeuer they that come bring with them, lett her receaue it of them, to bee deliuered to the depofitary, and what foeuer shee receaueth or deliuereth, lett her setr downe in writing, which writing euery one that entreth shall subscribe with their owne hand, of all which things they must dispose a litle before they make their profession.

4. She must haue care that the Nouices and Schollers haue a good methode in meditating deliuered vnto them, and shee must

*unless on account of the particu-
lar disposition of any nouice
the Confessor fudge otherwise.

ſee they bee taught how they may vſe vocall prayer fruytefully, shee is to teath them the Catechiſme and Chriſtian doctrine, and the manner how to examyne their Conſciences and the way how to roote out all Vices and to ouercome all euill habittes and Cuſtomes, and finally to mortify their Paſsions that togeather with the contempt of themſelues, they may increaſe in the loue of God.

5. After they are entred, shee shall declare vnto them, what they are to vndergoe, and what the Congregation expecteth at their hands, shee shall often reade vnto them thoſe Rules and Statutes which appertayne to them and belong to common diſciplyne; then shall they deliberate with themſelues (weying duly the forces of their bodyes and myndes) what is moſt expedient for them, and if they continue in their former purpoſe, then they are by holy meditations to prepare and arme themſelues for thoſe things, which they are to take vppon them, in the holy State of Religion.

6. Moreouer the Miſtriſſe of the Nouices muſt teach thoſe that are vnder her gouernment a Religious manner of carriage touching their ſtanding, going, looking, ſpeaking, eating, and all other ſuch Actions; that they shew therein a Religious decency
and

and comelynesse; to witt, that in their gate
they bee not two hasty, except vrgent necessity force them that in talking they vse
noe gestures with their hands, especially
whyle they speake to their Superiors, and
to Externes, but either they are to hould
them vnder their Scapulare, or within the
Sleeues of their great habbitt, that they altogeather fly and auoyde all affected speath,
and whatsoeuer may fauour of secularitie,
or Courtly Vanitie and Curiositie, which
alsoe in their outward behauiour they must
dilligently eschew. that they cast or fasten
not their eyes vppon the Countenances of
their Superiours, or of Externes, neither
houlding them to much vpward, or downe-
ward, that they speake not to lowde, or
burst out into to much intemperate laughter, especially when at the Grates they speake with Externes, the which liberty they
must vnderstand is seldome to bee granted
or permitted them; that they eate, not two
fast, to slowly, or to greedily, or that they
looke not about them whyle they eate, that
whyl they drinke they hould their cupp
with both their hands, that they seeke to
preuent euery one in doing them honour,
and Reuerence that they carry themselues
with grauitie, and staydnesse, that they haue
                                        a care

a care to keepe cleanelyneſſe in their Cells
and Garments ; and that in their Countenances they shew myrth and Alacritie,that
whyle they turne, they turne their body as
well as their heade ; and finally that they
carry themſelues gratefully and louingly to
all; and if their bee any thing vnhanſome
in their natures, Cuſtomes ; or Education,
lett the Miſtriſſe endeauour to reforme it,
and bring them to a better faſhion ; and lett
her haue a care to inſtruct them exactly, in
the holy Ceremonyes of the deuyne ſeruice ; and in all the Obſeruances of their Religious State.

7. If ſhee ſee any to bee Drawne to
doe their duty vppon feare, ſhee is to vnderſtand that ſuch are not very fitt for Reliligion, although a moderate feare (eſpecially
of God) doth not a litle healpe and conduce thereunto.

8. Shee muſt labour to encourage ſuch as
are deiected, and puſilaminous, yet if ſhee ſee
any to bee of ſufficient Spiritt and Courage,
ſhee muſt not for all that vrge them to
much ; lett her bee wary and Circumſpect
in all her proceedings towars them ; and
lett her perſwade them to diſcouer their difficulties to their Ghoſtly Father, that they
may the better bee grounded in their Voca-

tion , and consequently bee the more securely guyded and Directed in the Scope and end which they ought to ayme att.

9. The Nouices and Schollers must bee tryed in base and humble Exercises, soe often as may bee thought expedient, yet they shall not bee sent to the places appertayning to the charge of other Officers, except the sayd Officers consent thereunto ; and lett the sayd Schollers and Nouices bee warned, that the Conuent ought and will seeke to bee informed of their humilitie, Obedience, and desire of the Contempt of themselues.

10. Lett her not perswade or oblige any of them to any kinde of austeritie, but by the Counsel of the Abbesse.

11. She must beware that they bee not ouerthrowne and carryed away with their first feruour, whyle therein they passe the limitts of discretion , and therefore shee shall admonish the Ghostly Father hereof, if their happen any iust cause therein.

12. To the end all may bee the better informed of the natures and dispositions of the Scholers and Nouices, and that they that enter for such may better knowe the vnitie Charitie , modestie , and Religious manner of life which the Religious embrace and leade, the Mistrisse (by Commaundement from
the

the lady Abbesse) shall make choyce of such to conuerse and conferr with her Nouices and Schollers, whoe either by their beha- uiour, experience, or good example, are best able to edify instructe and helpe them.

13. The Mistris is to bee subiect in all thinges for domesticall disciplyne to the Prioresse, soe farr forth as shee bee not hin- dred from the Execution and accomplis- hing of her Office, where by shee is obliged to teach her Scollers, and Nouices, to sing, reade, pronounce a right, and the like; Soe alsoe the Nouices and Schollers in the Quier, Chapter house, Refectory, and in all such places, where the whole Conuent must bee subiect to the sayd Prioresse, wherefore the Mistresse may not commaunde them there in any matter, that there by shee may yeald the more Reuerence and respect to the Su- periour, and if any difficulty or inconueni- ence happen here by or that the Mistrisse bee hindred from the due Execution of her Office, lett her seeke to the Lady Abbesse, for the Remedy there of.

THE

THE VII. CHAPTER.

Of the Assistans.

1. LET such Assistants bee chosen, as vppon whose prudence, and Counsayle the Abbesse may very well rely, in such difficulties as may occurr : whoe alsoe may well Guyde and direct such Religious as come vnto them at any tyme for comfort, or would informe them of matters occurring according to the Statutes. Therefore they must bee very discreete and circumspect, noe ways headdy, free from all inordinate Passions, Zealous of the common good of the Conuent, which they ought to sett forward according to their best skill, and they ought to bee very care full mayntayners of whatsoeuer maketh for the peace and good disciplyne thereof.

2. For asmuch as the Prioresse is wont to bee admitted to the Consultations ; foure Assistants wilbee sufficient, and they are not to exceede the number of foure, and the younger professed among them, must first in Order deliuer her opinion , before the Abbesse declare her mynde, or what shee would haue concluded; lett them all well and maturely ponder the matter propounded

ded, and if soe bee that the matter may suffer delay, and bee of great Consequence, lett them haue longer tyme to discusse and consider it with themselues, that thereby it may bee the better determyned.

3. Once euery weeke or at least twise euery Moneth, they must bee called to Consultation at that houre which the Abbesse shall appoynte, where shee her selfe must alsoe preside, and bee present; and one of these Consulters and Assistants must euery weeke haue accesse to the Abbesse, to know of her when the Assistants are to bee called to Consultation. Before the Consultation begin, *Veni Creator Spiritus &c.* with the prayer. *Deus qui corda fidelium &c.* is to bee sayd, and the Consultation being ended; *Suscipe clementissime Deus &c.*

4. The things that are handled in Consultation most commonly are these, The Causes and Remedyes of disciplyne broken or neglected; the defects of Officers in their Offices; the trouble or disgust of any one conceaued against any Officer; want of health in any through indiscretion; dissentions, secretts meetings, and whisperings; what manner is to bee obserued in enioyning of Penances; the Receauing or deliuering of Messages or writings to Externes; the deposing

C 3

sing

sing of Officers ; or appointment of new
Officers; the Measure of their diett, to grea-
ther with the defect or excesse committed in
the same ; what persons are to bee propounded to the Conuent, and such like.

5.   Lett them permitt nothing that may
weaken disciplyne , and if they consult
about the enioyning of any Pennance, after
the thing hath beene maturely determyned,
lett them not afterwards interpose themselues for any moderation. But if vppon better
Information they finde the Case , to stand
other wise then when they consulted about-
it, and that thereby they feare any hurt or
inconuenience may ensue , they must make
it knowne to the Abbesse , and soe committ
it wholy to her discretion.

6.   Of those things that are propounded
vnto them they may not debate among themselues out of the place of Consultion , and
then noe otherwise then in the presence of
the Abbesse ; and soe in like manner of those
things about which they haue had Consultation. If they shall offend in the contrary,
they must endure the same penance, that the
other professed should incurr, if they offended in the like Case, much lesse may they
communicate vnto others , either within,
or without the Conuent, what hath passed
in

in Confultation , or which may any wife
touch any perfon of the Conuent; and if
any should vnderftand that Confultation
hath beene had about her felfe , yet none
shall tell her what refolution hath beene
taken about her , but they shall remitt it to
the Relation of the Abbeffe her felfe, except
the Abbeffe doth otherwife ordayne.

7. In their Iudgments lett them conforme themfelues to the Commaundement
of the Abbeffe neither may they contend
among themfelues , or ftand to ftubborne-
ly in their owne opinions , they muft an-
fweare each other with meaknesse , and
propofe their reafons with all humilitie,
yet alfoe with Religious freedome and liberty. Where vppon the lady Abbeffe muft
bee willing to heare their aduifes, and muft
permitt them to haue their neceffary liberty in fpeaking their mynds; yea moreouer
shee muft inuite rnd incourage them , that
herein they carefully doe their Office, and
duty, and if any thing chance to bee fpo-
ken by any of them , that may bee diftaft-
full to her , lett her rather winke thereat,
then that the Affiftants bee made afrayde
to deliuer with fredome their opinions, as
they are obliged to doe in matters appertayning to the common good : neither

C 4   ought

ought the Abbesse to departe from that
they all Counsayle her, but vppon sufficient
ground and reason.

8.   If nothing occurr whereof they
should consult yet the Abbesse ought to
call them togeather to see if her Consulters haue any thing to propound vnto her,
and if nothing of worth doe occurr they
may bee dismissed.

9.   When the Religious will declare to
the Assistants their mynds concerning those
things which they are not willing to declare
to the Abbesse her selfe, whereby shee
may bee the better informed, let the Assistants, (naming none) performe this with
all charitie, and sinceritie, and bring them
an answeare and resolution as the Case requireth.

10.   Euery one must know that they
may not deale about any matter with the
Assistants, but vppon this Condition, that
what they declare vnto them, should bee
made knowne vnto the Abbesse, neither
may they giue eare to any thing vnder Condition that it bee kept secrett and vnknowne to the Abbesse.

11.   After the Assistants leaue their Offices, yet they may not discouer to others in
any sort those things that haue beene done
                                                                OR

or vttered in their Confultations, except
onely fuch matters as by the Abbeffe were
made common be fore and imparted to o-
thers, and if they shalbee found faulty here
in, there by they shalbee difinabled to haue
this Office againe for euer after; and to the
end the affiftants may bee more free in deliuering their opinions, by the Statutes it is
for bidden, that the Abbeffe doe manifeft
vnto others, what was fayd or counfayled
her by any of the affiftants, but onely (as
the Cafe may require) shee may tell the
Conuent what was counfayled her, yet foe
that shee difcouer not vnto them, the name
of her that gaue her Counfayle or aduefe
there in.

THE VIII. CHAPTER.

Of the defpofitayre.

1. THE Office of the depofitayre is to
keepe all fuch things as belong to
the neceffary prouifion of the monaftery, as
Woolen, linnen, money, and the like: and
shee is to render an exact accompt of all Receipts and expenfes to the Abbeffe, whom
shee is to certify of all fuch things of moment which shee receaueth, or fpendeth,
and

and there in shee is to follow her order and and appoyntment.

2. Shee must haue a Chest with two lockes, one of the keyes the Abbesse must keepe, and shee the other, soe that it may not bee opened without them both. In this Chest all the money of the house must bee kept, and from thence it must bee taken as neede requireth, except the Abbesse will keepe by her some smale somme, for such vses as some tymes may occurr.

3. Shee must haue the keeping of the great Seale of the Conuent, and therewith shee may Seale nothing without the Consent of the Conuent, shee alsoe must keepe all Originalls and other writings, and Euidences in a Coffer with a double locke, where of the Abbesse must haue one key and shee another.

4. Once euery yeare the depositor togeather with the Guardroabe must see what euery one hath, and what they want, they must sett all downe in writing, that afterwards they may consult with the Abbesse, how they may prouide for the necessitie of eath one, and lett them labour to carry an euen hand to all; And to the end all Confusion may bee auoyded, a certayne hower must bee appoynted, at which tyme euery

euery day all the Officers and the Religious must repayre to the depositoryfor their Neneſſities.

5. When shee deliuereth by appoyntment of the Abbeſſe any thing to the Cellarier, Guardroabe, or Cater, lett her demaund a writing of the perſon that receaueth it, where in the Receipt is contayned, and lett her shew her ſelfe prompt and eaſy to execute thoſe things, vnto whichshee is bound by her Office, and in noe wiſe muſt shee shew her ſelfe wrangling or contentious; yet if in her opinion, shee thinketh that any thing may bee better done, or that shee eſpyeth, that any thing is more ſpent then ought to bee, lett her make Relatiõ there of to the Abbeſſe.

6. Lett her take care that all Prouiſions bee made in their due tymes; for which cauſe shee muſt ſome tymes conferr with the Abbeſſe, and Procurator of the Monaſtery, as alſoe with the Cellarier, conceruing thoſe things which are vnder her charge, and which shee is to vſe.

7. Shee muſt gather togeather all ould things of the Monaſtery, as the ould lockes ould Iron and ſuch like, alſoe shee muſt keepe an accompt of all the Reuenewes, and ſommes of all the perticuler debts, and of ſuch things as are owing to any; or by any

any to the Monaſtery, and what tyme the
ſayd payments are to bee made.

8. Once euery yeare ſhee ſhall render an
exact accompt of all her Receips and Ex-
penſes, where of ſhee is to deliuer a Coppy to the Abbeſſe, whoe ſhall alſoe writt
it downe in her booke, and ſhee muſt ſeeke to haue the Abbeſſe ſubſigne to her
yeare ly Reckonings, whereby it may appeare that ſhee hath approued all, and that
all things haue paſſed according to her Order and well liking.

THE IX. CHAPTER.

Of the Cellarier.

1.   THE Cellarier muſt often conferr with the Abbeſſe about thoſe
things which appertayne to her Office, and
ſhee muſt performe that both for quantitie
and qualitie of the meate, which ſhee ſhall
appoynte; ſhee muſt ſee that all things bee
well keept in the Spence and Buttery, that
nothing bee negligently ſpent or waſted
in meate drinke or any other thing committed to her charge, and with a ſpeciall
care ſhee muſt endeauour that what ſoeuer
belongeth to her Office, bee kept cleane
and

and hand some.

2. In the manner of dreſſing and ſeaſo-
ning her meate , ſhee muſt looke to that
which is moſt whole ſome, and lett her
auoyde all Curioſitie and exceſſe in all things
ill beeſeeming a Religious eſtate; yea if any
thing bee ſuperfluons lett her keepe it care
fully , to bee ſpent, and vſed in due tyme
and Seaſon.

3. Lett her foreſee what is to bee prouided for the day folluwing , and lett her
certify the Cater thereof, and that by writing , ſoe likewiſe lett her inquire in good
tyme of the Cooke , what ſhee wanteth,
that in due tyme Prouiſion may bee made
thereof; and if the depoſitair ſhallbee wanting to her in any thing , ſhee ſhall onely
ſignify it to the Abbeſſe.

4. If at any tyme any of the Profeſſed of
the Quier bee ſent vnto her for any thing,
ſhee is to deliuer vnto them that which they
haue neede of with all due Charitie and
ſweeteneſſe as her abilitie will permitt
her.

5. Shee muſt ſoe diſpoſe all her buſineſſes that ſhee may bee ſtill preſent at the
deuine Office, ſoe farr forth as ſhee can
poſſible.

6. The Conuerſe Siſters both Schollers,
Noui-

Nouices as alſo the profeſſed , and all the Seruantes of the houſe are vnder her charge , and shee muſt bee very watchfull to keepe them all in peace and Concord , directing them with all meakeneſſe and gentleneſſe , taking care that they bee not two much ouer charged with their labour , and that nothing bee wanting to their ſpirituall proffitt and good ; but eſpecially of her Conuerſe Siſters.

7. Shee muſt inſtruct her Conuerſe Siſters in the Catechiſme , and Chriſtian doctrine, and how to pray and make their Confeſſion, and to goe to the ſacreed Communion with fruyte and proffitt.

8. Lett her ſee that ſuch Conuerſe Siſters as are appaynted for ſundry Offices haue their directions written in their ſeuerall Offices , which shee muſt take care that once euery Moneth they bee read vnto them, shee muſt alſoe haue an Inuentory of all ſuch things, as euery one vnder her charge doth vſe , and shee muſt often viſitt them all, that shee may ſee that nothing bee broken or nede reparation.

9. Lett her not behaue her ſelfe contentionſly or diſtaſtfully to others , but rather endeauour to mayntayne both her ſelfe and all her charge in inward peace, and lett

her

her seeke by her Religious outward temperate gouernment, moderation, and manner of speach to giue edification to others, by the example of her vertuous and true religious life.

THE X. CHAPTER.

Of the Portreße.

1. IT is the Office of the Portreße to keepe the key of the Gate oft the Monastery, the locke where of must haue two keyes, foe that it may not bee opened without them both. One of these keyes must bee kept by the Abbeße, and when foeuer any perfon is to enter into the monaftery, or any thing is to bee brought in, fome one Religious is to bee fent by the Abbeße whoe may bring with her, her key, and there with open and shutt the fayd Gate, and foe carry it backe to the Abbeße againe.

2. If any are to enter into the Monaftery from abroade, the Portreße togeather with her Companion whom the Abbeße or the Superiour shall appoynte (for fewer then two shall neuer accompany them) must bring them to the place whether they are

to

to goe, and none may fpeake vnto thofe perfons but in a word or two, and as it weare, Obiter, or by the way, neither may the Portreffe permitt euery one to open the Gate, or deliuer her key to any, but to her whom the superiour shall appoynte.

3. If there shalbee more Gates to the Monaftery then one, euery one of them muft allwayes haue two keyes, where of the Abbeffe muft haue one, and the Portreffe another ; and the Portreffe muft bee very carefull to fee they bee allwayes well shutt; and that whofoeuer are lett into the Monaftery, doe allwayes enter and departe at full day light, except fome moft vrgent Caufes of neceffitie doe exact the contrary, and after Complyne shee is to giue vpp her keyes to the Cuftody and keeping of the Lady Abbeffe.

THE XI. CHAPTER.

Of the Thourier, or the Prefect of the speaking place.

1. THIS Officer muft haue a Cell neere vnto the speaking place, that

that shee may bee the readyer to answeare such as come, and to deliuer such messages as are requisitt.

2. Shee must demaunde the names of such persons as come to the speaking place (if shee know them not) and shee must endeauour to informe the Lady Abbesse, or Prioresse of the qualitie of such persons, as require to speake with any one.

3. Shee shall call noe Religious to speake with Externes at the Grate without the the lycence of the Prioresse at the least, and what soeuer shee receaueth of Externes, shee must deliuer it to the Abbesse or to the Prioresse soe soone as well shee may.

4. When the Religious are called to speake with Externes shee must notify vnto them the quality of the persons, that if they bee persons of qualitie they may goe vnto them in their great habitt, and when shee calleth any to the Parloy or speaking place, lett her signify vnto her what Companion shee is to haue, according as the Abbesse or Prioresse shall appointe; and if the Conuersation seeme to bee vn profitable or inconuenient lett either her Companion or the Prefect of the place prudently and discreetely call her thence.

5. If any Externe bee denyed to speake

D   with

with any, lett her in good Religious manner seeke to giue the person due satisfaction, by her yealding those reasons that
are for that purpose, and in her speeches,
or answeares, lett her haue care of edification, and religious Ciuilitie, and being by
the Bell called to the Parloyre, lett her make
hast to goe thither, and make answeare
to the person that called, and see that there
shee vse noe other talke, then that which
is necessary and conuenient.

6. Shee may not suffer any to execute
her Office, but onely that Religious whom
the Superiour shall appoynte.

7. Shee may receaue noe writing or
message to bee sent to any, except the
Abbesse, Prioresse, or Conuent bee ac-
quaynted ther with, except it bee to
bee sent and addressed to the Bishopp,
or Visitours, as hereafter in the third
parte, and first Chapter shalbee declared.

THE

THE XII. CHAPTER.

Of the Chantreſſe.

1. ALL the bookes that appertayne to the Quiar muſt bee in the Cuſtody of the Chauntreſſe, whoe muſt haue care that in their ſinging and reading, the hearers may bee edifyed, and euery weeke vppon Wednesday ſhee ſhall ſett vp a Paper, wherein there names are to bee written, that in the weeke following muſt ſing, or reade any thing in the Quiar, Shee muſt make choyce of the more ſkillfull according to the ſolemnitie of the Feaſts, and in all things lett her take that Courſe and methode in her proceedings, that ſhee bee not ouer greiueous or troubleſome to any.

2. Euery weeke vppon Saterday lett her ſett vpp in writing the Order of the Office for the weake following, and withall the extraordinary obligations, both for the liuing and the dead; for which cauſe ſhee muſt haue the keeping of that booke wherein the ſayd Obligations are contayned.

3.   Lett her bee very wary and Circumspect before shee begin to sing , or intone
any thing , and lett her vse the same war-
rynesse in euery thing els, that if any error
happen shee may seeke to amend it with
Zeale , yet without any signe of impatience, soe farr as shee can possibly.

4.   If they shall sing any thing in Musicke in the Church, those are to bee appoynted by her (or by some other who perhapps may bee fitter for this Office) that
must sing, neither may any other presume
to sing , but such, as by her are appoynted.

THE XIII. CHAPTER.

Of the Sacristane.

1.   THE Sacristane must bee very dilligent to see that what soeuer belongeth to the Church , Cloyster, Chapter
house , and Sacristy bee kept very carefully
and han somely.

2.   Lett her carefully prouide that the
wine which must serue for the most holy
Sacrifice, bee good and pure and drawne
the same day ; that the Chalices , Purifica-
                                    toryes,

toryes, Corporalls, Cruetts, Water, Towells and all the furniture and appurtenances of the Church, bee whole and very cleane, shee muſt carry holywater to the Cells, and the accuſtomed places of the Monaſtery, where euery weeke shee muſt put it into Veſſells, that there are appoynted to contayne the ſame.

3. Lett her appoynte the tyme when euery one is to goe to Confeſſion, by the aduiſe of the Abbeſſe, and lett her ſee that all the Maſſes bee ſayd in fitt tymes, if they haue ſundry Priſts to celebratt. Lett her make the hoſts as fayre as shee can poſſibly, which shee muſt prouide may bee ſufficient for the Maſſes, and the Communicants, and shee muſt ſee that shee allwayes haue them in readyneſſe, as neede may require.

4. Shee muſt kepe the kyes of the Turne, and Grate of the Church, or Sacriſty, neither may shee receaue or deliuer any thing by them, but onely ſuch things as appertayne to the Aultar, the holy Sacrifices, or Church, lett her ſee that this grate or Turne bee allwayes well shutt and locked, except in tymes of Communion, or when any thing is to bee deliuered, or receaned by the ſame.

5. Shee

5. Shee muſt not ſpeake or talke with any at the Grate, but onely about thoſe things that neceſſaryly appertayne to her Office and if any Externe demande any thing of her which concerneth not immediately the Church, lett her ſend him to the Tourier, and when shee ſpeaketh with any at her Turne or Grate, lett her doe it with a low voyce, and lett her bee ſtill ready to deliuer thoſe things, which belong to the Seruice of the Church.

6. Shee muſt deliuer euery Euening to the Abbeſſe, the keyes of her Office, and in the morning lett her demaunde them of her at a competent tyme.

7. See that with due care and Dilligence shee write downe in ſome booke all ſuch donations, as haue beene made to the Church, togeather with the names of the giuers, and shee muſt take an Inuentory of all ſuch things as are committed to her charge.

THE

THE XIV. CHAPTER.

Of the Infirmaire.

1. THE Infirmayre must assist the sicke with singuler Charitie, and seeke to procure their confort accordingly, wherefore shee must endeauour to performe all those things, that may tend to the ease and comfort of the diseased, with very great alacritie.

2. About the sicke all things must bee neat, and decent, and the Infirmaire must haue an Inuentory of all such things, as belong to her Office.

3. Shee must haue all medicinable things and what soeuer els are neceessary for the sicke in some conuenient place, and shee must often visitt them, to see that nothing bee corrupted, and to procure by Order from the Superiour that new bee had in due tyme.

4. If the disease soe require it, lett her send for the Phisition, yet with the consent of the Abbesse, and lett her punctually obserue his prescriptions, and ordinations, concerning the diett and Phisicke of the Patient, she

D 4   must

S

must alsoe haue certayne common Rule and instructions, according to which hee may proceede, when the disease seemeth not to require the presence or aduise of the Phisition.

5. If the disease increase lett the Abbesse bee certifyed there of, that other Phisitions bee sent for in due tyme, if it seeme needefull, or if the disease bee infectiue, that others bee for bidden to haue accesse to the diseased, or to conuerse with her.

6. If the Sicke bee in any danger shee must prouide that in fitt tyme they bee armed with the holy Sacraments, and assisted whith the deuoute prayers of the Religious and withall may bee excited with holy admonitions to endure patiently the greife of their disease, and willingly to embrace the will of almighty God in all things.

7. Some holy Pictures and Images must bee had in the Infirmary, and shee must see that a Table bee decently adorned and prepared when the most blessed Sacrament is to bee brought thither, and shee is to make it ready and to prepare all other necessaryes for the Communion of the sicke, soe often as the ghostly Father shall thinke it expedient, that they communicate.

8. Shee may not change or omitt any thing

thing that the Phifition hath appoynted, except fome euident reafon moue her to the contrary, and lett her haue a booke where in all muft bee fett downe that hee prefcribeth.

9. Whenfoeuer the Phifition or Surgeon commeth to the Monaftery, by fome figne the Conuent shalbee aduertifed of their comming, that if any haue neede of their helpe, by the Superiours licence they may come vnto them.

10. When the Ghoftly Father, the Phifition, or Surgeon enter the Infirmary, shee or fome other, with a Companion, muft bee prefent, who shall neuer departe out of the place, till they bee thence departed.

11. Shee muft not difmiffe thofe that are on their Recouery, till shee fee the ftrong and able to vndergoe their accuftomed labour.

12. Shee muft haue a Care that they obferue due modefty, whyle they are vnder her charge, left that whyle they feeke to reftore their corporall ftrenght, they loofe their Zeale and Spiritt, yet they shall not foe much imploy themfelues in their meditations and deuotions as before, vntill that they may bee able to retourne to their former Exercifes, in perfect health, and with-

D 5 out

out any inconuenience.

THE XV. CHAPTER.

Of the Guarderobe.

1. THE Guarderobe must keepe all such
Cloathes as the Religious doe not vse:
as alsoe all linnen, and woollen which are
applied to their bedding or to any other Monasticall vses, the which shee must dilli
gently looke vnto, as to those things which
are belonging to the poore.

2, Shee must keepe an accompt of all such
things that are vnder her charge, as of all
those things whereof the Religious haue the
vse, and if shee bee to make prouision for
any, either in linnen or in Woollen, lett he
acquainte the Lady Abbesse therewith, neither may shee deliuer to any a new garment, or any thing els that is new, without
the consent of the Lady Abbesse.

3. Lett her haue great care of cleanely-
nesse, and handsomenesse, and shee must
haue commodious places, to lay vpp those
things that appertayne to her custody, the
which shee must looke vnto, that by noe
meanes they bee spoyled.

4. Whe:

4. When shee deliuereth out any thing to bee washed, or which is already washed, shee muſt deliuer them by accompt, and by accompt shee muſt receaue them backe againe; alſoe all ſuch things as are deputed, for the vſe either of the Refectory or of the kitchin, and when shee deliuereth any linnen or Woollen to the Religious, shee muſt deliuer them on Saterday, and shee shall keepe written what and when, and to whom, any thing is deliuered, that euery one may receaue their neceſſaryes in due ſeaſon.

5. Lett her ſeperate and keepe a parte that which is new, from that which is ould, and put euery thing in their ſeuerall places, and diſtinguiſh by certeyne ſigures or numbers, what ſoeuer is granted for the perticuler vſe of each Religious. But if any thing cannot bee accommodated for the vſe of the Religious, lett her make the Abbeſſe know thereof, that shee may diſpoſe thereof accordingly.

6. Shee shall haue care to ſee that the Garments bee mended, and shee shall at the appoyntment of the Superiours deliuer them to bee mended by thoſe whom the Superiour shall pleaſe to name.

7. Shee muſt haue care of all their Shooes, and

and shee must see that they bee mended in
due tyme, and new must bee giuen to euery
one, according to their necessitie and as the
Superiour shall appoynte.

8. In her Office lett her carry her selfe
meeke and gentle, neither must shee suffer
any to endure any Want in Clothing and
Garments.

9. Shee must eschew and auoyde all no-
ueltie, secularitie, and Curiositie in all things
and therefore a certayne Patterne of their
habbits, Vayles, and other garments, must
bee made and prescribed, the which shee
must keepe in her Office of the Guardroabe,
shee and all the rest shall bee bound and
obliged to obserue this fashion, neither may
any bee soe bold, as to presume to make,
or fashion, or haue any thing but according
to the sayd Patterne, according vnto which
euery thing must bee præcisely made and
accommodated.

THE XVI. CHAPTER.

Of the Conuerse Sisters.

1. THE Conuerse Sisters are admitted
into this Congregation, that by their
pious labours they may serue their God and
Crea-

Creator, and that they may assist those, whoe haue dedicated themselues to his holy Seruice, and soe serue with them the selfe same soueraigne Lord, vnder the selfe same Statutes, Rules and Sacred Vowes; therefore they must endeauour to draw that spirituall proffitt and commoditie from their sayd Labours, in such sort that they may fully accomplish all their ymployments to the glory of almightie God, and to the Saluation of their omne Soules.

2. The Conuerse Sisters (being noe lesse Religious then are those of the Quier) must in like sort bee prouided for in all things that appertayne to ther spirituall and Corporall good : as both aliue and dead they enioy all those Graces, and prouiledges which the others enioy, onely those excepted, which speciall and perticuler exception is made in the Statutes, whereof, by reason of their sundry imployments, businesses, and impediments that are incident to their estate, they cannot bee capable.

3. They must know that all such Statutes, that any wise touch the Religious of the Quiar. doe alsoe appertayne vnto them, soe farr forth as by their State they may bee accommodated vnto them.

4. They vnto whom any perticular Offices

ces are inioyned must receaue their speciall
directions from their Superiour in writing,
the which they must haue sett vpp in the places of their Offices.

5. Euery day they must attend to mentall
and vocall prayer, for soe long a tyme as the
Superiour shall appoynte them, which may
bee longer or shorter as their Labours, and
businesses will permitt them, if they shall
perceaue that they are not soe apt for mentall prayer as they might wish, let them
acquaint their ghostly Father therewith that
they may imploy the tyme of prayer in some
other exercise of deuotion.

6.   Lett them pay to our Lord God a dayly taske and oblation of their Prayers, to witt
for their Nocturnes and Mattins, they shall
say thirty *Pater Nosters*, and soe many *Aue Marias*; for their Prime, Third, Sixt, None, and
Compline, for each of these seuen *Pater Nosters*, and seuen *Aue Marias*; and they shall recite the sayd *Pater nosters* and *Aue Marias* twlue
tymes ouer, in stead of their Euensong;
But they that are able, and can finde leisure
may say the Office of our blessed Lady, or of
the dead, or the seuen penitentiall Palmes,
with the Litanies, insteed of those *Pater nosters*
and *Aue Marias* prescribed.

7. They that are admitted for Conuerse
Sisters

Sisters, after they haue made their Profession, may neuer passe to the State of the
Professed of the Quier, and therefore they
may not learne to sing, read or write, nor
yet may they bee taught to doe the some.

8. They may vse all religious freedome
with their Superiours, for which cause they
may confidently repayre vnto them if they
want any thing, or in their labours finde
them selues ouercharged aboue ther streng-
thes, and both Superiour as alsoe all the
rest must loue them as their most deare Sisters, and carry them selues towards them
in all Charitie, beneuolence, and true louing affection.

9. If at any tyme the Nouices bee sent
by their Mistresse, or the Professed of the
Quiar by the Superiour to serue in the kitching or such like places, the Conuerse
must soe seeke to direct them in their labours, that withall they carry them selues
towards them with all religious gentlenesse
humilitie and discretion, neither may they
take more vppon them then is meete in their
proceedings or speeckes, but they must with
sweetnesse teach them, when they see any
rhing worthy to bee amended in them, but
in those things which appertayne not to
their Offices, lett them informe their Superiours

periours of them.

10. Let them auoyde all bitternesse among them selues, but rather lett them seeke to nourish that mutuall charitie, which bee seemeth them, lett them behaue themselues with all obedience towards their Superiours, whom they must reuerence in most humble manner, the Religious of the Quier they must honour and respect each one according to that Estate wherein shee is.

11. They must bee very dilligent and warry that there happen noe danger by their Fyre or Candle in the places of their Offices, they must see that all things bee neate and cleanely, they must haue a noate of all such things as are deliuered to their vse and Custody, that they may make a due accompt and reckoning of all things when it shall bee required of them.

12. They must bee very carefull and dilligent that nothing bee vnprofitably wasted or spoyled in their Offices, they must alsoe bee very great louers of Pouerty, and in all the places of their labours they must speake very sparingly, and for the most parte of things necessary, and then they must speake with a submissiue and lowe Voyce.

THE

THE XVII. CHAPTER.

Of those that are admitted in to the Monastery to receaue the Habitt, and to make holy Vowes, and Profession of Religion.

1. AS the Conditions and dispositions of those are, that are admitted into this Congregation, such alsoe will the whole Congregation bee, therefore with great choyce must they admitt such as offer themselues to the Congregation, lest by admitting such that are vnfitt their spirituall progresse and vigour of disciplyne fall and decay:

2. Therefore they are especially to bee admitted into this Congregation, whoe haue giuē some shew or proofe of their Vertuous life, in the places of their education and former Conuersation, and whose reputation was alwayes held for good, whyle they liued in the World.

3. They that are notably defectiue either in body or mynde may not bee admitted,

E nor

nor they that are in danger of continuall ficknesse, the Abbesse and the Conuent must bee Iudges whether they bee in these things defectiue: but yet where there may bee any doubt or question, they must seeke for the Counsayle of those, whose Iudgment and experience may assist them in these matters.

4.   Widdowes, Sisters, or such as are neere of bloode, may not bee receaued without great, Cause, nor they very easely whoe haue had gouerment ouer others in the world, and were subordinate to none, because such are not gouerned but with great difficultie.

5.   They that are entred into the lawfull bond of Matrimony, although they haue not consummated the same; may not obtayne admittance without very great warynesse and deliberation, nor they whoe haue beene suspected to take vppon them this State of life, by the hard and vnkinde vsage and dealing of their Frends, wherefore if any such shall enter, and shall conceale these things, they must know that they cannot continew in the Monastery, if these things doe afterwards come to light; but if the Conuent shall see any somewhat constrayned here vnto, and proceede afterwards

according

according to a true and an assured spiritt
of Religion, shee may bee admitted, after
shee hath yealded due profe and experi-
menteof her sincere Vocation.

6. Shee that is vnlawfully begotten or is
held for such, ought not to bee admitted,
except some reason of especiall moment
may bee alleadged for her, which reason
must bee aproued by the most Voyces of
the Religious, before shee bee permitted
to enter in.

7. Shee that is in debt or in Processe,
may not enter, vntill the debt bee payed,
and the Processe ended.

8. Shee that hath receaued the Habitt of
another Religious Order, or hath liued in
any Monastery of this Order, that obserue
not these Statutes and hath there receaued
the Habitt of Religion may not bee taken
into this Congregation, except vppon most
important Reasons.

9. None may easely bee receaued that
are aboue seuen and twentie yeares old, yet
if they bee such that are expert in reading
and song, and are knowne to bee of strong
and healthy bodys, they may bee admitted,
although they bee thirty yeares ould.

10. For as much as the impediments of
those that seeke to enter among you may

E 2   bee

bee often very fecrett, and hard to bee
knowne, lett her that offereth her felfe to
this Congregation bee demaunded, if fhee
haue any fuch impediments, whether fhee
bee able to paffe with the common dyett,
whether fhee bee often or feldome ficke,
and what fickneffe that may bee, of what
health or ftrenght fhee findeth her felfe
for the prefent, whether their parents had
any difeafe, which may bee feared to bee
hereditary vnto her, whether fhee bee fubiect to any Obligation vppon any contract
whatfoeuer; whether fhee hath publikely
celebrated any fpowfales, or plighted her
promife of mariage to any man, of all which
the Congregation muft bee planely and perticulerly informed.

11. Further more fhee muft bee demaunded what it was that induced her to haue
this defire, why fhee rather defireth to bee
in this Conuent then of another. If perhap-
pes, for that fhee hath here of her kindred,
or fome Sifter, or Cozens in the Congregation, who might much inclyne her here
vnto, or for the place, Country, or Education, moreouer it muft Bee inquired of her
whether fhee bee content to bee ymployed
in the bafer fort of labours, and to bee
perpetually exercifed there in according to
                                        her

her State and degree, whether shee bee
refolued to endure thofe things which may
helpe to bring her to humilitie, patience,
and contempt of her felfe, what qualities
shee hath, what difficulties shee hath fuf-
fred in making her Refolution, finally what
shee hath to difpofe of, and what fatisfac-
tion shee hath giuen to her Frends, out of
all which, if the Abbeffe and Prioreffe
(whoe are both feuerally to examine thofe
that would enter) can draw any thing that
may feeme worthy of great deliberation,
they shall remitt it to the Iudgement of the
whole Conuent.

12. They that after their entrance giue
litle hope of their good proceeding in Spirritt, muft bee difmiffed in good tyme, but
with great Charitie, but they that yeald
fome hope, and yet not foe certayne and
affured as may bee wished, their clothing
may bee foe long deferred vntill the Conuent bee fufficiently fatisfied, yet the Conuent is not bound vppon Charitie to retayne,
and mayntayne fuch among them whoe
may rather bee a burthen vnto them then
that they are like to make that proffitt in fpirit which they should.

13. A certayne number of Religious as
alfoe of the whole family muft bee appoynted,

E 3

ted, according to their certayne temporall meanes and Reuenewes, neither may they admitt more then their Ordinary Reuenewes or Almes are able well to entertayne and nourish.

14. None may bee admitted to bee either of the Quier, or a Conuerse, vppon indiscreete pitty and Compassion ; as neither that person ought to bee admitted to bee of the Conuent, whoe hath not a mynde to vndergoe, and endure what soeuer is according to Religion.

15. The Schollers muft haue a Vayle deliuered them, before they can bee permitted to come to the Quiar, or Refectory as alfoe a certayne kinde of habitt conuenient to the state and Vocation.

16. Such as are admitted muft ordinarely haue a whole yeare before they receaue the holy Habitt of Religion, if it happen otherwife that this tyme bee either preuented or prolonged, lett the Conuent approue the Caufe and Reafon, that afterwares it may not happen to bee turned in to a Cuftome.

17. Shee that is admitted may not vrge, or bee to erneft to receaue the Habitt, but lett her onely shew her propension, and good defire to proceede in her holy courfe, and
leaue

leaue the reſt to the diſpoſition of the Conuent.

18. They ſhall admitt none-to receaue the
holy habitt of Religion, before ſhee bee
twelue yeares ould, nor may they permitt
her to make her Profeſſion before ſhee
bee ſixteene yeares old full compleate
according to that which is decreed in
the holy Counſayle of Trent, in the twentie
fift Seſſion and in the fourth Chapter ; and
ordinarily lett none bee receaued, that after
two yeares cannot make her Profeſſion.

19. The Schollers and Nouices muſt liue
in ſilence ſeperated from the reſt, at leſt for
the ſpace of eight dayes before their Cloathing and Profeſſion that they may ſeriouſly
and maturely conſider of the greatneſſe of
the matter they are to take in hand ; againe
after three dayes are expired after their cloathing, they muſt retourne to their former
ſilence, for at leſt eight dayes more, that
they may well ponder and caſt with them,
by what meanes they may beſt with fruyte
vſe that benefitt of god his holy Grace and
fauour which hee hath beſtowed vppon
them and how they may Zealouſly accom-
pliſh thoſe things, which to the honor and
ſeruice of God they had before purpoſed
and determyned with themſelues.

E 4   20. The

20. The place of Recreation for the Schollers and Nouices muſt bee different from that of the profeſſed; neither yet may they conuerſe with thoſe, whoe álthough they liue in the Monaſtery, yet are not there with intention and purpoſe to bee Religious, except for ſometyme the Abbeſſe ordayne otherwiſe.

21. They muſt not ordinaryly bee admitted to make their Profeſſion before they bee eighteene yeares ould, although reaſon may ſometyme perſwade the contrary; as when their Iugdments and forwardneſſe may ſupply the defect of their yeares, and ſhee that after the yeare of her Probation is found vnfitt muſt bee diſmiſſed.

22. All the Religious muſt receaue from the Miſtris of the Nouices information, concerning the diſpoſitions, Vertues, and aptneſſe, of the Schollers, and Nouices, eſpecially when otherwiſe they cannot haue ſufficient notice and knowledge thereof; But as touching the Conuerſe Siſters, they muſt inquire of the Celarier, concerning what ſoeuer may occur touching them.

23. When the Religious deliberate among themſelues in Chapter concerning the admiſſion of any either to the habiti or profeſſion the Siſter or kinſewoman of the party within the third degree (yea although it bee

the

the Abbesse her selfe) may not bee present, as neither the Mistris of the Nouices, or Cellarier , whyle the Religious doe there debate among themselues concerning those that are vnder their seuerall charges , yet they must bee present when by balloting they all are to deliuer their suffrages and Voyces. The Suffrages of the Religious for those that are to bee admitted for cloathing or Profession , must not bee deliuered by writing , but by Bowles , and they that are to bee admitted must haue more then halfe the Voyces of the Couent, and the Couent must giue these their Voyces some six Weekes before their Cloathing ãd Professió, but especially before the Professió, that the LordBishopp or his deputy may bee certifyed in fitt tyme of those that are to bee admitted, that hee may examyne thē according to that which is decreed in the fife ãd twētySessió of the holyCounsell of Trent.

24. They must dispose of al things that any wyse appertayne vnto them , before the day of their Profession, and if they shall not bee found fitt , all what soeuer was any wayes bestowed vppon the Monastery must bee rendred to them backe againe, as in the holy Counsayle of Trent, in the 25. Session and 16. Chapter is enacted .

25. After the Profession the Mistris shall

E 5 in

informe the Prioreffe of their natures and difpofitions, foe farr forth as it is conuenient for her to know them, and after their Nouitiate shee shall ordinarely leaue them to the Prioreffe to difpofe of them and to bee fubiect vnto her in all things, in fuch fort as the reft of the Profefted for the Quier are.

26. If at any tyme young Children bee receaued into the Monaftery, for their education, let that bee done with great choyce and in regard of a greater good, and whofe good education (in regard of thofe things which paffe in Religion) may proue to aduance them to a greater good: they may not bee receaued before they are feuen yeares old, and they may not bee retayned in the Monaftery after they are paft fifteene, they may not bee admitted with any burthen to the Monaftery, excepted it bee otherwife fufficiently prouided for.

27. Whyle thefe Children liue in the Monaftery they may not bee curioufly cloathed or adorned, but the Habitt which they are to vfe muft bee decent, and fitly beefeeming the place; they may not conuerfe with the Schollers, Nouices, or Profeffed, but as the Lady Abbeffe and Prioreffe shall giue them leaue, neither may they fpeake or

haue

haue any Conuerſation with ſuch as come vnto them from abroade, and when this latter ſhalbee permitted them, lett them doe it at a certayne Grate, that muſt bee peeuliarely appoynted for them, and they muſt allwayes haue there ſome graue Religious ordinarely to accompany them, and to bee preſent with them.

THE THIRD
PARTE.

OF THOSE MATTERS
that are more extrinsecally and
externally appertayning to the
Congregation, and Monastery, and
are belonging to the Temporalities
of the same.

AT GANT.

Printed by Ioos Dooms. 1632.

THE FIRST. CHAP:

Of the Visitor, and Visitation of the Monastery.

1. THE Abbesse with her Conuent shall propose to the Bishopp, that hee would vouchsafe to appoynte and constitute some one Visitor of the Monastery, whose authoritie shall wholly in all things depend of the Bishopp; and the place of his ordinary residence must bee at the most but one dayes Iourney from the Monastery, and he must yearely make a visitation of the monastery and that must bee within the Feasts of S. Iohn Baptist, and of the Assumption of the blessed Virgin Mary, if it can possibly bee soe.

2. If at any tyme the Visitation cannot bee made at the ordinary appoynted tymes, the Abbesse shall certify the Conuent of the hindrance, and when the tyme of the Visitation approacheth; shee must vse that forme of writing to the Visitour which is sett downe in the booke of Ceremonyes.

3. The

3.   The Conuent muſt chouſe one that is
skillfull in the practiſe of Religion, and is
a Religious man, who may aſſiſt at the Viſitation. And becauſe the Abbeſſe is likelyeſt
beſt to know who may bee moſt fitt
for this purpoſe, after shee hath deliberated
of the matter with her Aſſiſtants, shee shall
propoſe two or three to the Conuent, leauing free vnto them to chuſe one of them
or ſome other, as may ſeeme meeteſt to
them.

4.   During the Viſitation all muſt yeald
their accuſtomed obedience to the Abbeſſe,
and other Superiors, in thoſe things that appertayne to ordinary diſciplyne, neither may
they require of the Viſitor leaue to doe any
thing before they haue firſt warned the Abbeſſe thereof.

5.   The Abbeſſe muſt deliuer a noate of
all the names of her Religious and Family
to the Bishopp or Viſitor, when hee commeth to viſitt, and shee muſt write downe
what Office, euery one beareth in the Monaſtery.

6.   To the end that euery one with better aduiſe may declare to the Viſitor their
mynds, and difficulties, they shall deliuer
vnto him in writing what they would ſay
vnto him. And all muſt haue free acceſſe

to

to the Visitor, that in any sort appertayne to the Monastery. But they that cannot write, may explicate to him their myndes by word of Mouth.

7. They shall auoyde and fly all kinde of exagerations in those things that they write and propounde, and they shall onely make a naked Relation of the matter, and they must maturely ponder with themselues, whether their Superiors could not haue sufficiently of themselues amended and reformed those things which they declare vnto the Visitor or whether at least wise the Superiors vnderstoode the case, that they might thereby haue prouided some remedy for it.

8. Those things that are to bee conferred about whith the Visitor (besides that which of himselfe he may enquire or examen) may bee reduced to these heads. The defects of good obseruation of the Rule, or Statutes, those things that belong to Chastitie, Pouerty, Obedience, and Clausure. to much Conuersation with seculer people, danger of scandale, occasion either offered or permitted of breach of peace, and disunion of myndes, want of necessaryes for their life and dyett, comming from those whoe of duty should haue mad due

A 3   proui-

prouifion , vnprofitable expences and ex-
cefle in any thing : notable defectes in the
Abbefle, ghoftly Father, Chaplaynes, or in
the reft of the Superiours, Officers , and
whatfoeuer els may feeme to bee greatly hurtfull to the good of the Monaftery.

9. The bookes of accomptes, and the
fome of the Prouifion they haue made, muft
bee shewed to the Vifitor, as vnto him alfoe muft bee declared , what is lett , and
in what manner and by whofe ayde and
affiftance, more ouer hee muft fee the Orders left them by former Vifitours, and efpecially thofe of the laft Vifitation (if any
thing were left in writing) all which their
Orders and Ordinations are to bee committed to writing , but yet they may not bee
ioyned to the Statutes , becaufe they are to
bee thought onely fuch things, as are onely
accommodated to certayne tymes and perfons.

10. If any would deliuer her Complaynte
to the Vifitor ; lett her fee that shee doe
it vppon a good ground, freing her mynde
from all Paffion, and shee muft onely mention thofe things that are of moment. If
any thing bee found to bee deuifed, or to
difcouer in them any notable Paffion , the
offendor

offendor muſt expeɕ a good Pennance
(which the Viſitour is to impoſe) according to her deſertes.

11. If any Complaynte ſhould bee deliuered vpp againſt the Abbeſſe , or any of
the Superiors , or of the Religious , the accuſed may neither direɕly or indireɕly , goe
about to finde out the Authors of the ſayd
Complaynte ; neither may ſhee ſhew any ſi-
gne of any greife or diſguſt againſt any , if
by any circumſtances ſhe may thinke that
ſhe haue diſcouered the Author thereof.

12. When the Viſitor entreth in to the
Incloſure the Abbeſſe ; Prioreſſe , and Aſſiſtants ſhall allwayes accompany him , whyle there hee remayneth , neither may they
conceale any thing from him , which hee
ought to ſee , or wherewith hee ought to bee
acquainted.

13. None may tell vnto any other any
thing that the Viſitor inquired of her ; or
where of hee examined , neither ſhall ſhee
ſignify her ſuſpicion of any thing that
was ſayd , or done with the Viſitor, and if
by any meanes the ſayings , or doings of
others ſhall happen to come to her knowledge , ſhee may not bewray it to any other,
except the Viſitor giue her leaue , vnder

payne of being diſabled to all offices afterwards and of other puniſhment which the
Viſitor ſhall pleaſe to enioyne.

14. What ſoeuer ſhallbee ſuggeſted or
ordayned by the Viſitour the Abbeſſe and
Conuent muſt receaue with due reuerence:
neither may they directly or indirectly make
their recourſe to any other ſeculer or eccleſiaſticall perſon, but to him ſelfe or his
Aſſiſtant (before named) or to the Biſhopp,
or his Superior; and if at any tyme any
ſhall dare to ſeeke for remedy of thoſe
things, that belong to the Office of the Viſitour and Biſhopp, by ſeeking to any ſeculer or Eccleſiaſticall Princes, or Magiſtra-
tes, the Abbeſſe and Conuent ſhall iudge
and condemne ſuch for vnquiett perſons,
for as much as they trouble the common
peace of the Conuent, and ſoe puniſh them
by ſeparating and debarring them from the
Conuerſation of the reſt.

15. If any of the Profeſſed would at any
tyme write to the Biſhopp or Viſitour, ſhee
ſhall haue free liberty to doe the ſame, and
ſhee may deliuer her letters to the Thourier,
who may not (vnder payne of loſſe of actiue and paſſiue Voyce for euer, and of other
puniſhments which by the Chapter may bee
enioyned her) diſcouer to any, that euer
shee

shee receaued any such letters to bee addressed vnto them, except the Religious that deliuered them vnto her, doe leaue it in her freedome and discretion; what shee receaued to bee sent vnto them, shee must see that shee deliuereth to a fayth full Messenger, or to him whoe is esteemed such an one, soe that it will not bee likely that the sending of such letters will euer come to the notice of the Superiors, or of others by his meanes.

16. Neither may the Abbesse or any other Superiors either Directly, by any wayes, signes or outward shew of Countenances, hinder the free writing of their Religious to their Superiors (to witt the Bishopp or Visitour) vnder payne of suspention from their Offices, and other greater penalties to bee inflicted on them by the Bishopp.

THE II. CHAPTER.

Of the Family of the Monastery and of such as liue out of the Inclosure.

1. THE Monastery must haue for their Ghostly Fathers such as are modest, prudent, and learned, and first the Conuent must bee well informed of their

A 5   suffifufficiency, Vertue, and honefty before they are to bee admitted; alfoe their Chaplaynes, Phifitions, and Chirurgions, muft bee of modeft life and good fame.

2. The Conuent muft entertayne noe feruant that is not modeft, or is noted for any perticuler cryme, or in his apparell and outward cariage is lighter then reafon would.

3. All thefe Seruants muft goe to Confeffion and the holy Communion once euery Moneth, and they muft obferue all fuch Ordinances, as they fhall receaue from the Abbeffe, Vifitor, or the Cellarier.

4. Noe woman of what foeuer State, dignitie or Condition fhee may bee, can bee permitted to liue or dwell with thofe of the family: that all occafion of ill fufpition and badd toungs may bee wholly takē away.

5. Hee that is chofen for the Steward or Procurator of the Monaftery by the Conuent, muft bee fuch a one, as is graue, godly, prudent, and hee muft not bee charged with wife, or Children, hee muft dilligently attend to the Affayres of the Monaftery, procuring ftill the proffitt thereof, with the good edification of fuch abroade as hee dealeth with all and the Abbeffe and the Conuent muft bee affured of his honefty,

sty, and fidelitie, in those things that are committed to his care and disposition.

6. Hee must bee obedient in all things to those Officers that haue authoritie from the Abbesse to commaunde him, and hee must haue some certayne howers, where in hee must repayre vnto them, but especially to the depositair, and Cellarier, vnto whom the care of the dayly prouisiones doe principally belong.

7. Hee must haue a booke where in hee is to sett downe all his receipts and expences, and once a weeke hee must receaue of the depositair, that which shall suffice for the necessary prouisions of that weeke; and when hee receaueth any money, hee must deliuer her a Bill where in hee shall acknowledge the receipt and for what vse hee receaued it.

8. Hee is to vnderstand that hee can take nothing vppon creditt, without the leaue of the Abbesse deliuered him in writing, except for some matter of litle moment, and hee shall incontinently pay for what hee receaueth, or take care that it bee payd, neither may hee euer bee debtor for aboue twentie Florens, except the Abbesse and dispositayre bee consenting there vnto.

9. If hee shall receaue any money due

to the Monaſtery, vppon what title ſoeuer,
hee muſt deliuer it vpp preſently to the de-
poſitayre and of her receaue an Acquittan.
ce for the receipt there of.

10. Hee may not vndertake noe Proceſſe
or call any into law without the knowledge of the Abbeſſe and Conuent; and if att
any tyme hee ſhall vndertake any ſuch matter, hee muſt demaund the Counſayle of
ſuch as are skillfull, whoſe aduiſe hee may
follow, and before any Suytes bee com-
menced (hauing firſt acquainted the Superiour there with) lett him offer to put the
matter to agreement, and Compremiſe.

11. Hee muſt often render an accompt
to the Abbeſſe of thoſe things, where in
hee dealeth, and hee muſt like a good and
faythfull Seruant in forme her of all ſuch
things, as hee thinketh wilbee profitable
for the Monaſtery, and hee muſt ſuggeſt
vnto her at what tymes all Prouiſions are
to bee made, that by theſe meanes, Coſts
and Charges may bee moderated; and lett
him ſee that what hee buyeth bee good
and profitable for the Monaſtery.

12. Hee ſhall certify the Abbeſſe of whatſoeuer hee findeth to want neede of reparation; and if hee ſhall thinke any thing fitt
to bee ſould, or otherwiſe to bee imployed,
                                    lett

lett him not attempt any such thing without her knowledge, or in lesser matters, without at least the knowledge of the depositayre.

13. Lett none bee admitted to eate with the Chaplaynes or Seruants without the Consent of the Abbesse, who must not grant easely hospitalitie to seculer people (except some singuler obligation require the same) and then lett it bee done in some place without the Bowndes and Circuit of the Monastery, where notwithstanding due regard and care must bee hadd of religious Frugalitie.

14. The Steward must not permitt that any thing bee vnprofitably spent and consumed, and if any thing bee ouerplus, lett him take care that it bee brought backe againe, to bee kept for those vses the Superiors shall approue; and hee must haue care of all the Seruants, and must dilligently see that euery one doe their duty and that they liue not idlely.

15. At what tyme soeuer hee requireth of the depositayre any Originall Writings, Registers, Charters, or other Instruments, lett him sett downe in writing that hee receaued them from her, vppon such a day, which writing shee must deliuer againe

vnto

vnto him, when hee hath reſtored the affore
ſayd things.

THE III. CHAPTER.

Of beſtowing and letting the Goods of the Monaſtery.

1. WHatſoeuer is giuen to the Monaſteryes vſe, through the pious li-
beralitie of good people, is to bee eſteemed
as applyed to Chriſt our Lord, or to the
Religious as his poore membres, that there
by being freed from all care of temporall
mattets, they may the better attend to the
Seruice of his diuine Maieſty; and therefore they muſt interprett that whatſoeuer
temporall goods they haue, or receaue, they
muſt imploy in ſuch ſort as may beſt ſtand
with the honour of God, and may ſeeme
to bee moſt agreable to the Intention of
the giuers.

2. If the Rents of the Monaſtery, and
donations of good people ſhould grow to
that greateneſſe, that, (the number of the
perſons liuing in the Monaſtery, and the
difficulties which may happen well conſi-
dered) they may ſeeme ſuperfluons or not
neceſ-

necessary, nor decent for a Religious State; then the Abbesse with the consent of the Conuent may apply them to some pious vses, as to the sustentation of poore families, bringing vpp of poore Schollers in learning and all such like godly workes, as may best aduance the good of Religion and seruice of God.

3. The Abbesse her selfe and by her owne authority, may dispose of those things that are of lesser valew, or giue some things in way of gratitude, yet shall shee sett downe in a booke, what, to whom, and to what end, shee hath giuen any thing, that it may bee shewed to the Visitor if it should seeme necessary.

4 The Abbesse may not giue vppon colour and prætext of Seruice done, more then Iustice beeseeming a Religious State may exact. And if at any tyme any peculier Consideration bee to bee had of some perticuler person, and that some notable thing is to bee added to his wages, lett that bee done by the consent of the Conuent.

5. The Abbesse must haue in her keeping a Register of all the Lord shipps, landes, and possessions of the Monastery, and of the yearely Reuenew which shee draweth from euery one of them, what was receaued
when

when they were laſt let, whether any poſſeſ-
ſion bee lett for terme of yeares, together
with the names of ſuch perſons as occupy
them.

6. The Abbeſſe may not lett any poſſeſ-
ſions of the Monaſtery, without the conſent
of the Conuent, whom ſhee muſt in forme
how much they yeald yearely, and what
the opinion of thoſe that are moſt practicall
in ſuch aſſayres is here in, and lett ſuch
men bee herd by the Abbeſſe, Prioreſſe, and
depoſitary, who are skillfull and of good
Iudgment in ſuch aſſayres, that the Conuent
may bee the more fully informed, and ſoe
may the better iudge there of, and let the
Conuent vſe ſuch perſons, whom none may
ſuſpect that they will draw any thing to
their owne priuate lucre, and gaine, or to
the benefitt of their Frends.

7. They muſt vnderſtand that noe Eccleſiaſticall goods can bee lett aboue the terme
of nyne yeares, without the obſeruation of
ſuch ſolemnities, as according to law are
required, in the alienation of the Church
goods, neither may any letting bee renued
during the tyme of the former leaſe, more
then for one yeare for the Tythes, and at
moſt for three yeares in reſpect of other
proffitts, before the end of the Rent that
                                    runneth,

runneth, neither may they take more then six Florens for an earnest penny, for renewing of the sayd Rent.

8. If any lettings of such goods should bee made by anticipating the Rent before hand, they may noe wayes binde ther Successours, as is d creed in the 11. Chap. of the 25. Session of the Counsayle of Trent. Therefore if the Monastery will lett forth their possessions for any long tyme , or bynde themselues for any money receaued ; it must bee done by them whoe according to law are able to grant it.

9. In the Monastery nothing may bee made by the Religious to bee sould , except ther pouerty want or necessitie driue the thereto.

10. If their Originall writings, Registers, Instruments , and monuments should happen through ouldnesse, Rottennesse , or euill keeping to bee spoyled or corrupted, the Abbesse and depositayre must take Care to haue them authentically coppyed out , and well kept , and if it happen that the sayd writings are to bee communicated or shewed to any lett him testify vnder his hand and writting what hee hath receaued ; neither may the Abbesse and depositayre deliuer to any the sayd publicke Instruments whithout the Conuent bee alsoe assenting there vnto.

B   11. Those

11. Thofe that are to per vfe their writings muft bee very fayth full, of whofe honefty and fidelitie there may bee noe doubt; and the Conuent muft haue certayne trufty Frends whom they may vfe in this matter, neither is it conuenient that they committ their affayres and State, onely to hyrelings.

THE IV. CHAPTER.

Of the tranflation of the Religious from one Monaftery to another.

1. THE tranflation or change of the Religious from one Monaftery to another may not bee made, except very great reafons perfwade the fame; and the fayd reafons muft bee allowed by the Bifhopp and by the Conuent, from which they are fent, as alfoe by that Conuent whether they are to goe, and it muft bee very profitable for the peace and quiett, or at leftwife for the fpirituall good of both.

2. None may deale either directly or indirectly: with any perfon about her owne tranflation; but onely with her Superiors, and that, onely by propofing the matter vnto them, but noe wayes vrging there vnto, that foe they may leaue it in their full libertie

tie to determyne therein, what they shall
thinke good.

3. When any new Monastery is to bee be-
gunn, it shall ly in the power of the Abbesse
and Conuent to make choyce of those persons
that are to bee sent to the beginning there of.

4. When any of the Religious are sent to
supply the want of another Monastery, it
must bee done with the consent of the Bishopp, Abbesse, and Conuent, from whence
they are taken, and when but one is granted,
shee shall haue an other Religious to accompany her thither, and with her some graue
matrone; with whom the sayd Religious
may retourne backe againe, if shee bee to
retourne backe againe.

5. When they are to goe from one Monastery to another, they must receaue in
writing from the Bishopp, or the Visitor
by what way they are to passe, neither may
they goe out of that way, and they must
allwayes repayre to the Rellgious houses
especially of their owne Order and Congregation, if conueniently they may.

6. The Religious that is sent from one
Monastery to another of the same Order
and Congregation, shall make her Vou of
Obedience in Chapter to the Bishopp and
Abbesse where shee shall reside, and there

B 2   shee

shee shall obferue all the laudable Cuftomes of the fame place.

7. Shee that is fent shall haue her place in the Conuent according to the tyme of her Profeffion, and shee shall participate of all the priuiledges of the Monaftery to which shee is fent; and if the day of her Profeffion, fall vppon the fame in which fome of the Monaftery were profeffed, the, profeffed of that Monaftery shall prefide and haue the Prioritie.

8. Shee that is tranflated to another Monaftery may not fpeake of any of the defects of any of that Conuent from which shee was tranflated, neither may shee extoll the Religious of one Conuent, that shee may feeme there by to detract or diminish any thing from the Creditt of the other, and if shee perceaue any thing to bee in vfe and obferuation in the other Monaftery, which is not obferued in the Monaftery where shee dwelleth, shee may propofe it to the Vifitor, Abbeffe, or Superior but shee may neither directly or indirectly fpeake there of to the other Religious except from the affore fayd Superiors shee haue licence to doe the fame.

9. Shee that for her greater peace and more perfection is fent to another Mona-

ftery

ſtery. ifſhee trouble the peace and quiett
of that Monaſtery, and carry her ſelfe in
trouble ſome manner, ſhee muſt bee ſent
backe againe to her former Conuent, that
there the Superiours may ſoe diſpoſe of her
as in our Lord they ſhall thinke beſt for
her owne good, as alſoe for the good of
the Conuent.

THE V. CHAPTER.

*Of the ʋnion and Combination of the
Monaſteryes of this Cougregation
amongſt themſelues.*

1. **A** Combination and vnion of diuers
Monaſteryes liuing vnder the ſame
Rules and Statutes doth make very much
for the increaſe of Religion, good diſcipline, and true Charity amongſt thoſe that
liue in them; Therefore the Superiours of
the ſeuerall Monaſteryes of this Congregation muſt endeauour to nouriſh among thē-
ſelues by their often mutuall correſpon-
dence, writing, and letters this pious Con-
iunction and charitable affection, whereby
it will come to paſſe that where as the ſeuerall Conuents of this Congregation will

make one body among themselues by meanes of this Combination soe will they alsoe be made partakers of all those priuiledges, graces and such like holy meritorious workes, which the rest either ioyntly or seuerally doe enioy or exercise.

2. Therefore these Monasteries liuing ynder the same Rule and Statutes, shall healpe and assist each the other, when they suffer any necessitie; as may happen through plagge, fier, vniust persecution, and the like; yet that must bee performed herein by each Monastery, which by the Iudgment of the right reuerend Lord Bishopp, and Visitor shalbee appoynted and determyned.

3. When soeuer any Monastery of this Congregation shall chance to bee vniustly wronged or oppressed, the rest shalbee obliged ioyntely to defend their right, and in the their common good; and they must dilgently labor that what soeuer may appertayne to the spirituall or temporall good there of, they may by any good manner deliuer from the vniust assaults and oppressions of others.

4. The Religious by those Conuents with whom they haue this Society, must bee intertayned in their Monasteries, and they shall bee subiect to the Abbesse or Superior, soe long as they remayne therein.

5. If

5. If any Religious in this fort intertayned in any Monaftery, should chance there to end her life, let that bee there performed concerning her buriall, which is accuftomed to bee performed to thofe, that are refident in the fame Monaftery ; But the Monaftery from whence shee came, muft fullfill thofe Maffes, and fuffrages for her Soule, which it doth for others.

6. When in any Monaftery of the Congregation an Abbeffe is to bee chofen, the other Monaftaries whoe shall haue notice of this election, shall fing or caufe to bee fayd a Maffe of the holy Ghoft for the fame; and the Superiours shall write one to the other of the deceafe of fuch Religious as depart this life in their feuerall Monafteryes, that there by they may bee made partakers of the merits, and deuoute prayers of their fellow Sifters.

7. Who foeuer is chofen Abbeffe of any Monaftery, muft with all conuenient expedition write to the other Abbeffes of this Congregation; and shall offer them her affiftance in all thofe things, that may any wayes concerne the fpirituall and tempor all common good of the whole Congregation.

8. All the Monafteryes muft depend vppon the firft Monaftery, from whence they

B 4   firft

firſt proceeded, or to which they were conioyned by the admiſſion of the ſame Statutes; ſoe that they muſt deferr the prioritie to the ſame, and they ſhall beare it a peculier reſpect, and whatſoeuer (concerning Religious perfection) is done there in , the reſt muſt follow and performe the ſame, framing and forming themſelues to the imitation and gouernment there of.

9. If any Monaſtery by not obſeruing fully the Statutes ſhalbe notably altred, and changed from the firſt, and ſoe from the reſt, It ſhall bee depriued and looſe all thoſe priuiledges , which is enioyed by reaſon of this Vnion, recept it recall and reforme it ſelfe.

10. If the firſt Monaſtery ſhould notably fayle in diſciplyne and Spirrit (which God for didd) it ſhalbee depriued of the priuiledge of priority ouer the reſt, and the prioritie ſhalbee transferred to the ſecond, and if that ſhould in like ſort proue defective then it muſt goe to the Third, and thus in all the reſt; otherwiſe the prioritie muſt ſtand according to the antiquitie of the Monaſteryes, and of their vnion and Combination with the reſt.

11. Theſe are the Statutes and Conſtitutions of this holy Congregation , compi-

led

led for the more perfect and better obseruation and keepeing of the most holy Rule
of the most glorious Father and Patriarch
Sainte BENEDICT, which all though
they ought to bee of highe esteeme and
authoritie with the Religious, and Children
of this Sodalitie, and consequently to bee
præcisely kept by them, soe farr forth as
their diuers and sundry regular imployments may require, or occasion may bee
offered, yet they impose not further obligation vppon their Consciences, then the
very nature of the things, and reason it
selfe shall require or in force, yet they are
greatly obliged in Conscience to obserue
those things that are appoynted touching
the Election and deposition of the Abbesse
as alsoe those things that concerne the
Correction of most greueous faultes, where
by any may deserue to bee seperated from
the Company of the rest; moreouer euery
one is obliged neuer to require or to permitt that more liberty bee admitted, then
the Rule and the Statutes will yeald vnto:
but if any thing bee brought in, or prac-
tised, which is not sett downe in the Rule
or Statutes, that must bee to greater perfection and austeritie; and it shall onely belong to the right Reuerend the Lord Bis-
B 5   hopp,

hopp, or Visitor, to explicate the sense
and meaning of the words and Clauses contayned there in, if there may happen any
doubt or Controuersy there in; to whose
Verdict and Iudgment euery one must stand
in this matter; therefore for as much as all
the professed Religious in this Congregation ought to obserue all the Statutes according to that sense and me aning which
the Bishopp or Visitor shall admitt (as hath
beene sayd) none may bee suffered to make their Profession amoug you, whoe shall
not first promise in the Chapter house (according to a certayne forme of writing
seet downe in the booke of Ceremonyes)
that they will accept of any reformation,
proceeding from the Bishopp corformable
and agreable to the Rule and Statutes, and
that they will not admitt any greater liberty, then the Rule and Statutes will permitt,
and this their purpose sett downe in writting they shall confirme with their owne
hand, and deliuer it to bee kept in the place of their other principall writings and
monuments.

The End of the Statutes.

THE

CONFIRMATION

OF

THE STATVTES.

MATHIAS *by the grace of God, and of the holy Sea Apostolike Arch Bishopp of Machlin to our welbe loued Daughters in Christ the Abbesse and Conuent of the Blessed Virgin Mary of the Order of S^t. Benedict residing in the Citty of Bruxelles subiect to vs by ordinary right health in our Lord. Although the Rule of the holy Father Saint Benedict which you professe bee written, and sett downe with a certayne kinde of deuine prudence,*

and

and ,wifedome, foe that it truly defer-
ueth, and ought to bee eftemed euen of
it felfe to bee an abfolute and perfect
guide and directory of good life, to fuch
as follaw the fame; Yet for as much as
diuers præcepts there of are fome what
generall, and therefore are diuerfly
vnderftoode, and obferued by diuers,
according to the diuerfitie of their natures, and Countrayes, your piety and
zeale of perfection was fuch, that you
made vour humble fupplication to the holy
Father the Soueraigne Bifhopp of Rome,
that by vs you might haue certayne
Statutes and Conftitutions, in perticuler
de termining the fayd Rule, to bee by vs
deliuered to you, confirmed for you, and
by our Commaundment to bee impofed
vppon you that (as by the motion of
Gods fpiritt you vehemently defire) you
                                        may

*may by them bee directed to the exact
and vniforme obseruation of the sayd
Rule; But wee knowing right well our
owne imperfection, would not trust only
to our selues in this matter, but wee would
vse the helpe and Counsayle of diuers
men well seene and experienced in Monasticall manner of life, for the best com-
piling of these Statutes, yea and when
they were soe compiled, wee would not
soe hastely commaunde you to keepe them
except that first you had fully tryed for
more then the space of a whole yeare,
whethere your humane and naturall infirmitie could obserue them; after which
your triall, when you had declared and
made knowne to vs your promptitude
and willing myndes, wee thought good
to confirme them by the authoritie of the
sayd holy Fater delegated vnto vs for*

this

this mater by a speciall Breue directed to vs, as by these our present letters wee doe now confirme them; Commaunding both you, and all your Successors to obserue and keepe them perpetually and purely. In truth where of wee haue subsigned and firmed these with our hund and Seale in Bruxelles the seuen and twentith of Iuly Anno Dñi. 1612.

MATHIAS Archiepiscopus
Mechliniensis.

NOTE

NOTE that the wordes inter-
liued in a diuers Carecter are
onely obferued by this monaftery
of Gand, by grant of his lordshipp
whoe att left for the prefent iudged it
fitter. For vs to finge our office ouer
night and keepe onely one refectory
though fome for health are ordained
to eate flesh when the comunity
eateth fish.